FOOTSOLDIERS: POLITICAL PARTY MEMBERSHIP IN THE 21ST CENTURY

This accessible, rigorously researched and highly revealing book lifts the lid on political party membership. It represents the first in-depth study of six of the UK's biggest parties – Labour, the Conservatives, the Scottish National Party, the Liberal Democrats, UK Independence Party and the Greens – carried out simultaneously, thereby providing invaluable new insights into members' social characteristics, attitudes, activities and campaigning, reasons for joining and leaving, and views on how their parties should be run and who should represent them. In short, at a time of great pressure on, and change across parties, this book helps us discover not only what members want out of their parties but also what parties want out of their members.

This text is essential reading for those interested in political parties, party membership, elections and campaigning, representation, and political participation, be they scholars and students of British and comparative politics, or politicians, journalists and party members – in short, anyone who cares about the future of representative democracy.

Tim Bale is Professor of Politics at Queen Mary University of London, UK.

Paul Webb is Professor of Politics at the University of Sussex, UK.

Monica Poletti is Social Researcher in the UK Civil Service, following a Research Fellowship at Queen Mary University of London, UK.

"When so many say the UK's political system is broken, who are the party members who effectively choose who become our Prime Ministers? In this vital book the authors draw on the latest comprehensive research to dig down to the grassroots where politics is shaped for all of us. It will confirm some prejudices. It will shock as well."

– Adam Boulton, All Out Politics, *SkyNews.*

"Are the current political parties fit for purpose? As both Theresa May and Jeremy Corbyn struggle with the question of whether they are really in charge of their respective parties, both would be wise to turn to *Footsoldiers*. Who joins, why they join and where the balance of power lies are all explored in this thoroughly researched and acutely observed new book."

– Sam Coates, Deputy Political Editor, SkyNews.

"We hear far too much about the generals. *Footsoldiers* tells you everything you wanted to know about British party politics' poor bloody infantry. It busts myth after myth after myth, taking a subject you thought you knew all about and shows why you are completely wrong."

– Philip Cowley, author of The British General Election of 2017.

"It's a brilliant analysis of current trends and the authors' conclusions should be read by anyone who wants to understand why some parties are increasing their memberships while others are on a seemingly never-ending decline."

– Iain Dale, LBC Radio Presenter.

"*Footsoldiers* shines a light on the little platoons of citizens whose voluntary contributions of time, resources and energy, giving up their evenings and weekends to doorstep canvassing and branch meetings, keep our political parties functioning day to day. The authors exploit an impressive mass of data on the memberships of six parties to paint a clear and vivid picture of democracy's volunteer corps - who they are, what motivates them, and how they serve and shape our political parties. Vital reading for anyone interested in the inner workings and health of British party democracy."

– Rob Ford, Manchester University, UK, and co-author of Revolt on the Right.

"This is a book that needs to be read by anyone who is interested in the future of representative democracy in the United Kingdom. At a time when political parties are under siege, Webb, Bale and Poletti offer an unparalleled study of UK party members and supporters across the political spectrum. Why do people join parties? Who are they and what do they do? What motivates them and why do they leave? Answering these important questions through new survey and interview data, this book provides a timely and original analysis of the role of members in modern party organisations. Highlighting the challenges that parties face in recruiting members that reflect the general population and satisfying their demands once they join, the authors show that maintaining a vibrant and engaged base of supporters is no easy task for modern parties."

– Anika Gauja, University of Sydney, Australia.

"Party memberships are the seed beds of political leadership and this is a brilliantly well-timed drill down into who they are, why they join and how they affect our politics. We talk about activists and party members but desperately needed an up to date study on exactly who they are, why they join and with what effects. Here it is, assembled by the best academics in the business. Whether it is Labour grassroots and the Corbyn story, Tory grassroots shaping Brexit or the smaller party memberships surging and shrinking, our politics has rarely been more influenced by the activist base. This book is essential reading for all who want to understand what underpins our political parties and where the memberships might take them."

— *Gary Gibbon, Political Editor, Channel 4 News, UK.*

"If you want to understand British politics, you need to understand party members. And if you want to understand party members, you absolutely need to read this book. Party members have enormous influence on Britain's political parties. They are influential in some of the most important twists and turns in Brexit, in the changes and divisions in our major political parties, in who – ultimately – becomes Prime Minister. *Footsoldiers* is vital reading for understanding British democracy. For the first time we comprehensively see just how different the people who become members of different political parties are from the electorate those parties seek to represent."

— *Jane Green, University of Oxford, UK.*

"A fascinating, timely, and accessibly written book. Using original data from repeated surveys of party members, it tackles head on the crisis facing political parties via a detailed examination of the people who make them tick – their members. Required reading for anyone interested in contemporary politics, and particularly the fraught party politics of the UK."

— *Anand Menon, King's College London, UK.*

"This is a brilliantly insightful study. If you think you already know all about why people join parties, why they get active and what they think of the organisation they've joined, then either you are (a) fooling yourself, or (b) one of the book's authors. For the rest of us interested in how politics really works, it's a must-read."

— *Mark Pack, Editor,* Liberal Democrat Newswire.

"This is the perfect guide to the activist (and not-so-active) party members who are shaping our politics today. The team behind it combine academic rigour and down-to-earth common sense, and are well-known for helping provide clarity on the confusion that mires our politics."

— *George Parker, Political Editor,* Financial Times.

"Bale, Webb and Poletti are the leading authorities on what has been happening to membership of our political parties and who the members are. Which means they're the leading authorities on those who are bossing our confused and anxious MPs. This book is for anyone who wants a deeper understanding of why our politics has become so dysfunctional."

— *Robert Peston, Political Editor, ITV.*

"Want to get inside the head of a political activist? This is your guide. We hear so much about party membership numbers and the store that leaders put by them. But who are these members? What are their social characteristics and why have they joined? How long do they stay? And crucially what influence do they really have on the choices made by those at the top of their chosen political homes? *Footsoldiers* seeks to provide the answers in a lively and accessible way – with enough data, anecdotes and cool hard facts backed up by the most up to date research to satisfy the voracious political reader, the student, the activist or the journalist. In these turbulent political times I am sure it will become a well-thumbed indispensable guide."

– Carolyn Quinn, Host of BBC Radio 4's Westminster Hour.

"At a time of seismic change in British politics this forensically researched and illuminating book is a must-read. Every page shines light on the UK's parties while exploring the historic implications of their epic fragilities and precarious strengths."

– Steve Richards, Writer and Broadcaster.

"*Footsoldiers* is an indispensable guide to the demographics of Labour members and their policy positions, plus their motivations for joining in the first place and how likely they are to rip up their membership cards. Full of compelling data presented in an accessible way, this is a must-read for anyone interested in the Labour Party and where it's going next."

– Sienna Rodgers, Editor, LabourList.

"This timely study is a must-read for anyone who wants to understand the opportunities and challenges of making UK party politics more grassroots oriented. Presenting evidence from surveys of members, supporters and representatives of six UK parties, it illuminates the ideals and aims that inspire today's British citizens to get involved in – and to drop out of – party politics."

– Susan Scarrow, University of Houston, USA, and
author of Beyond Party Members.

"This is a fascinating study of an essential topic, by the leading experts in the field. Dispelling myths about the nature and function of the political parties, and shedding light on the reality of party politics in 21st Century Britain, is a valuable service for anyone hoping to understand what's happening at every level of our politics. Whether you love them or loathe them, the fate of major and insurgent parties is bound up with the future of our country, and this book lifts the lid on how they work."

– Mark Wallace, Executive Editor, ConservativeHome

"Clear-sighted and concise, this invaluable study shines a forensic light on an area of modern politics that gets all too little attention. With party members playing an increasingly assertive role, from deselections of MPs to shaping policy on Brexit and even picking Prime Ministers, a thoroughly researched analysis like this is well overdue."

– Paul Waugh, Political Editor, HuffPost UK.

FOOTSOLDIERS: POLITICAL PARTY MEMBERSHIP IN THE 21ST CENTURY

Tim Bale, Paul Webb and Monica Poletti

Routledge
Taylor & Francis Group

LONDON AND NEW YORK

First published 2020
by Routledge
2 Park Square, Milton Park, Abingdon, Oxon OX14 4RN

and by Routledge
52 Vanderbilt Avenue, New York, NY 10017

Routledge is an imprint of the Taylor & Francis Group, an informa business

British Library Cataloguing-in-Publication Data
A catalogue record for this book is available from the British Library

Library of Congress Cataloging-in-Publication Data
A catalog record for this book has been requested

ISBN: 978-1-138-30245-7 (hbk)
ISBN: 978-1-138-30246-4 (pbk)
ISBN: 978-0-203-73176-5 (ebk)

Typeset in Bembo
by Apex CoVantage, LLC

CONTENTS

FIGURES

TABLES

ACKNOWLEDGEMENTS

This book would not have been possible without the generous support of the Economic and Social Research Council's (ESRC's) research grant ES/M007537/1. In persuading the ESRC to entrust us with its money we were assisted by the invaluable feedback of a number of colleagues, including Elin Allern, Lynn Bennie, Nicole Bolleyer, Rosie Campbell, Philip Cowley, Anika Gauja, Lee Jones, Andrew Loveland, Mike Kenny, Karina Kosiara-Pedersen, Laura Morales, Wolfgang Rüdig, Susan Scarrow, Emilie van Haute and Paul Whiteley. Along the way, many more have contributed constructive and helpful comments and criticisms at conferences and workshops where we have presented drafts of work that has eventually found its way into various published papers and the chapters of this book; the individual names are too many to mention (or, at least, for us to recall) but they were among participants at academic events staged at Sussex, Queen Mary University of London, Exeter, Oxford, Berkeley, Chicago, Brighton, Cardiff, Gothenburg, Brussels, Prague, Glasgow, Aberdeen, Nottingham, Birkbeck University, Brisbane and Royal Holloway, University of London. In addition, we benefitted greatly from engaging with those most directly touched by our research outside the academy, whether they were politicians, party officials, party members, or delegates at party conference fringe events in which we participated. Likewise, the many journalists and media commentators who have been kind enough to take an interest in, and to write and talk about, our findings. A number of think tanks and organizations provided important opportunities to present our findings and ideas, including the Social Market Foundation, the McDougall Trust, the Electoral Reform Society, the Institute for Government, the Mile End Institute, the British Academy, the Palace of Westminster and the House of Commons Library. Full details of these events and many other aspects of the Party Members Project can be found at https://esrcparty membersproject.org We are also grateful to the editors and anonymous reviewers of the academic journals in which some of our work has appeared since we began thinking about and then carrying out this project – the *British Journal of Politics and International Relations*, *Electoral Studies*, *International Political Science Review*, *Party Politics*, *Politics*, *Political Insight*, *Political Studies*, and *West European Politics*. And we owe a huge debt of gratitude to Anthony Wells, Chris Curtis and Matthew Smith at YouGov, as well as Joe Twyman, now at DeltaPoll.

As ever, it is important not to overlook the support of those who are closest to us in our daily lives – our families and loved ones. They have put up with numerous absences while we have been engaged on the research and dissemination activities that have contributed to the making of this book. For that and many other more important things besides, we shall always be grateful.

TPB, PW, MP
Summer 2019

1

INTRODUCTION

Few, if any, of the world's democracies function without political parties. Parties package up myriad ideas and interests into more or less digestible manifestos and programmes, enabling us as citizens to cut through what would otherwise be bewildering complexity and to hold our governments to account. Parties also help recruit and train the politicians whom we allow to run the country on our behalf.

Yet parties are in trouble almost everywhere. In the UK, as in most other European countries, they are less and less trusted to do the right thing.[1] They find it harder and harder to command the loyalty of voters, many of whom tell pollsters that there's no real difference between politicians and that they are only in it forthemselves. And although some parties have recently managed (temporarily at least) to buck what is a long-term, European-wide, downward trend, others struggle both to attract and to hold on to members.

Unless we are willing to see parties become essentially elitist, 'hollowed-out' institutions, these developments should give us serious cause for concern. In a truly healthy representative democracy, parties cannot simply be brands run by elites for their own and for our collective convenience. They do not need to be, or to behave like, social movements – even if enthusiasts for a more participatory form of democracy in the Labour Party, for instance, have taken to arguing that they should.[2] But they do need to be rooted in, rather than disconnected from, society. Their programmes need to reflect meaningful differences between competing visions, be they idealistic or pragmatic, or both. And their leaders and candidates are best chosen by competitive election rather than appointment or inheritance.

Party members cannot, of course, guarantee that all this occurs all by themselves. But they can certainly help – both by demanding that their party's policies bear at least some relation to its professed ideals and by demanding at least some say on who represents it. They are also important because they can make the difference between their party winning or losing an election – perhaps by picking the right or the wrong leader, perhaps by insisting that leader adopt popular or unpopular measures or perhaps simply by working hard at election time in close-fought contests. In short, although leadership matters, so does membership, and, to be successful, parties need to achieve the right balance between the two.

In spite of all this, we do not know as much as we might do about party members in the twenty-first-century UK. True, we ourselves helped carry out surveys of the Conservative Party's membership in 2009 and 2013.[3] However, the last fully comprehensive survey of Labour members was carried out back in 1997, and the last such survey of Liberal Democrat members was completed in 1999. Just as important, there has never been a study of the members of several parties carried out concurrently, thereby enabling us to ask them all exactly the same questions about who they are, what they think, and what they do for their parties, at exactly the same time. Nor has there ever been any systematic study of those who are strong supporters of parties but don't actually join them or, indeed, of those who do join but then leave – people who, given the difficulties some parties seem to have in retaining as well as recruiting members, are surely worth looking at, too.

Of course, it is one thing to want to conduct this sort of survey research and quite another to work out the best way of doing it – especially at a time when many parties are understandably reticent about allowing researchers access to their membership lists, not just because of concerns about the embarrassment that some of the findings might cause them but also worries about data protection. Fortunately, that reticence is no longer the obstacle it once was, as long, that is, as one is able to navigate around it – something we were able to do thanks to a grant from the UK's Economic and Social Research Council.[4] That is because, nowadays, internet panels of the kind painstakingly assembled and maintained by the commercial opinion research company YouGov make it possible to independently obtain large samples of members of the six parties we focus on in this book – Labour, the Conservatives, the Scottish National Party (SNP), the Liberal Democrats, the Green Party of England and Wales, and the UK Independence Party (UKIP).[5]

In the early summer of 2015, then, we surveyed members of all those parties, along with people who felt a strong affinity with each of the parties but were not currently members of them, as well as members of Labour-affiliated trade unions. We surveyed party members again in the early summer of 2017, some (but not all) of whom we had spoken to two years previously. We also surveyed people who had been but were no longer members of political parties. In between, in the spring of 2016, we surveyed people who had joined the Labour Party after the 2015 general election, many of them as part of the so-called Corbyn surge, which, for obvious reasons, we were keen to explore and explain. Finally, just before Christmas in 2018, we surveyed members of Britain's two main parties, Labour and the Conservatives, in order to explore their views on the central – and possibly realigning – issue of our age, Brexit.

Approaching members in this way gave us complete freedom to ask them whatever questions we wanted to ask – and without the nagging fear that one or other of the parties would change their mind and veto the project at the last moment.

The panel constructed by YouGov, which is also used by the British Election Survey, allowed us to directly compare actual and potential joiners, members and voters, as well as those members who stick with their party and those who leave. And, whereas previous surveys of party members were carried out years apart, we were able to conduct a simultaneous survey of members from several parties, allowing us to compare and contrast them to an extent that has never before proved possible. Moreover, because we, as opposed to the parties themselves, had control of the timing of the surveys, we were able to conduct them very shortly after not just one but two general elections – when members' memories of what they did (or perhaps did not do) during the campaign were fresh.

'Fresh', of course, does not necessarily mean completely accurate or honest. Indeed, party members are surely no less prone to the 'social desirability bias' that leads all sorts of survey respondents to give answers that reflect well on them rather than tell the absolute truth – even when their anonymity is guaranteed and they are inputting those answers into a machine rather talking face-to-face to a human being. Moreover, this is far from being the only limitation faced by survey research. Another is that respondents can only do their best when selecting from a predetermined set of answers to a host of questions which may never have occurred to them and may seem pointless, even stupid, particularly towards the end of a long questionnaire. Obviously, by building on previous surveys that seemed to have worked reasonably well, by pre-testing questions, by consulting with other professionals, and by providing respondents with an opportunity to write in more expansive, free-form responses, one can attempt to minimize those problems.[6] But one can never eliminate them altogether – any more than one can be sure that one's carefully crafted questions are actually able to measure what they're intended to measure. More frustrating still, however, are the questions that – goodness only knows why – we didn't think of asking at the time but now seem so painfully obvious, especially when compared with questions that once seemed important but which time and chance have rendered pretty much irrelevant.

Even leaving these caveats and qualifications aside, a study of party members based solely on surveying them would still lack something crucial. Surveying them gives us an insight into what one might call the 'supply side' of membership – in other words, into those willing (or, in some cases, no longer willing) to offer parties their money and maybe their time. But what about the 'demand side' – the parties who, we assume, need those resources? How do they understand membership, and what do they want out of their members? Are they changing the way they do things, turning themselves into what one academic has called 'multi-speed membership parties' by creating novel, possibly less demanding (and less expensive) categories of affiliation so as to attract the support of people with varying levels of commitment?[7] These are questions that, because their staffers and elected representatives are much harder to sample and survey, can only really be addressed by more qualitative means – studying and interpreting documents and, where possible, conducting interviews. That, therefore, is precisely what we have done, talking (off the record so as to encourage candour) with staffers, activists and politicians.

Our aim is to produce a book that will appeal both to an academic and a general audience. Scholars around the world who are interested in parties (and in elections and campaigning, representation and participation) will, we hope, gain valuable new insights into members' social characteristics, their attitudes, activities, and campaigning; their reasons for joining and leaving; and their views on how their parties should be run and who should represent them – as well as learning something about how their parties are coping with the challenges of recruitment and retention in an era in which loyalty and commitment can no longer be taken for granted. But by making a determined effort to ensure the book is an accessible, even enjoyable read – one reason why we have confined any advanced statistical material to its appendix and to journal articles cited in its endnotes – we hope it will also be read by people outside the so-called ivory tower, not least by party members themselves. Ideally, it will serve as a go-to resource on membership and one based on hard data rather than on hearsay and half-truths about parties, including, most obviously, the common wisdom that they are all the same these days.

After Chapter 2 takes a look at what the existing research tells us about membership and the number of people who belong to parties, we begin in earnest, in Chapters 3 and 4, by exploring the demographic and attitudinal profiles of party members. Just how unusual – socio-economically, educationally, and ideologically – are they? Are they really so unrepresentative? How much does all this vary between parties? And how much do the members of the six parties constitute different, relatively distinct and cohesive 'tribes'?

In Chapter 5, we look at why people join parties – something that's particularly fascinating in an era where the widespread assumption that fewer and fewer people were bound to want to do so seems questionable, if not downright mistaken. We ask what distinguishes those who do join from those who don't? We also take a look at why so many British parties, including those which have recently experienced defeat, enjoyed a surge in members recently – and is this likely to be a permanent or temporary phenomenon? Chapter 6 looks at precisely what (if anything) members actually do for their party – both between and during general elections. Does activism differ much according to which party's members we're looking at? And what might explain it in the first place?

Chapter 7 looks at what members think about how their party is – and should be – run and organized. What rights and obligations, and how much influence, do the members of different parties have? What are their attitudes towards their leaders and party headquarters? Do they feel that their party is sufficiently democratic? Do they feel listened to, valued and respected? What do they think of intra-party processes and reforms, particularly with regard to policy-making, leadership and parliamentary candidate selection (and deselection)?

Until very recently, the long-term trend in membership was clearly one of decline rather than growth. Even now 'churn'/turnover may be more common than many imagine. And, of course, recent surges enjoyed by several British parties may ultimately prove temporary. Chapter 8 addresses the factors that lead people to leave parties. What are the most common reasons given for quitting? How do they relate to their reasons for joining? How do those who leave differ attitudinally and demographically (and in terms of activism and feelings about intra-party processes) from those who stay? Can we predict who'll stay and who'll go?

Chapter 9 switches gear by drawing on off-the-record interviews to look at the demand rather than the supply side. Why do parties still seem keen to recruit and sustain mass memberships? How do party professionals and elected representatives regard their rank and file? How important do they think they are, for example, in terms of campaigning? What costs and benefits do they bring? How much influence do they think members have (and should have)? And what are parties today doing in order to retain members, recruit new, younger and less traditional members, and manage their demands and activities?

In Chapter 10 we recap our major findings and arguments, and we look ahead, perhaps paradoxically, by recalling some perennial tensions between party members and their leaders.

We begin, however, by summarizing in Chapter 2, what we think we already know about party members and party membership in the light of decades' worth of research on them, both in the UK and elsewhere.

Notes

1 See Dommett, Kate and Temple, Luke (2019) *What People Want to See in Parties Today* (Sheffield: University of Sheffield), available online at www.katedommett.com/uploads/1/1/2/7/112786573/final_-_what_people_want_from_parties_today.pdf.

2 See Fielding, Steven (2018) 'Labour: Why Jeremy Corbyn still struggles to turn his dream of a social movement into reality', *The Conversation*, 23 September, available online at https://theconversation.com/labour-why-jeremy-corbyn-still-struggles-to-turn-his-dream-of-a-social-movement-into-reality-103315. Of course, many party members, for more or less instrumental reasons, are already involved in other, supposedly non-partisan, social movements – in addition to rather than instead of their involvement in their party: see Giugni, Marco and Grasso, Maria (forthcoming) 'Party membership and social movement activism: A macro-micro analysis', *Party Politics* and Wauters, Bram (2018) 'Which party members participate in direct political action? A cross-national analysis', *International Political Science Review*, 39 (2), pp. 225–241.

3 Childs, Sarah and Webb, Paul (2012) *Sex, Gender and the Conservative Party: From Iron Lady to Kitten Heels* (Basingstoke: Palgrave) and Bale, Tim and Webb, Paul (2013) 'Members only: Views of the Conservative Party's rank-and-file', *Political Insight*, 4, pp. 4–8.

4 This book, like all our work on party members since 2015, has been made possible by the support of the Economic and Social Research Council's grant ES/M007537/1. We gratefully acknowledge the support of the ESRC.

5 These are the six largest mainland British parties in terms of vote share, except for Plaid Cymru, which gained more voters than the Green Party of England and Wales in 2015 and 2017. Unfortunately, there are not enough Plaid Cymru members in the YouGov panel of respondents to generate a representative sample, so we were unable to include this party in our analysis. YouGov recruited the survey respondents from a panel of around 300,000 volunteers who are offered a small reward for completing a survey. Upon joining the YouGov panel, volunteers complete a survey asking a broad range of demographic questions which are subsequently used to recruit respondents matching desired demographic quotas for surveys. Potential respondents for the party member survey were identified from questions asking respondents if they were members of any of a list of large membership organizations, including the political parties. Results reported are not weighted in any way since there

are no known official population parameters for the various party memberships. However, previous YouGov party membership surveys using unweighted data have generated predictions for party leadership contests that came very close to (that is within 1 per cent of) the final official outcome, which gives us confidence in the quality of the data. Moreover, our respondents look very like the members of the SNP and UKIP who responded to recent surveys conducted with the cooperation of those parties. See Bennie, Lynn, Mitchell, James and Johns, Rob (2017) 'New members, new parties? Causes and consequences of surging party membership following the Scottish Independence Survey', Paper presented at the Annual Conference of the Political Studies Association, Glasgow; and Clarke, Harold, Goodwin, Matthew and Whiteley, Paul (2017) *Brexit: Why Britain Voted to Leave the European Union* (Cambridge: Cambridge University Press).

6 Particular thanks here should go to Anthony Wells and to Chris Curtis from YouGov for their consistently excellent, timely and helpful advice.

7 See Scarrow, Susan E. (2015) *Beyond Party Members: Changing Approaches to Political Mobilization* (Oxford: Oxford University Press).

2
PARTY MEMBERS

What we think we already know

Just as it is difficult to imagine representative democracy without political parties, it is difficult, if not necessarily impossible, to imagine political parties without members.[1] Party members are no less, then, than the footsoldiers and the lifeblood of democracy. Without their campaigning, parties would find it difficult – and certainly a lot more costly – to fight elections. Members also help connect parties to society, lend them a degree of legitimacy, anchor them ideologically and provide them with both funds and a pool of candidates. Moreover, they play a big part in choosing those candidates, as well as their parties' leaders. So what do we think we know about them already?

Quite a lot, it turns out – thanks in no small part to academics throughout Europe who have been carrying out research on members, often through surveys, since the early 1990s.[2] As a result of their work, we know a fair bit about the social and demographic composition of party membership in this country and elsewhere. We also believe we know something about why people join parties and what they do for them once they've joined. Not only that, but we also reckon we know quite a bit by now about what they think – in terms of ideology, in terms of policy and in terms of their views on how their party should be run. And we know the extent of the say afforded to those members – something that varies considerably both over time and between parties.

One thing we know with some degree of accuracy is just how many people belong to political parties, at least in the UK. That is because most (though not all) parties nowadays are willing and able to produce reasonably accurate figures, with many of them voluntarily reporting them to the Electoral Commission along with the financial accounts they are obliged to file every year. It is these figures that are used in the excellent updates put together as briefing notes by researchers at the House of Commons Library. Parties which find that their membership appears to be growing also like to share the good news with the media, providing observers with the chance to keep a running, more 'real-time' tally. Should that growth go into reverse, however, parties become rather more reticent.

This chapter, then, aims to give readers an idea of the state of play when it comes to numbers and of 'the state of the art' when it comes to academic research – not just on party members themselves but also on how parties are trying to attract and hold onto them.

Numbers

Not so long ago, the UK fit comfortably into the dominant narrative on political party membership in Europe (see Figure 2.1) which holds – perhaps a little too pessimistically given the sometimes surprising differences between parties and fluctuations over time – that it is declining pretty much everywhere, even if that decline

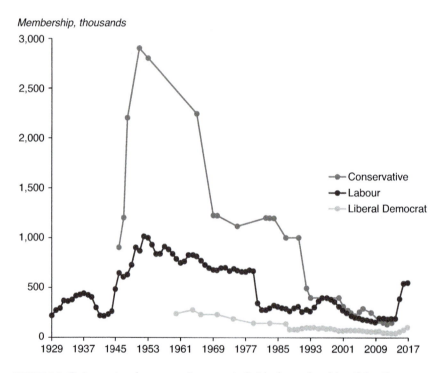

FIGURE 2.1 Going, going, but not quite gone: individual membership of the Conservative, Labour and Liberal/Liberal Democrat* parties, 1929–2017

Source: Parliamentary Library/Electoral Commission (https://researchbriefings.parliament.uk/Research Briefing/Summary/SN05125)

Contains Parliamentary information licensed under the Open Parliament Licence v3.0

Note: Labour Party membership figures include party members and affiliated supporters but exclude registered supporters.

* Including predecessor parties.

may be beginning at last to bottom out.[3] Until very recently (and aside from the odd blip like the 'Blair bounce' experienced by Labour in the mid-1990s) party membership in the UK seemed to be falling inexorably from the post-war highs of the 1950s – a fall that is routinely put down to a combination of factors, some on the demand side (i.e., how enthusiastic parties are about recruiting members) and some on the supply side (i.e., how enthusiastic people are about joining them).[4]

For instance, on the demand side, bigger, older parties might take their eye off the ball once they establish themselves and realize they can secure funding and win elections without mass memberships. Moving into government, too, might encourage them to adopt less distinct policy platforms with less appeal to those to whom ideological differences are important. Newer, smaller parties might be able to cater for them, of course, and might still be interested in recruiting as many people as possible to their cause: after all, a growing membership hints at, and may even facilitate, burgeoning popularity and badly needed legitimacy. On the other hand, less established parties may conclude (like some of their more established rivals) that members – especially of the formal, 'card-carrying' type who demand a say in party policy and candidate selection but don't really contribute much money compared to what corporate donations or state funding could bring in – are a drag and a distraction, the loss of which they are fairly relaxed about, at least in private.

All this can be overstated, of course. For one thing, although comparative research suggests that parties can lose members and yet continue to appeal to a much larger pool of supporters (at least some of whom can be persuaded to muck in at election time), they don't ever seem to have given up on trying to stem and even reverse the outflow of traditional paid-up members.[5] For another, even if there were a discernible link between, say, the availability of state funding and falling membership (there isn't), then the relative lack of the former in the UK would hardly explain the latter.[6] And anyway, as we shall go on to point out later, local ground campaigns do seem to make a difference to election outcomes – something that parties themselves are well aware of.

Meanwhile, when we think about the supply side (i.e., the extent to which people might want to volunteer their time), there have been massive economic, social and cultural changes which have seen a decline in the extent to which people identify both with particular parties (a development known as 'partisan dealignment') and a decline of some of the institutions and habits that reinforced such identification, such as trade unions and regular church attendance.[7] Those same changes rapidly began to offer people a hitherto undreamt-of array of individual and collective leisure opportunities against which the activities associated with party membership rather paled in comparison. They also began to provide anyone with an interest in politics with alternative forms of expression, ranging from single-issue pressure groups through to petitions, all of which expanded still further on the back of the digital and social media revolution that has up-ended so much of what used to be taken for granted. Meanwhile, at least in most liberal democracies, the fashion for increased transparency has meant there is no longer much point in formally enrolling in a party in order, for instance, to improve one's chances of securing a job, a government contract, or just the odd favour. And trust in politicians and parties has fallen sharply over time, making it less likely, perhaps, that people will want to join organizations dedicated to their promotion and election – especially if they no longer perceive them to be sufficiently different from each other.[8]

For all these reasons, and maybe others, party membership in Britain seemed set on an inexorable slide from the heights it reached in the early 1950s. But, as the twentieth century turned into the twenty-first, growing interest in and support for smaller, more radical parties such as the Greens and the right-wing populist UKIP began to see those parties recruit more members, albeit from a relatively low base (see Figure 2.2).[9] Then, in Scotland, the independence referendum held in late 2014 (notwithstanding the defeat of those wanting to break away from Britain) helped provide a massive boost to the membership of the SNP – part of a surge in support that saw it take an amazing 56 of the 59 Scottish seats in the House of Commons at the 2015 general election. The SNP reported to the Electoral Commission that it had 25,245 members at the end of 2013, the year before the referendum. In its next set of accounts, it reported that '[b]y 31 December 2014 [i.e., some three months after the independence referendum], the party had 93,045 members compared with 25,642 on 18 September [the day of the referendum itself]. And by June 2015, it had risen to over 110,000'. Perhaps inevitably, such incredible momentum could not be sustained, but by the end of 2016, membership had nevertheless increased to 118,959. At the end of 2018 it stood at 125,500 but is thought to have dipped a little since.

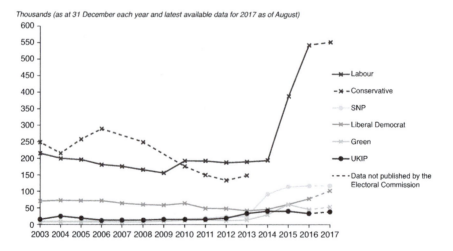

Thousands (as at 31 December each year and latest available data for 2017 as of August)

FIGURE 2.2 Uptick? Party membership in Great Britain, 2002–2017

Source: Parliamentary Library/Electoral Commission (https://researchbriefings.parliament.uk/Research Briefing/Summary/SN05125)

Contains Parliamentary information licensed under the Open Parliament Licence v3.0

Note: Labour Party membership figures for 2015 and 2016 include party members and affiliated supporters but exclude registered supporters.

Most of the SNP's electoral gains in 2015 were at the expense of a Labour Party which, in the UK as a whole, came nowhere near as close to regaining office as opinion polls had suggested it might. Instead, Labour, under Ed Miliband, finished a fairly distant second to David Cameron's Conservative Party, whose newly minted overall majority of 12 parliamentary seats allowed it to move on from five years of uneasy coalition with the centrist Liberal Democrats and govern on its own for the first time in nearly 20 years – to the unbridled joy of its members, who, while they regarded coalition as a price worth paying for power, made no secret of their desire to escape its constraints.[10]

Labour's membership, even if it hadn't exactly ballooned under Miliband, had remained relatively healthy during its five years in opposition between 2010 and 2015: the party reported to the Electoral Commission that at the end of December 2014, it had 193,754 individual members, up slightly from the 189,531 it had reported the previous year, although virtually the same as at the end of 2010 following a significant surge in membership after the party lost office that year. But the crushing disappointment the party experienced at the 2015 general election prompted many at the grassroots to wonder whether it was time for a more radical departure from the Blair/Brown 'New Labour' years than Miliband had been able (or, indeed, willing) to provide.[11] Rather surprisingly, they got what they wanted when a number of centrist Labour members of Parliament (MPs), in order to ensure a broad-based contest, agreed to nominate veteran left-wing rebel, Jeremy Corbyn, never dreaming for a moment he might actually go on to win. Yet win he did (and convincingly so) after thousands of people, some of them inspired by the grassroots campaign that went on to become Momentum, joined the party, either as full members or '£3 supporters', in order to back him, boosting membership from 201,000 on the eve of the 2015 general election to 293,000 just before Corbyn was elected leader.[12] And once he was installed, even more people flocked to his standard so that by the end of the year, Labour was reporting to the Electoral Commission that it had an astounding 388,262 members. This continued to rise, reaching a peak, in the latter months of 2017, of over 568,000. It has, some suggest, fallen since then to below (some Corbyn sceptics say well below) half a million, although even the publicly available figures are contested.[13]

But Labour, it turned out, was not the only party that experienced a post-2015 growth in membership. For the Liberal Democrats, five years of coalition with the Conservatives between 2010 and 2015 had proved disastrous in terms of votes: they had gone into government with 23 per cent of the vote and 57 MPs; they left it with just 7.9 per cent and 8 MPs. Coalition had done them few favours when it came to membership either, although the decline at the grassroots was by no means as calamitous as it was at Westminster. That said, however, Liberal Democrat membership, according to the party's accounts submitted to the Electoral Commission, had dropped from 65,038 at the end of 2010 to 45,771 by the end of 2014. What happened, then, however, is interesting. Rather than leaving a sinking ship when they saw how badly the party had fared at the general election, a significant number of Liberal Democrat sympathizers decided they had to jump on board in order to steady it.[14] As a result, membership began to increase, and was subsequently boosted even further by the decision of the British people in the referendum held in June 2016 to leave the EU – a decision which left the Liberal Democrats (historically the most 'Europhile' force in parliament) the only UK-wide party appealing directly to 'remainers' who wished somehow to stop Brexit. By May 2017, they were boasting that their membership had risen to 102,000 – their highest ever total and one achieved in part by some 50,000 new members having joined since the EU referendum.[15] The question, given the uncertainties surrounding Brexit and the party's failure to rise significantly in the opinion polls, is whether they will stick around. At the beginning of 2018, the party had 103,000 members.[16] By the spring of 2019 it was apparently still hovering around the 100,000 mark.

Other parties, however, were beginning to show that what goes up must (or at least can) come down. The Conservatives may have broken free of their coalition partners after winning the 2015 election outright but, notwithstanding research that suggests that election success often has a positive effect on membership, there was no evidence that it did them any good in that respect.[17] In September 2014, the party claimed it had almost 150,000 members, apparently up from the 134,000 it reported in December 2013 (although, given that 253,689 were eligible to vote in the 2005 leadership contest won by Cameron, this supposed increase was perhaps less impressive than it sounded and should be qualified, perhaps, by recalling that, by the time of the 2015 election, nearly 300 local associations had fewer than 100 members, with only about 50 boasting more than 500).[18] However, the party's reluctance to release figures has made it difficult to tell how things have gone in the meantime; it is hard, however, to believe that any party would refrain from shouting its membership figures from the rooftops if the trend were up rather than down. Sadly, any hopes that the leadership contest triggered by David Cameron's post-EU referendum resignation in June 2016 might provide some official data were swiftly dashed: following the withdrawal of all other candidates, his successor, Theresa May, was installed as leader without the Tory grassroots being asked to vote. Hardly surprising, given all this, then, that rumours in the new year, 2018, that Tory membership had fallen below 100,000 and possibly as low as 70,000 were taken seriously by journalists even though that fall was not consistent with suggestions (confirmed by numerous interviews we did, incidentally) that the party had enjoyed a surge of tens of thousands of new members in the aftermath of the EU referendum in June 2016.[19] Indeed, this was one reason why Brandon Lewis, appointed by Theresa May as the party's new chairman in January 2018, decided to take a shot at compiling and releasing a more accurate figure two months later. The Conservative Party, it was reported in mid-March 2018, actually had 124,000 members – a figure that rose to 160,000 by June 2019, partly in anticipation of the leadership contest which finally began that month.[20]

The accuracy, and certainly the comparability, of that figure is open to question, however – not because of any chicanery on Mr Lewis's part but because for an organization that is normally Britain's most comfortably well-off political party, the Tories are hardly a model of efficiency. And this is especially the case when it comes to servicing and even recording its membership. Partly because of a long history of tension and turf wars between local constituency associations and Conservative Campaign Headquarters (CCHQ; and its predecessor, Central Office), the Conservative Party has lacked the kind of robust, exhaustive and exclusive centralized system which allows its rivals (most obviously, perhaps, the Liberal Democrats) to file accurate and up-to-date membership totals with the Electoral Commission along with their annual accounts – something the Tories singularly fail to do year after year. Ever since the party's then leader, William Hague, announced his so-called *Fresh Future* reforms in the late 1990s, the Conservatives have aspired to introduce a truly national membership system. But it is an aspiration that, until now perhaps, and despite various initiatives down the years, has never been fully realized. Accordingly, it has not been altogether clear exactly where (centrally, locally or both) the details of those who join (or, indeed, those who subsequently leave) the Tory Party are held. As a result, there may still be both missing and duplicated data in the figure released, despite CCHQ's best efforts. Nor is it likely that its latest exercise was conducted using precisely the same methods that were used three or four years previously, meaning that any attempt to identify a trend is fraught with danger.

The party's inability to accurately count or even contact all its members, however, could not, in the end, be allowed to prevent it holding a leadership contest involving its members, thereby forcing it to produce an apparently definitive figure.[21] More important, the very anticipation of that leadership contest precipitated an influx of new members, thereby ensuring that the party could claim, at last, that it was growing rather than shrinking or at best standing still.[22] That influx was in many ways wholly predictable: Labour's experience in 2015 suggested that leadership contests can make excellent recruiting sergeants, and this, after all, was a contest that everyone knew was bound to happen sooner or later, encouraging anyone who wanted to take part to join so as to ensure that, by being a member for three months by the time the ballot closed, they would be entitled to vote in it.

Moving on from, and to the right of, the Conservative Party, Theresa May's insistence as UK prime minister that not only would the country be leaving the EU but that it would also be leaving the single market and the customs union seems to have done for UKIP – along, that is, with its evident (and, at times, excruciatingly embarrassing) failure to find a leader capable of replacing the 'bad boy of Brexit' and now leader of the Brexit Party, Nigel Farage. Admittedly, the early general election that Mrs May called in the summer of 2017 turned out badly for the Conservatives, who lost their overall majority and so, as a minority government, had to turn for support to the Democratic Unionist Party of Northern Ireland. But it was possibly even more disastrous for UKIP, which went from winning 3.88 million votes (or 12.6 per cent of the vote share) in 2015 to winning just 0.59 million votes (1.8 per cent). And it wasn't just voters UKIP was losing, but members, too: at the end of 2014, the party had reported to the Electoral Commission that it 'had started the year with 32,447 members and ended it with 42,163, an increase of 30% after the impressive increase the year before [i.e., December 2012–December 2013] of 60%', but at the end of September 2017, when Henry Bolton became (it turned out only briefly) the party's third leader since Farage had stepped down in 2015, some 33,000 members were apparently balloted, but only 13,000 took part. Its return to the Electoral Commission put its membership at 24,000 – enough it seems, after the party launched a financial appeal in early 2018, to maintain it, just about, as a going concern. In December 2018, its interim leader, Gerard Batten, was boasting that, after a further fall, it had rebounded under his leadership to nearer 30,000 by the spring of 2019, although many of those who had by then abandoned the party (and then perhaps joined the Brexit Party) were claiming that those who'd replaced them were far-right followers of Stephen Yaxley-Lennon, aka Tommy Robinson, of whom Batten was a clearly a big fan.[23]

At the other end of the ideological spectrum, the Greens have also suffered recently. They too experienced a decline in support at the 2017 general election, going from 3.6 per cent of the vote in 2015 to a meagre 1.6 per cent, although they did manage to hold on to their one parliamentary seat in Brighton Pavilion. This setback was widely put down to a fair proportion of the party's erstwhile support-ers, many of whom were as much (if not more) left-wingers as they were ecologists, switching to Labour in the wake of it electing Jeremy Corbyn as its leader in 2015 and then re-electing him (when he was precipitately challenged by panicked Labour MPs) in 2016. As with UKIP, a loss of electoral support was accompanied by a loss of membership. The party had reported a membership of 30,900 to the Electoral Commission as of 31 December 2014 (a very impressive increase on the previous year's total of 13,809), and at the end of 2015, this had risen as high as 63,219.[24] But by the end of 2016 (by which time Corbyn had been Labour leader for well over a year), it had fallen back to 45,643. In the spring of 2019, it stood at 36,379 but this represented an increase of nearly 5 per cent on the figure six months previously, suggesting any decline had, at the very least, levelled off.[25]

In sum, then, the Conservatives are by some distance the larger of the two main parties in terms of parliamentary seats at Westminster, but Labour, primarily because of the huge surge it has enjoyed since 2015, is (by an even greater distance) the big-ger of the two in terms of ordinary members. Indeed, so low did the Conservative Party membership shrink that it may have come close to dropping below that of Britain's traditional 'third party,' the Liberal Democrats, and that of the country's actual third party (in terms of seats at Westminster anyway), the SNP, both of which have grown markedly in the last three to four years. The picture for the coun-try's more radical alternatives, the Greens and UKIP – parties which at times have enjoyed considerable voter support but find it almost impossible to win parliamen-tary seats because of the UK's first-past-the-post electoral system – is more mixed. After enjoying growth before the 2015 election, both have struggled, although the Greens now seemed to have staged a recovery.

Motives

So we have a pretty good idea about how many people belong to political parties, both in the UK and elsewhere. But what do we think we know about why they join in the first place? Quite a lot, it turns out, not least because this is just about the most commonly asked research question among academics studying party members. This is especially the case among those using survey methods to do it, most of whom broadly agree with what has become known as 'the General Incentives Model'.[26] The consensus is that, in most cases, members sign up not because they think doing so will make them personally better off or secure them a career in politics but because they believe that it will help promote the principles and policies advocated by their party and, of course, counter those advocated by its political opponents.[27] There may be other factors (or, to use the language political scientists have borrowed from economists, incentives) involved, such as the opportunities offered by membership to meet like-minded people and get involved in meetings and other tasks which (believe it or not!) some people simply enjoy for their own sake. But, for the most part, the incentives that seem to matter – in the sense of making membership worthwhile despite the costs (in terms of time and money) and despite the fact that the benefits of that party winning elections and governing aren't only enjoyed by its members – are ideological and collective rather than instrumental and individual.[28]

The qualifiers 'for the most part' and 'seem to' are important, however. Obviously, motives vary – some, to borrow the terms employed by some fairly recent comparative research into young members, may well be *moral-minded* (driven by ideology and the desire to make the world a better place), some more *social-minded* (driven by wanting to meet up with like-minded people) and others more *professional-minded* (those hoping for a career in politics). Moreover, as the same study noted 'behind each new membership, there is a unique alchemy of family and social history, intellectual predisposition and interaction with the events and social realities that shape the politics of [particular] countries'.[29] Contingency, and 'catalytic moments' can also play a part: a particular issue flaring up or a particular candidate standing for and winning the leadership, may persuade some people to join who might otherwise not have bothered.[30] And, of course, levels of loyalty and commitment vary: most members agree with their party most of the time but, especially in the larger so-called *catch-all* parties, not all of them do – and, for some, the differences they have with their party can lead them not just to think about joining another party but to vote for it, too.[31]

Furthermore, all the preceding is based on what party members themselves say motivated them to join, which is problematic in two ways: first, joining was a decision they may have made years, even decades, previously; second, some answers (in this case, claiming to have joined on a point of principle rather than for personal gain or advancement) are doubtless more socially acceptable than others – a perennial problem in survey research, even when that research is conducted over the anonymity of the web rather than face-to-face with an interviewer holding a clipboard. True, the gap between the proportion of members claiming nobler over baser motives is so big that one would have to posit a truly staggering level of dishonesty or self-delusion in order to suppose that, in reality, self-interest trumps idealism. Nevertheless, the caveat is worth mentioning not least because, as one recent study of party members (albeit not British party members) found, in some ways rather amusingly, they are much more cynical about the reasons why others join than they are about their own![32]

Other caveats are also worth noting. For instance, it may well be the case that, just as living in a particular place makes people more or less likely to vote for a particular party, it could be that the same goes for joining it – in other words, people who otherwise might not have bothered may do so if they come from somewhere where the party they join boasts a particularly strong legacy and tradition.[33] Even more important, and something that has preoccupied political scientists interested in participation more generally, is the fact that people are much more likely to join a party (just as they are more likely, for instance, to vote or to get involved in a pressure group or almost any other form of political activity) if they share the following characteristics: if they are male; if they are members of the ethnic majority; if they are better educated, better off and older than most of their compatriots; and if they are interested in politics and relatively confident that they can make a difference (i.e., they have a sense of 'political efficacy') – all of which brings us neatly to what we think we know about both the social and the ideological characteristics of members.

What do party members look like?

As is the case when it comes to reasons for joining, there is something of a consensus among researchers when it comes to the socio-demographic composition of party membership, whether we're talking about the UK or other European countries.[34] Members are clearly odd – not in the sense of being bizarre people (although as one study of young activists notes they are often made to feel that way by friends and acquaintances) but in the sense of being involved in something that most 'normal' people wouldn't dream of doing.[35] Obviously, in reality, there is no such thing as a 'typical' or 'average' member: after all, there is (and probably always has been) huge variation not just between but also within parties.[36] On the other hand, membership as a whole is clearly skewed one way rather than another. Members, especially if they belong to centre-right parties, tend to be men. They tend to be white. They tend to be middle class. They tend to have been through further and higher education.[37] And they tend to be middle-aged. However, apart from some evidence that the age gap between people who do and don't join parties may be widening, there is little evidence, at least from cross-national comparative studies, that members are somehow becoming even less like non-members as time goes on.[38] Nor, it seems, are they becoming less and less socially representative of their parties' supporters in the wider electorate.[39]

If that comes as a surprise, so (because it runs contrary to so much common wisdom) will the following: people who belong to a party may be a little more ideological than those who simply support it, but they are not wildly so, nor, it seems, are they becoming more so. Admittedly, the average member of a centre-left party will probably be a little more left-wing than someone who normally votes for it, but he or she is unlikely to be the hard-line Stalinist of media imagination – and the same probably goes even for those who belong to smaller left-wing alternatives. Likewise, most members of centre-right parties don't actually make Genghis Kahn look like a bleeding-heart liberal or Margaret Thatcher look like a passionate advocate of state control and union perks. By the same token, members of nationalist parties might be even keener on regaining sovereignty than those who merely vote for them, but they are not necessarily desperate to see all resident foreigners instantly repatriated. And members of Green parties might be more enthusiastic about environmental regulation than the average Green voter but they don't envisage returning the country to some sort of Stone Age existence. Perhaps even more surprisingly, party members (even so-called activists) aren't generally more radical than the parliamentary elites whom they hope to see elected – indeed, if anything, the opposite may well be the case: MPs are often some of the most zealous members of a political party, while a fair few of its most radical rank-and-file members are among those least likely to step forward when volunteers are called for.[40] None of this should allow us to forget, however, one very simple truth that, while it may seem obvious, nevertheless bears repeating since research bears it out – namely, that, notwithstanding an inevitable degree of overlap at the edges, members of different parties tend to have different values and priorities.[41]

Activism

One thing research on all sorts of parties in all sorts of countries also makes clear is that many of their members do little or nothing for their parties beyond joining and, presumably, paying their subscriptions and perhaps donating extra sums of money on an ad hoc basis.[42] Indeed, the latest cross-national research suggests that, although there are variations between countries and parties (with parties on the left evincing slightly higher levels of activism than those on the right), as many as half of all members give up no time at all to help their party.[43] Understanding why the other half (who may consequently wield more influence) do, however, has been one of the main goals of researchers, most of whom turn to the same General Incentives Model that, as we have already noted, they use to explain why people join in the first place.[44]

As with joining, cross-national research also suggests that having certain characteristics or resources makes it more likely that people will campaign for the party they identify with: for instance, men are more likely to do more than women, as are graduates and the middle-aged.[45] Other things, of course, can reduce activism: one study suggests, for instance, that even in Denmark, where child-care provision is much better than it is in the UK, having young children has a negative impact on how much members do for their parties.[46]

Studies also suggest that members may be doing rather less for their parties than used to be the case, although the lack of longitudinal and panel studies makes it difficult to know for sure quite how significant any decline over the long term has been.[47] That also makes it hard to know precisely which of the various explanations of decline – the increased availability of alternative forms of participation combined with falling party identification, say, or greater state regulation ensuring that getting involved is more of a chore than it used to be – is the most convincing.[48] Researchers – rightly or wrongly – are rather more confident about the main reason behind short-term fluctuations in electoral activity, however: losing an election, they argue, can see a party sucked into a 'spiral of demobilization' in which a decline in local activity leads to further losses, whereas winning (and therefore needing to defend seats that have been won) can sometimes work wonders.[49]

If members are becoming less active, should we presume that it's necessarily a problem, at least, for their parties? In all probability, yes. A whole host of studies, most of them conducted in the UK and the US where results in single-member constituencies really matter, have concluded that local campaigning, and, in particular, doorstep canvassing, helps get out parties' voters – although the success of such efforts may partly depend on there not being too big a mismatch between volunteers and voters.[50] Research on how valuable volunteers are to parties as campaigning begins to move online, however, is (understandably) in its infancy. We are not even in a position to say with any certainty whether time spent by members promoting their party online will take time away from their efforts 'in real life' or whether their activity on, say, Twitter or Facebook, will occur in addition to (as opposed to instead of) more traditional activities like canvassing or leafletting. We can say with some confidence, however, that the move toward online campaigning is going to challenge the centralized, command and control model that has generally been the norm offline: parties are going to have to get used to members doing it for themselves – creating memes and messages organically as well as sharing those which are produced by party HQ; by the same token, the ease with which people can get involved in such activity may well blur the distinction between 'fully paid up' or 'card-carrying' members, on one hand, and supporters on the other.[51] Right now, research suggests that the former do more for their parties at election time than the latter, although the work done by the latter should not be sniffed at: and in the future, who knows?[52]

Parties: recruitment, retention and reform

In fact, many researchers would argue that the distinction between these two groups is already blurred, not least because parties, anxious about declining numbers and commitment and keen to retain the legitimacy (and voluntary labour) that a healthy membership brings with it, have begun to encourage looser forms of affiliation for people who may wish to signal their support without going so far as to join as a traditional member and who are prepared to accept fewer rights and privileges (often for a reduced fee or sometimes no fee at all).[53] Indeed, some researchers argue that we have now entered an era of what one has labelled 'multi-speed membership parties' in which different forms of affiliation are increasingly centralized (because people affiliate directly to the central, rather than their local, party), digital (in that they are facilitated by electronic communications technology) and accessible (since they are easy to exercise at low cost). All of this, it is argued, theoretically means we should recognise six different classes of party adherent, any combination of which might be found empirically in a multi-speed party: full members, 'light' members, 'cyber' members, 'financial sustainers', 'followers and friends' and 'party sympathisers'.[54]

These moves are relatively recent compared to another trend, namely the grant-ing of greater rights to members (and sometimes a wider circle of supporters, too) to determine party policy, select candidates and elect the party leader – reforms that have been widely pursued, at least in part, to boost recruitment (and therefore legitimacy and electoral strength) by making members feel they have more of a say in the direction their party takes.[55] This growth of intra-party democracy is controversial in the sense that some researchers suggest that there is both less and more to it than meets the eye: by granting a say to so many individuals, only a few of whom are engaged or knowledgeable enough to exercise that say effectively (if at all), party leaders have cleverly bypassed and marginalized potentially awkward activists; as a result, even if they have lost some control over candidate and leader-ship selection, those at the top still tend to determine the overall direction of the party.[56] This might be a little too sceptical, however: there is a great deal of variation between parties in this respect (not all of it rooted in whether they are right-wing or left-wing), and whatever the results so far, the increased rights afforded members (and, in some cases, supporters) nevertheless have at the very least the potential to cause upsets – the election of Jeremy Corbyn in 2015, following the Labour Party's decision in 2014 to change the way it went about choosing its leader, is an obvious case in point.

Corbyn's election, and what has happened to the composition of the Labour Party's membership as a result of it, prompts an obvious question. Does the intro-duction of additional ways for people to signal support for their favourite party (the so-called dilution of membership or 'membership-lite') and greater opportu-nities for them to influence policy and candidate/leadership selection help parties boost enrolment and maybe even influence the type of individual who enrols? And, relatedly, what about varying the cost of membership? Does charging people less and expecting less of them in terms of a time commitment, for instance, bring in more people? On the other hand, does charging them more and expecting more of them bring in fewer but, relatively speaking, more active members – and if so, are members now less representative of their parties' voters than they used to be, both demographically and ideologically?

The answer (if it can be called an answer) to all these questions, at least when we look at the latest comparative research, is 'maybe but maybe not' – unsurprisingly, perhaps, if one treats declining membership figures not simply as an inevitable symptom of wider socio-economic and cultural changes but also as the product of a myriad of incentive-based choices by thousands, even hundreds of thousands of individuals.[57]

If we take the last question (the extent to which parties have become less repre-sentative) first, then, as we have already noted, it is clear that parties' memberships are, in general, older, better-off, and better-educated than voters, although different parties tend to have different demographics. For instance, although things can vary considerably both between and within countries, left-of-centre parties (including Green parties) tend to find it easier to attract female members than their right-wing counterparts, while older, long-established parties tend to have older members than their newer rivals do. However, it also appears to be the case that, contrary to conventional wisdom perhaps, this overrepresentation of certain groups and under-representation of others has not become more acute as party membership overall has declined over the decades and may actually have improved when it comes to gender – possibly, at least in part, because there seems to be a link between the intro-duction (and the success) of measures to increase the number of female candidates and legislators and the number of women joining (and, indeed, getting active in) political parties.[58] Interestingly, the same can be said when we move from demog-raphy to ideology: although parties' members do tend to be more radical than their voters, this doesn't appear to be any more the case now than it ever was.[59]

But even if parties don't have to worry too much on this score, they still need to think hard about how to attract more members and, given potentially high levels of frustration some research has detected among existing members, retaining those who have already joined.[60] Research suggests that members and potential members are price-sensitive, but subscription costs are already relatively low, meaning that lowering them further is unlikely to bring in lots more people. Raising the cost of joining does have an effect, however, although it appears to have more of an effect on socio-demographic than on ideological representation – poorer, less educated and female supporters are more likely to be put off by higher dues, but it's not only parties' most radical supporters who are prepared to swallow any hike and join anyway. In the end, upping the benefits available (for which read strengthen-ing intra-party democracy and offering a bigger say to a wider pool of supporters) also appears to make the most difference.[61] But parties need to strike a balance. For instance, existing members – particularly those who are wary of their party dilut-ing its ideology – might be happy to see it create new 'membership-lite' categories, such as 'registered supporters', but only if those who take up the offer aren't granted exactly the same rights as full members when it comes to influencing policy, choos-ing candidates and electing leaders.[62] On the other hand, given that support for extending internal party democracy may well be strongest among a party's most radical members, giving the grassroots a greater say on policy making and/or candi-date and leadership selection could prove risky for any outfit worried about straying too far from where voters are, especially, perhaps, if giving members and supporters a greater say leads (as it sometimes does) to disputes and division within the party.[63]

Interestingly, for parties desperate to make up for a drop in membership, these organizational changes may well be a more attractive option than, say, signalling a big policy shift in order to persuade ideologically convinced supporters to join or re-join – possibly because adopting a more radical stance might mean alienating more moderate voters. On the other hand, if such shifts do occur and appear to have done the trick, then, then there is research evidence to suggest that parties will try to repeat it by shifting still further in whatever direction appears to have brought it more members: once again the Labour Party under Jeremy Corbyn may well be a case in point.[64]

We should remember, however, that the phenomenal increases in membership that Labour (and, indeed, the SNP) have recently experienced, and the more modest, sometimes temporary, but nonetheless significant increases experienced over the last five years by the Liberal Democrats, the Greens, and UKIP, are unusual, to say the least. As we noted right at the start of this chapter, most parties in most countries, at least in Europe, are finding things much tougher. This doesn't mean that they have given up: a recent cross-national study, for instance, points to 'the reluctance of political parties . . . to depart from the modern party as anything but a membership organization' – indeed, it found that parties 'both celebrated and maintained a commitment to the continued importance and role of party members in both public discourse and that designed for internal party consumption'.[65] That said, many of them have already tried, building perhaps on the idea of a 'multi-speed' party that acknowledges and even promotes different levels of affiliation and commitment, to make prospective supporters a better offer (whether it be cheaper and/or looser forms of affiliation, bolder policies or more influence) but all to no avail. In those circumstances, it seems that some of them are more or less reluctantly scaling back their local presence but spending more nationally, employing more paid (but not always well-paid) staff back at HQ, and simply doing less between general elections than they would have done before.[66]

This counsel of despair does not appear to apply – at least not quite and not for the moment anyway – to the parties on whose members we focus here, beginning in the next chapter with a look at who they are. And we hope, for democracy's sake, that it never does.

Notes

1 See Mazzoleni, Oscar and Voerman, Gerrit (2017) 'Memberless parties: Beyond the business-firm party model?', *Party Politics*, 23 (6), pp. 783–792. See also Cirhan, Tomas and Stauber, Jakub, 'Online supporter and registered sympathiser as alternatives to a regular party member', *East European Politics*, 34 (4), pp. 458–482.

2 For more on this research, see the homepage of the *Members and Activists of Political Parties* network at www.projectmapp.eu/. A recent insight into party members in the Balkans and Eastern Europe is provided by Gherghina, Sergiu, Iancu, Alexandra and Soare, Sorina (2018) *Party Members and Their Importance in Non-EU Countries: A Comparative Analysis* (Abingdon: Routledge).

3 See Kölln, Ann-Kristin (2016) 'Party membership in Europe: Testing party-level explanations of decline', *Party Politics*, 22 (4) pp. 465–477. See also Van Haute, Emilie, Paulis, Emilien and Sierens, Vivien (2018) 'Assessing party membership figures: The MAPP dataset', *European Political Science*, 17 (3), pp. 366–377.

4 See van Biezen, Ingrid, Mair, Peter and Poguntke, Thomas (2012) 'Going, going, . . . gone? The decline of party membership in contemporary Europe', *European Journal of Political Research*, 51 (1), pp. 24–56; and van Biezen, Ingrid and Poguntke, Thomas (2014) 'The decline of membership-based politics', *Party Politics*, 20 (2), pp. 205–216. See also Pemberton, Hugh and Wickham-Jones, Mark (2013) 'Labour's lost grassroots: The rise and fall of party membership', *British Politics*, 8 (2), pp. 181–206.

5 See Hooghe, Marc and Kern, Anna (2015) 'Party membership and closeness and the development of trust in political institutions: An analysis of the European Social Survey, 2002–2010', *Party Politics*, 21 (6), pp. 944–956; Ponce, Aldo and Scarrow, Susan (2016) 'Which members? Using cross-national surveys to study party membership', *Party Politics*, 22 (6), pp. 679–690; and Gauja, Anika (2015) 'The construction of party membership', *European Journal of Political Research*, 54 (2), pp. 232–248.

6 See Van Biezen, Ingrid and Kopecky, Petr (2017) 'The paradox of party funding: The limited impact of state subsidies on party membership', in Scarrow, Susan, Webb, Paul and Poguntke, Thomas (eds.) *Organizing Political Parties: Participation, Representation and Power* (Oxford: Oxford University Press), pp. 84–105. They actually find a positive relationship between state funding and membership and suggest (pp. 100–101) that 'precisely because parties are now so well-endowed by the state', it is possible that they can make 'investments that keep their membership organizations afloat'.

7 See Dalton, Russell J. and Wattenberg, Martin P., eds. (2000) *Parties Without Partisans: Political Change in Advanced Industrial Democracies* (Oxford: Oxford University Press). See also also Allern, Elin Haugsgjerd and Bale, Tim, eds. (2017) *Left-of-Centre Parties and Trade Unions in the Twenty-First Century* (Oxford: Oxford University Press).

8 See Uslaner, Eric M., ed. (2018) *The Oxford Handbook of Social and Political Trust* (Oxford: Oxford University Press).

9 Unless otherwise indicated, all recent year-end/year-beginning figures are taken from the parties' annual accounts which are available on the Electoral Commission's website. Most but not all parties include (on a voluntary basis) a figure for their membership, although differences in the way each of them treats those members in arrears means the figures aren't strictly comparable – and, of course, the Conservative Party does not tradtionally provide such a figure. See www.electoralcommission.org.uk/find-information-by-subject/political-parties-campaigning-and-donations/political-parties-annual-accounts/details-of-accounts.

10 Bale, Tim and Webb, Paul (2016) 'Not as bad as we feared or even worse than we imagined? Assessing and explaining Conservative Party members' views on coalition', *Political Studies*, 64 (1), pp. 123–142.

11 See Bale, Tim (2015) *Five Year Mission: The Labour Party Under Ed Miliband* (Oxford: Oxford University Press) and Goes, Eunice (2016) *The Labour Party Under Ed Miliband: Trying But Failing to Renew Social Democracy* (Manchester: Manchester University Press).

12 See Nunns, Alex (2018) *The Candidate: Jeremy Corbyn's Improbable Path to Power* (London: OR Books) and Prince, Rosa (2018) *Comrade Corbyn* (London: Biteback). See also Pickard, Sarah (2018) 'Momentum and the Movementist "Corbynistas": Young People Regenerating the Labour Party in Britain', in S. Pickard and J. Bessant (eds.) *Young People Re-Generating Politics in Times of Crises* (London: Palgrave Macmillan). Figures for Labour membership, collated from publicly available sources, kindly provided by Stan Anson. For graph, see https://twitter.com/moutajup/status/1039784326060273664.

13 See Lee, Georgina (2019) 'Are Labour inflating their membership figures?', *Channel 4 Fact Check*, 24 January, available online at www.channel4.com/news/factcheck/factcheck-are-labour-inflating-their-membership-figures.

14 Speed, Barbara (2015) 'What does the Lib Dem membership surge mean for the struggling party?', *New Statesman*, 17 June, available online at www.newstatesman.com/politics/2015/06/what-does-lib-dem-membership-surge-mean-struggling-party.

15 Liberal Democrats (2018) 'Liberal Democrats hit highest ever membership on eve of local elections', 3 May, available online at https://web.archive.org/web/20170503110530/www.libdems.org.uk/liberal-democrats-highest-membership-local-elections.

16 See Pack, Mark (2018) 'Liberal democrat membership figures', 8 October, available online at www.markpack.org.uk/143767/liberal-democrat-membership-figures/.

17 See Paulis, Emilien, Sierens, Vivien and Van Haute, Emilie (2015) 'Jumping on the bandwagon? Explaining fluctuations in party membership levels in Europe', PSA Conference Paper, Glasgow, 10–12 April, 2017. See also Fisher, Justin, Denver, David and Hands,

Gordon (2006) 'Party membership and campaign activity in Britain: The impact of electoral performance', *Party Politics*, 12 (4), pp. 505–519.

18 Wallace, Mark (2014) 'Conservative party membership has risen to 149,800 – up 11.7 per cent', *ConservativeHome*, 28 September, available online at www.conservativehome.com/thetorydiary/2014/09/conference-survey-and-membership-figures.html. See also Strafford, John (2017) 'My proposals to change the party's constitution for the better', *ConservativeHome*, 16 April, available online at www.conservativehome.com/platform/2017/04/john-strafford-my-proposals-to-change-the-partys-constitution-for-the-better.html.

19 See Wheeler, Brian (2018) 'Tories must come clean on membership figures – Ex-chairman', *BBC*, 5 January, available online at www.bbc.co.uk/news/uk-politics-42565294. We were reliably informed, in an interview conducted in CCHQ on 1 February 2017 that the period between 23 June and 'the back-end of October' had seen 50,000 people joining, some of them presumably in anticipation of a leadership contest that never happened (and in which, according to party rules, they would have been ineligible to participate, having joined too recently to qualify). See also Kennedy, Andrew (2016) 'The remarkable story of a post-referendum surge in membership – The most intense I can remember', 18 July, available online at www.conservativehome.com/thecolumnists/2016/07/andrew-kennedy-the-remarkable-story-of-a-post-referendum-surge-in-conservative-membership-the-most-intense-i-can-remember.html.

20 Yorke, Harry (2018) 'Conservative party nearly twice the size originally thought, new figures show', *Daily Telegraph*, 17 March.

21 This had already happened on a smaller scale in September 2018 when the party's primary for the London mayoralty produced a turnout of just 7,321, which apparently constituted 47.8 per cent of Tory members and implied a total membership of about 15,000 in a city (admittedly a Labour-leaning one) containing more than 5 million voters eligible to vote for its mayor. Bartlett, Nicola (2018) 'Shaun Bailey named London mayor candidate for Tories', *Daily Mirror*, 28 September, available online at www.mirror.co.uk/news/politics/shaun-bailey-named-london-mayor-13324186.

22 Newton Dunn, Tom (2019) 'BLUKIP Senior Tories fear thousands of Brexit activists are infiltrating the Conservative Party to have a say on who the next PM will be', *Sun*, 15 April, available online at www.thesun.co.uk/news/politics/8870950/.

23 Casalicchio, Emilio (2018) 'How Ukip became the party of Tommy Robinson', *PoliticsHome*, 6 December, available online at www.politicshome.com/news/uk/political-parties/uk-independence-party/nigel-farage/opinion/politicshome/100395/long-read Figure for membership kindly provided by UKIP was 28,200 in April 2019.

24 For more detail, see Poletti, Monica and Dennison, James (2016) 'The Green Surge and how it changed the membership of the Party', *LSE British Politics and Policy*, 3 March, available online at http://blogs.lse.ac.uk/politicsandpolicy/the-green-surge-and-how-it-changed-the-membership-of-the-party/.

25 Figure for March 2019 kindly provided by the Green Party of England and Wales.

26 This model was first developed by British political scientists, Patrick Seyd and Paul Whiteley, whose books on party members – the first of which, published in 1992, was *Labour's Grass Roots: The Politics of Party Membership* (Oxford: Clarendon) – are widely recognized as seminal contributions to our understanding. For an admirably concise list of possible motives for joining a party – rational and individualistic, expressive and social – see also Katz, Richard (2015) 'Should we believe that improved intra-party democracy would arrest party decline?', in William Cross and Richard Katz (eds.) (2013) *The Challenges of Intra-Party Democracy* (Oxford: Oxford University Press), pp. 49–64.

27 See van Haute, Emilie and Gauja, Anika, eds. (2015) *Party Members and Activists* (Abingdon: Routledge).

28 In some ways this is all the more remarkable because as one researcher notes, there is surely a risk that 'respondents invited to talk about individual reasons to mobilise or about individual actions tend to respond in terms of individualism and individualised practices

at the expense of collective forms of political participation'. See Faucher, Florence (2015) 'New forms of political participation: Changing demands or changing opportunities to participate in political parties?', *Comparative European Politics*, 13 (4), p. 419.

29 Bruter, Michael and Harrison, Sarah (2009) *The Future of Our Democracies: Young Party Members in Europe* (Basingstoke: Palgrave), p. 65. The study, which brilliantly combines over 500 semi-structured interviews with a survey of nearly 3,000 members from six countries, suggests that moral minded members made up 40 per cent of young members, social-minded 34 per cent and professional-minded 26 per cent. The figures for young party members in the UK were 47.5, 22.5 and 30 per cent, respectively.

30 Jeremy Corbyn standing for the Labour leadership is an obvious example. Note that in Canada, where people can often join parties just prior to leadership and nomination contests, those contests can see a big influx of members only to see membership fall precipitately in the following years – something that has not, so far anyway, happened to Labour. See Cross, William (2015) 'Party Membership in Canada', in Emilie van Haute and Anika Gauja (eds.) *Party Members and Activists* (Abingdon: Routledge), pp. 50–65.

31 Kölln, Ann-Kristin and Polk, Jonathan (2017) 'Emancipated party members: Examining ideological incongruence within political parties', *Party Politics*, 23 (1), pp. 18–29. See also de Vet, Benjamin, Poletti, Monica and Wauters, Benjamin (forthcoming) 'The party (un) faithful: Explaining party members' defecting voting behaviour in different contexts (Belgium and Britain)', *Party Politics*. Interestingly, it may well be the case that less active members are more likely to disagree with their party than their more active counterparts. See also Lisi, Marco and Cancela, João (forthcoming) 'Types of party members and their implications: Results from a survey of Portuguese party members', *Party Politics*.

32 Kenig, Ofer, Philippov, Michael and Rahat, Gideon (2013) 'Party membership in Israel: An overview', *Israel Studies Review*, 28 (1), pp. 8–32.

33 Goodwin, Matthew, Ford, Robert and Cutts, David (2012) 'Extreme right foot soldiers, legacy effects and deprivation: A contextual analysis of the leaked British National Party (BNP) membership list', *Party Politics*, 19 (6), pp. 887–906.

34 See van Haute, Emilie and Gauja, Anika, eds. (2015) *Party Members and Activists* (Abingdon: Routledge) which covers 77 parties in ten countries.

35 See Bruter, Michael and Harrison, Sarah (2009) *The Future of Our Democracies: Young Party Members in Europe* (Basingstoke: Palgrave), pp. 130–135.

36 For a portrait of Conservative, Labour and Liberal grassroots members between the wars, see Ball, Stuart, Thorpe, Andrew and Worley, Matthew (2017) 'Elections, leaflets and whist drives: Constituency party members in Britain between the wars', in Matthew Worley (ed.) *Labour's Grass Roots: Essays on the Activities of Local Labour Parties and Members, 1918–45* (Abingdon: Routledge).

37 Note that these effects may be indirect. For instance, some research suggests that is not the content of education or even the generic skills it endows people with but the social networks to which it grants them access which are most important: see Persson, Mikael (2014) 'Social network position mediates the effect of education on active political party membership', *Party Politics*, 20 (5), pp. 724–739. Note, too, that various characteristics interact, the most obvious example being education and age: parties with the oldest members also tend to have the least educated members because, when they were young, fewer people went to university.

38 Scarrow, Susan and Gezgor, Burcu (2010) 'Declining memberships, changing members? European political party members in a new era', *Party Politics*, 16 (6), pp. 823–843.

39 See Heidar, Knut and Wauters, Bram (2019) *Do Parties Still Represent? An Analysis of the Representativeness of Political Parties in Western Democracies* (Abingdon: Routledge). See also Gauja, Anika and Jackson, Stewart (2016) 'Australian Greens party members and supporters: Their profiles and activities', *Environmental Politics*, 25 (2), pp. 359–379.

40 See Van Holsteyn, Joop, Den Ridder, Josje and Koole, Ruud (2017) 'From May's Laws to May's legacy: On the opinion structure within political parties', *Party Politics*, 23 (5), pp. 471–486; see also, for particular examples, Faucher, Florence and Boy, Daniel (2018)

'Fifty Shades of Green? Political differences between elites, members and supporters of Europe Ecologie Les Verts', *Environmental Politics*, 27 (1), pp. 161–185 and, of course, Norris, Pippa (1995) 'May's law of curvilinear disparity revisited: Leaders, officers, members and voters in British political parties', *Party Politics*, 1 (1), pp. 29–47. On do-nothing radicals, see van Haute, Emilie and Carty, R. Kenneth (2012) 'Ideological misfits: A distinctive class of party members', *Party Politics*, 18 (6), pp. 885–895.

41 See, for example, Whiteley, Paul and Seyd, Patrick (2002) *High Intensity Participation: The Dynamics of Party Activism in Britain* (Ann Arbor: University of Michigan Press), pp. 20–21.

42 Anyone thinking that members who are supposedly too busy to help out will make up for it by donating more cash instead are likely to be disappointed. It seems as if those who are least generous with their time are also least generous with their money (and vice versa). See, for example, Gauja, Anika and Jackson, Stewart (2016) 'Australian Greens party members and supporters: Their profiles and activities', *Environmental Politics*, 25 (2), pp. 359–379.

43 See van Haute, Emilie and Gauja, Anika, eds. (2015) *Party Members and Activists* (Abingdon: Routledge), p. 197.

44 On the greater influence of the activist minority (which appears to bother the passive majority less than it bothers some leaders and many observers), see Gauja, Anika (2013) *The Politics of Party Policy: From Members to Legislators* (Houndsmills: Palgrave Macmillan).

45 Kernell, Georgia (2015) 'Party nomination rules and campaign participation', *Comparative Political Studies*, 48 (13), pp. 1814–1843. On younger people being less involved in politics more generally, see Sloam, James (2013) '"Voice and equality": Young people's politics in the European Union', *West European Politics*, 36 (4), pp. 836–858. Note, however, that one cross-national study of young party members (aged 18–25) saw them report far higher levels of activism than studies of party members overall have found, with about three-quarters of them classifying themselves as very or quite active: the interviews conducted for the study, however, revealed a lot of moans about everything being done by (or left to) a small hard core of 'party-holics'. See Bruter, Michael and Harrison, Sarah (2009) *The Future of Our Democracies: Young Party Members in Europe* (Basingstoke: Palgrave), pp. 68, 72, 159–160.

46 Kosiara-Pedersen, Karina (2014) 'The impact of having children on party member activism', *Copernicus Journal of Political Studies*, 1 (5), pp. 87–100. Interestingly, the findings apply irrespective of whether the members are male or female.

47 See Whiteley, Paul (2011) 'Is the party over? The decline of party activism and membership across the democratic world', *Party Politics*, 17 (1), pp. 21–44. See also Whiteley, Paul and Seyd, Patrick (2002) *High Intensity Participation: The Dynamics of Party Activism in Britain* (Ann Arbor: University of Michigan Press).

48 Ponce, Aldo and Scarrow, Susan (2016) 'Which members? Using cross-national surveys to study party membership', *Party Politics*, 22 (6), p. 686ff.

49 Whiteley, Paul and Seyd, Patrick (1998) 'The dynamics of party activism in Britain: A spiral of demobilization?', *British Journal of Political Science*, 28 (1), pp. 113–137.

50 See, for example, the following: Pattie, Charles and Johnston, Ron (2003) 'Hanging on the telephone? Doorstep and telephone canvassing at the British General Election of 1997', *British Journal of Political Science*, 33 (2), pp. 303–322; Johnston, Ron, Pattie, Charles, Scully, Roger and Cutts, David (2016) 'Constituency campaigning and canvassing for support at the 2011 National Assembly of Wales election', *Politics*, 36 (1), pp. 49–62; Karp, Jeffrey, Banducci, Susan and Bowler, Shaun (2008) 'Getting out the vote: Party mobilization in a comparative perspective', *British Journal of Political Science*, 38 (1), pp. 91–112; and Townsley, Joshua (forthcoming) 'Is it worth door-knocking? Evidence from a United Kingdom-based Get Out The Vote (GOTV) field experiment on the effect of party leaflets and canvass visits on voter turnout', *Political Science Research and Methods*. See also Enos, Ryan and Hersh, Eitan (2015) 'Party activists as campaign advertisers: The ground campaign as a principal-agent problem', *American Political Science Review*, 109 (2), pp. 252–278.

51 See Chadwick, Andrew and Stromer-Galley, Jennifer (2016) 'Digital media, power, and democracy in parties and election campaigns: Party decline or party renewal?', *International Journal of Press Politics*, 21 (3), pp. 283–293 and Vaccari, Cristian and Valeriani, Augusto (2016) 'Party campaigners or citizen campaigners? How social media deepen and broaden party-related engagement', *The International Journal of Press/Politics*, 21 (3), pp. 294–312. See also Dommett, Katharine and Temple, Luke (2018) 'Digital campaigning: The rise of Facebook and satellite campaigns', *Parliamentary Affairs*, 71 (suppl_1), pp. 189–202 and Gibson, Rachel, Greffet, Fabienne and Cantijoch, Marta (2017) 'Friend or foe? Digital technologies and the changing nature of party membership', *Political Communication*, 34 (1), pp. 89–111. And see Hooghe, Marc and Kölln, Ann-Kristin (forthcoming) 'Types of party affiliation and the multi-speed party: What kind of party support is functionally equivalent to party membership?', *Party Politics*.
52 Fisher, Justin, Fieldhouse, Edward and Cutts, David (2014) 'Members are not the only fruit: Volunteer activity in British political parties at the 2010 general election', *The British Journal of Politics & International Relations*, 16 (1), pp. 75–95.
53 See Gauja, Anika (2015) 'The construction of party membership', *European Journal of Political Research*, 54 (2), pp. 232–248 and Kosiara-Pedersen, Karina, Scarrow, Susan and van Haute, Emilie (2017) 'Rules of engagement? Party membership costs, new forms of party affiliation and partisan participation', in Scarrow, Susan, Webb, Paul, Poguntke, Thomas (eds.) *Organizing Political Parties: Participation, Representation and Power* (Oxford: Oxford University Press), pp. 234–258. See also Sandri, Giulia and Seddone, Antonella (2015) 'Sense or sensibility? Political attitudes and voting behaviour of party members, voters, and supporters of the Italian centre-left', *Italian Political Science Review/Rivista Italiana di Scienza Politica*, 45 (1), pp. 25–51, Cross, William and Gauja, Anika (2014) 'Evolving membership strategies in Australian political parties', *Australian Journal of Political Science*, 49 (4), pp. 611–625 and Gauja, Anika (2017) *Party Reform: The Causes, Challenges, and Consequences of Organizational Change* (Oxford: Oxford University Press).
54 Scarrow, Susan (2015) *Beyond Party Members: Changing Approaches to Political Mobilization* (Oxford: Oxford University Press). See also Mjelde, Hilmar (2015) 'Non-member participation in political parties: A framework for analysis and selected empirical examples from Scandinavia', *Representation*, 51 (3), pp. 299–310 and Gauja, Anika and Grömping, Max (forthcoming) 'The expanding party universe: Patterns of partisan engagement in Australia and the United Kingdom', *Party Politics*.
55 For the most comprehensive discussion of all this, see Gauja, Anika (2017) *Party Reform: The Causes, Challenges, and Consequences of Organizational Change* (Oxford: Oxford University Press). See also Cross, William and Katz, Richard, eds. (2013) *The Challenges of Intra-Party Democracy* (Oxford: Oxford University Press) and especially Chapter 5 on 'Party members and intra-party democracy' (pp. 65–80) by Lisa Young.
56 The *locus classicus* for this point of view is Katz, Richard and Mair, Peter (1995) 'Changing models of party organization and party democracy: The emergence of the cartel party', *Party Politics*, 1 (1), pp. 5–28. For more recent variations on the theme, see Faucher, Florence (2015) 'New forms of political participation: Changing demands or changing opportunities to participate in political parties?', *Comparative European Politics*, 13 (4), pp. 405–429; Schumacher, Gijs and Giger, Nathalie (2017) 'Who leads the party? On membership size, selectorates and party oligarchy', *Political Studies*, 65 (suppl_1), pp. 162–181. See also Koo, Sejin (forthcoming) 'Can intraparty democracy save party activism? Evidence from Korea', *Party Politics*.
57 See Seyd, Patrick and Whiteley, Paul (2004) 'British party members: An overview', *Party Politics*, 10 (4), pp. 355–366.
58 See Ponce, Aldo, Scarrow, Susan and Achury, Susan (2019) 'Quotas, women's leadership, and grassroots women activists: Bringing women into the party', Unpublished MS.
59 For more on all this, see Heidar, Knut and Wauters, Bram, eds. (2019) *Do Parties Still Represent?: An Analysis of the Representativeness of Political Parties in Western Democracies* (Abingdon: Routledge). On female representation, see Childs, Sarah (2013) 'Intra-party democracy: A gendered critique and a feminist agenda', in Cross William and Richard

Katz (eds.) *The Challenges of Intra-Party Democracy* (Oxford: Oxford University Press), pp. 81–99.

60 See Bruter, Michael and Harrison, Sarah (2009) *The Future of our Democracies: Young Party Members in Europe* (Basingstoke: Palgrave).

61 Achury, Susan, Scarrow, Susan, Kosiara-Pedersen, Karina and van Haute, Emilie (forthcoming) 'The consequences of membership incentives: Do greater political benefits attract different kinds of members?', *Party Politics* and Kosiara-Pedersen, Karina, Scarrow, Susan and van Haute, Emilie (2017) 'Rules of engagement? Party membership costs, new forms of party affiliation and partisan participation', in Scarrow, Susan, Webb, Paul and Poguntke, Thomas (eds.) *Organizing Political Parties: Participation, Representation and Power* (Oxford: Oxford University Press), pp. 234–258.

62 Gauja, Anika and Jackson, Stewart (2016) 'Australian Greens party members and supporters: Their profiles and activities', *Environmental Politics*, 25 (2), pp. 359–379.

63 See Spies, Dennis and Kaiser, André (2014) 'Does the mode of candidate selection affect the representativeness of parties?', *Party Politics*, 20 (4), pp. 576–590 and Kernell, Georgia (2015) 'Party nomination rules and campaign participation', *Comparative Political Studies*, 48 (13), pp. 1814–1843. See also Rüdig, Wolfgang and Sajuria, Javier (forthcoming) 'Green party members and grassroots democracy: A comparative analysis', *Party Politics*.

64 Rohlfing, Ingo (2015) 'Asset or liability? An analysis of the effect of changes in party membership on partisan ideological change', *Party Politics*, 21 (1), pp. 17–27.

65 Gauja, Anika (2017) *Party Reform: The Causes, Challenges, and Consequences of Organizational Change* (Oxford: Oxford University Press), p. 183, p. 30.

66 Kölln, Ann-Kristin (2015) 'The effects of membership decline on party organisations in Europe', *European Journal of Political Research*, 54 (4), pp. 707–725.

3

WHO ARE THE MEMBERS?

According to the nation's favourite fictional civil servant, Sir Humphrey Appleby, its parliamentarians 'aren't chosen by the people. They're chosen by their local party: thirty-five men in grubby raincoats or thirty-five women in silly hats'.[1] His remarks were probably a little unfair even in the days when people actually wore raincoats and hats, and they would certainly be unfair today. Yet Sir Humphry had a point – namely, that people who belong to political parties are, in the strictest sense of the word, abnormal. True, an awful lot of people in the UK are members of a party – getting on for one million, in fact. But that leaves tens of millions who don't currently belong to one and who, in most cases, would probably never dream of joining one either.[2] Still, the fact that those who *have* decided to join constitute a very small minority of their fellow citizens doesn't necessarily make them as weird and way-out as their media stereotypes might suggest. Not every grassroots Conservative is a blue-rinsed dragon or a Colonel Blimp – or, for that matter, an oleaginous 'Tory Boy' (or girl). Likewise, not every Labour member is a middle-class, Corbyn-supporting 'Trot' or a salt-of-the-earth trade unionist. Not all members of the Scottish National Party (SNP) are merciless and monomaniacal 'cybernats'. Liberal Democrats don't necessarily sport bushy beards and open-toed sandals. Greens aren't all tree-hugging eco-warriors with white dreads and a dog on a string. And to characterize UKIP's membership, as 'a bunch of . . . fruitcakes and loonies and closet racists' (to quote former Tory leader David Cameron) might be similarly unfair.

In this chapter we try to get behind the stereotypes to see what members of six of the country's biggest parties actually look like. Are they really so very different from the 'average Brit'? Do they resemble each other more than they resemble the rest of us? Or are members of the different parties actually very different from each other – not only when it comes to what they believe but also, for instance, when it comes to how old or how well-educated or how well-off they are?

Class

Half a century ago, the political scientist Peter Pulzer famously asserted that '[c]lass is the basis of British party politics; all else is embellishment and detail'.[3] That may well be less true now than it was back then, not least because Britain's class structure has become more complex as the economy has moved further away from manufacturing and towards services, and society has become ethnically and culturally more diverse. However, as studies which try to take account of those changes and their impact on electoral politics show, people's backgrounds nevertheless continue to influence their life chances, their attitudes, and their preferences.[4] Research also shows that they continue to influence their political participation, too. Put bluntly, the better off (and the better educated) you are, the more likely you are to get involved, whether that means, say, turning out to vote or else joining organizations and campaigns aimed at getting what you want by persuading or putting pressure on the powers that be.[5] It is not perhaps surprising, then, that the nation's party members are, on balance, a pretty middle-class bunch.

The 'social grade' classifications that will be familiar to many readers, not least because market researchers and the media make such widespread use of them, divide people according to the occupation of the 'head of household'.[6] ABC1 comprises three subgroups, namely, 'higher managerial, administrative or professional' (A); 'intermediate managerial, administrative or professional' (B); and 'supervisory or clerical and junior managerial, administrative or professional' (C1) – people who are widely seen as middle class. C2DE is generally equated with the working class and comprises the following three subgroups: 'skilled manual workers' (the C2s that we often hear so much about when it comes to floating voters who supposedly decide elections), 'semi-skilled and unskilled manual workers' (D) and a rather disparate group comprising 'casual or lowest grade workers, pensioners, and others who depend on the welfare state for their income' (E).

Table 3.1 compares the social grades of the members of Britain's parties with those who vote for those parties and covers the elections of both 2015 and in 2017 (when there were some changes in the kind of voters the parties attracted, although far fewer changes in the composition of their memberships). For ease of comparison, it also includes a column for each party showing the extent of the class differences between its members and its voters. The 'M–V' scores for each party, then, measure the extent of the differences between members and voters. In each and every case, we can see that party memberships are proportionately more middle class than working class in both 2015 and 2017. In short, members are rather more well-heeled than voters – and, given the fact that more middle-class than working-class people vote, probably even more middle class than the population as a whole.[7]

When we look at individual parties, we see some even bigger disparities – and not just with voters in general but also with the voters who vote for the parties which members belong to. Take the Conservative Party in 2017: some 86 per cent of its members are middle class compared to 63 per cent of its voters – a gap of 23 percentage points. Staying on the right of the political spectrum and in 2017,

TABLE 3.1 Occupational class profiles of party members and voters

	Conservative		Labour		Liberal Democrat		UKIP		Green		SNP	
	Memb	*Voters*	*Memb*	*Voters*	*Memb*	*Voters*	*Memb*	*Voters*	*Memb*	*Voters*	*Memb*	*Voters*
2015												
ABC1	85	67	78	59	86	70	66	48	78	68	71	59
C2DE	15	33	22	41	14	30	34	52	22	32	29	41
MC–WC	70	34	56	18	72	40	32	–4	56	36	42	18
M–V	18		19		16		18		10		12	
2017												
ABC1	86	63	77	60	88	72	66	43	80	67	72	60
C2DE	14	37	23	40	12	28	34	57	20	33	28	40
MC–WC	72	26	54	20	76	44	32	–14	60	34	44	20
M–V	23		17		16		23		13		12	

Note: All figures percentages of column categories. MC–WC = gap between percentages of ABC1 and C2DE supporting each party. M–V = gap between percentages of members and voters supporting each party. Membership sample: N = 5694 (2015) and 5219 (2017). Electorate sample: N = 26078 (2015) and 25821 (2017).

we can see that UKIP's members, although less well-heeled than Tory members, are still pretty middle class (66 per cent are ABC1), and because fewer of its voters are middle class (i.e., some 43 per cent compared to 63 per cent of Tory voters), there is a similarly big gap (23 percentage points) between members and voters. Other parties have smaller gaps, most obviously the SNP, the Greens, and the Liberal Democrats – in the case of the latter because both their membership and their voters are even more middle class than the Tories'. Labour sits somewhere in the middle: interestingly for a party that began life as the parliamentary representative of working people, some 77 per cent of its members are now middle class, as are 60 per cent of its voters, making for a class gap between Labour's members and its voters of 17 percentage points.

This prompts a couple of questions. First, has this changed much, and second (and perhaps more important), does it matter? As far as the first question goes, we can go back to some of the pioneering surveys of some of the larger parties and make some comparisons, albeit broad ones because they used different categories.[8] With that caveat in mind, it looks as if both the Conservatives and the Liberal Democrats may actually have slightly (but only slightly) more working-class members as a proportion of their total memberships than they did back in the 1990s. Labour, on the other hand, has about the same proportion of working-class members as it did back in the late 1980s, moving from just over a quarter then to just under a quarter now, which, interestingly enough, is, if anything, a larger share than it was in the late 1990s.[9] Moreover, the difference between Labour's membership and its voters has actually narrowed considerably since the 1980s and 1990s as its voters have become significantly more middle class (albeit not quite as middle class as its members) in recent years. The survey of the Green Party in the 1990s used yet another set of categories, but (with the same caveats applying) it would appear that there hasn't been much change in the class composition of that party's membership, with only about a fifth of members both then and now being, broadly speaking, working class.[10]

On the second question (namely, does it matter?), the answer is that it may. Given that the UK likes to think of itself as not only a liberal but also a *representative* democracy, it cannot be right that there are so few working-class people who belong to the parties that play such a vital role in it, especially when one of the functions that those parties perform is the selection of candidates for Parliament – something we explore in a later chapter.[11] It may be no accident, given how thoroughly middle class this *selectorate* has become, that there are so few working-class MPs at Westminster nowadays.

True, the seemingly unstoppable professionalization of politics means that the skills required are similar if not identical to those required in the well-networked, graduate-type careers that many parliamentarians pursue before they are elected, making it more difficult than ever for 'ordinary' people to join the so-called political class.[12] True, too, that the decline of trade unions, particularly in the private and industrial sectors of the economy, has reduced the supply of supposedly 'horny-handed sons of toil', while recent research shows that those unions which are still important players in the Labour Party focus more on getting ideologically congenial rather than working-class candidates into winnable seats.[13] But it is hard to believe that party members are any less prone than the rest of us to favour people like ourselves – with the result that anyone who is not middle class ends up looking at our politicians (always assuming they haven't given up looking altogether) and sees hardly anyone who thinks and behaves, or at least speaks, as they do.

Potentially, and perhaps actually, this creates a vicious circle: the fewer working-class politicians there are, the less working-class people are inclined to participate in politics either by joining parties or simply by voting, and so the fewer working class politicians there are, and so on and so on. What academics call '*descriptive* representation' (the extent to which the elected are demographically like those who elect them) may also have an impact on '*substantive* representation' (the extent to which they act in their interests).[14] But it doesn't take a rocket scientist, let alone a political scientist, to see that the distributional consequences of an entire class being underrepresented among party members, and even more so in the parliament for which those party members are effectively gatekeepers, could be very serious indeed.

So, of course, could be the electoral consequences – at least for one party in particular. Labour has had to cope, over the course of the last 50 years, with the shrinkage of its traditional voter base, namely, the industrial working class. It has managed, as in some ways it simply had to do, by reaching out to middle-class voters, especially those whose liberal-progressive cultural values (and perhaps, too, their employment in the public sector) make them less inclined than they might otherwise be to vote for the Conservatives. Ideally, this would not come at the cost of alienating working-class voters – something electorally successful Labour leaders like Harold Wilson and Tony Blair were keen to stress. However, over time, and particularly during the latter's time in charge, it seems to have done so.[15] Widespread concerns about rapid immigration and the cultural changes it brings about helped push working-class voters towards parties with less 'cosmopolitan' views on such matters like the Conservative Party (particularly before and following David Cameron's time as leader) and, even more obviously, UKIP. Quite how Labour should respond to such a challenge – one faced by its sister parties all over the continent, of course – is debatable.[16] But the fact that about three-quarters of its members probably live very different lives to those lived by the voters who have deserted it may well play a part in its decisions – even more so now that the leadership claims it values members' views more than its supposedly 'Blairite' predecessors ever did. Certainly, it is possible to argue that, because of this, Labour needs to worry more than the Conservatives (whose members do not have any formal say on policy) about a membership that doesn't look or sound much like the electorate.

Gender

Concerns about underrepresentation are not, of course, limited to class. That we sometimes hear a lot more about other types of discrimination than we do about the comparative absence of working-class people does not make them any less egregious. Take women, for instance. Table 3.2 reveals a significant gender gap. At

TABLE 3.2 Gender profiles of party members and voters

	Conservative	Labour	Liberal Democrat	UKIP	Green	SNP	All parties
2015							
Members	29	38	32	24	42	44	35
Voters	52	55	52	43	57	45	51
M-V	–23	–17	–20	–19	–15	–1	–16
2017							
Members	30	48	38	26	48	43	39
Voters	49	55	47	42	53	44	48
M-V	–19	–8	–9	–16	–5	–1	–9

Note: All figures = percentages of column categories who are women. M-V = gap between percentages of women members and women voters supporting each party.

the far end, we can see that, in 2017, women made up 48 per cent of the voters of Britain's six biggest parties but only 39 per cent of their party members. True, that represents an advance on 2015, where the gap was even wider, partly because more women voted for those parties then but partly because they had even fewer female members in their ranks. However, the noticeable increase in female members between 2015 and 2017 did not occur evenly across all parties. In 2017, just 30 per cent of grassroots Tories were women – virtually the same as was the case in 2015. There wasn't much change over time in the SNP (44 per cent in 2015 and 43 per cent in 2017) or UKIP (24 per cent in 2015 and 26 per cent in 2017) either, although clearly the SNP's membership was far more gender-balanced than the other two to start with.

All this points to an obvious pattern that emerges from our data, namely that, nowadays anyway, the more left-leaning or so-called progressive parties tend to attract more female members (and, indeed, more female voters) than do their counterparts on the right.[17] The data also suggest that, in the case of the Liberal Democrats, the Greens and especially Labour, this is even more the case now than it was a few years ago. The Liberal Democrats, for instance, had nowhere near the number of female members as it had female voters in 2015, but they improved matters by 2017, by which time some 38 per cent of Lib Dems were women, up 6 percentage points from two years previously – the same rise the Greens experienced, albeit from a higher base, going from 42 per cent to near gender parity at 48 per cent. Perhaps the most impressive shift, however, came in the Labour Party, almost certainly as a result of more women than men joining the party to support Jeremy Corbyn: consequently, by the 2017 election, Labour, only 38 per cent of whose members were female two years previously, could boast that nearly half (48 per cent) of its members were women – not altogether surprisingly, some would argue, since women, who are considerably more likely than men to be primary carers and to work in the public sector, had borne the brunt of the austerity on which Labour took a much stronger line after 2015.[18]

As for changes over the longer term, comparison with the pioneering surveys shows the following: (a) that the Conservatives have lost a significant number of women since they were surveyed in the early 1990s, moving from a situation in which half of all their members were female to one in which only a third are, resulting in a significantly greater gender gap between Tory voters and Tory members than existed two or three decades ago; (b) that the Liberal Democrats also appear to have suffered in the same way, albeit not quite as badly – having come somewhere near parity in the late 1990s, since when they have dropped back to around four in ten of their members being women; (c) that the trend in Labour has gone in the opposite direction since, back in both the late 1980s and the late 1990s, the ratio of men to women was roughly 60:40 and now it is nearly 50:50, resulting in a significantly smaller gender gap between the party's voters and its members than existed two or three decades ago; and (d) that the situation in the Greens is pretty much the same as it was in the early 1990s, with the party not far off parity both then and now.[19]

How all this affects policy and candidate selection (see Chapter 7) will be interesting to see. In parties where members (theoretically anyway) have some serious influence on policy – most obviously the Liberal Democrats and the Greens but also Labour and the SNP – then a greater proportion of women may result in a shift in priorities and stances. Likewise, it may make them even more likely, if that gender balance is maintained, to pick women to represent them at elections. Rather more pessimistically, if, that is, one believes in greater equality, one cannot help but notice that the Conservative Party, notwithstanding some recent increases in its female representation at Westminster, has made little or no progress in attracting women to join it at the grassroots level. Given that recent research into both the demand for, and supply of, female candidates suggests party members are crucial in both respects, this does not bode well for the future.[20]

Age

Talk of the future brings us naturally to the question of age. In terms of average ages, the parties aren't actually as different from each other as is often thought – partly because the average Tory member, at 57, isn't quite as ancient as is sometimes assumed while the average Labour member, at 53 years old, isn't quite a young as the frequently seen photos and footage of Jeremy Corbyn playing to crowds of teenagers and twenty-somethings imply. The average age of other party members varies, of course, but not perhaps as much as one might imagine, coming in at 50 for the Liberal Democrats, 52 for the SNP, 56 for UKIP and 41 for the Greens. Generally speaking, then, party membership is not only a middle-class but also a middle-aged game.

But averages can be misleading. Accordingly, Table 3.3 provides a breakdown of the age *structure* of the membership of Britain's six biggest parties in 2015 and

TABLE 3.3 Age profiles of party members and voters

	Cons		Labour		Liberal Democrat		UKIP		Green		SNP		All parties	
	Mem	Vot	Mem	Vot	Mem	Vot	Mem	Vot	Mem	Vot	Mem	Vot	Mem	Vot
2015														
18–25	12	11	8	14	11	14	5	7	18	31	7	13	10	13
26–35	11	16	14	18	16	18	5	11	22	23	14	17	13	16
36–45	9	14	13	16	13	15	8	14	18	16	18	19	13	15
46–55	13	17	17	19	13	16	17	23	17	13	24	20	17	18
56–65	17	23	27	20	17	20	27	27	17	12	23	21	21	22
66+	40	20	20	13	31	17	38	19	8	6	14	9	25	16
2017														
18–25	7	8	6	13	8	11	3	5	9	29	6	8	6	11
26–35	10	11	12	14	15	14	3	7	21	17	9	12	12	12
36–45	11	13	13	16	19	14	5	13	19	15	15	18	14	15
46–55	17	18	16	20	15	17	14	22	18	15	21	22	17	19
56–65	18	25	29	22	20	23	29	30	19	15	29	27	24	24
66+	38	24	26	14	24	19	47	23	14	7	21	13	27	18

Note: All figures percentages of column categories. Mem = party members; Vot = party voters. Not all columns sum to 100 due to rounding.

2017 and compares that to the age structure of voters at the elections which took place in those years. What is immediately apparent, if we look at the far end of both tables, which shows the age structure for the members of all parties combined and all voters combined, is that, overall, the parties have an issue at each end of the age range: there are proportionately more young voters (i.e., those aged between 18 and 25) than there are young party members, while there are proportionately far more party members of pensionable age than there are voters. Generally, only one in 20 members of Britain's political parties is aged 25 or younger, compared to one in ten of the adult population. A glance along the table, however, shows that some parties have more of an 'age problem' than others – and a comparison with previous research suggests that this has long been the case. In the early 1990s, the average age of the Conservative rank and file, for instance, was 62, with nearly half of them aged over 65 and only 5 per cent aged under 35. In contrast, only one in five Labour members in the late 1980s was over 65, whereas just over 20 per cent were under 35, with the average age running at 48 (although ten years later, notwithstanding more young people joining the party after Tony Blair became leader, this had increased to 52). Liberal Democrat members surveyed in the late 1990s, were actually quite old, their average age being 59, with over a third of them over 65 and just under 20 per cent under 35. Members of the Greens, on the other hand, at least when they were surveyed in 1990, were quite young – only 44 on average.[21]

Still, the differences between the ages of parties' members and their voters nowadays can be quite subtle. For instance, the Conservative Party's membership may not be particularly representative of voters as a whole, but it is not that unrepresentative of people who vote Tory – and if anything it became more so in 2017 compared to 2015, although only because an apparent fall in the number of members in the younger age brackets (covering ages 18–45) was more than matched by the much-discussed decline in support at the ballot box from people of the same age. In fact, it seems to be Conservative Party voters in their late 50s and early 60s who are least well represented at the Tory grassroots. In contrast, voters in their late sixties are clearly overrepresented in the party's membership: in 2017 some 38 per cent (i.e., well over a third) of Tory members were aged over 66, compared to 24 per cent of those who voted Conservative that year and just 18 per cent of voters as a whole. All this tallies with anecdotal evidence: as one of our interviewees – who became a constituency chairman at an unusually young age – told us,

> [t]here were probably less than twenty [members] who were under 35 in the whole of the 200–220-odd in the whole time I was there. . . . I remember going to the Christmas dinner . . . and I was the youngest person there by thirty years. . . . There were fifty people in the room and they were all of pensionable age apart from me [and the MP and his wife].[22]

Labour, on the other hand, is clearly finding it more difficult to attract younger members than it is younger voters. Not only is there a gap of 7 percentage points between the proportion of Labour Party members aged between 18 and 25 and the proportion of Labour voters of the same age in 2017, but there is also a gap, albeit a smaller one in each of the age brackets until we reach the 56–65 group. In contrast to what we see at the Tory grassroots, people in their late 50s and early 60s (a fair few of whom rejoined Labour to support Jeremy Corbyn after leaving the party under Tony Blair or Gordon Brown) are actually overrepresented among its membership. But so, too, as in the Conservative Party, are people of pensionable age: those aged 66 and over made up 18 per cent of all voters in 2017 and 14 per cent of Labour voters, but they made up just over a quarter (26 per cent) of Labour members. That does not, of course, mean that Labour has fewer younger members than its rivals: indeed, because it now has so many more members than other parties, it actually has far more young people in its ranks than they do.

Perhaps predictably, given that older people tend to be more Eurosceptic and younger people more socially liberal, cosmopolitan, and environmentally conscious, it is UKIP which has the highest proportion of members of pensionable age (around four in ten) and the Green Party (very few of whose voters are elderly) which has the lowest (about one in ten).[23] The Liberal Democrats and the SNP seem to have the closest match between members and voters in terms of age, but even their memberships tend toward overrepresenting older people, too.

Whether this skewed age distribution represents a problem is a moot point. If what we see is what social scientists refer to as a 'life-cycle' (or an 'ageing' or 'seasoning') effect, then there shouldn't be too much to worry about: parties may always have struggled to recruit young people, but, as those young people get older, they will join parties in greater numbers. Generally speaking, as we noted, it does not look as if the age structure of parties has changed that much in two or three decades: they have always tended to attract older rather than younger people, so perhaps they shouldn't worry too much if they still find it difficult to persuade younger people to join; they may well do so when they're good and ready. If, on the other hand, what we see is a 'cohort effect' then the prospects for parties are rather bleaker: as seems to be the case with voting, where low turnout among young people doesn't seem to right itself as they get older, it may be that they are less and less likely to join parties and that their lack of interest in doing so will continue throughout their lifetimes; if so, then parties will gradually shrink as the members they have now eventually shuffle off this mortal coil.[24] This would be a real generational shift.

Education

Age, of course, intersects with education, not least because younger people will have been obliged to stay on at school later than older people (some of whom would have been allowed to leave before their 16th birthday) and because far more of them will have graduated with a tertiary qualification (normally a university degree or its equivalent) than was the case in their parents' or grandparents' generation. Educational opportunities are also influenced, as is the case with life chances in general, by social class. As a result, although it is true to say that party members overall are better educated than voters, it is truer of the members of some parties than others. Again, this has long been the case. In the late 1980s, the proportion of the population who were graduates was far, far lower than it is today (in fact, it was just under 10 per cent), but it was true of nearly 30 per cent of Labour Party members (a proportion that had risen to just over one-third a decade later). Surveyed in the early 1990s, only one in ten Tory members had a degree, however – probably a reflection of the fact that so many of them, being relatively old, were brought up when getting a degree was unusual (and unnecessary) even for many middle-class people. On the other hand, Liberal Democrat members, more of whom were middle-aged rather than retired, were just as well educated as Labour's grassroots. Meanwhile, a survey of Green Party members in the 1990s found that 55 per cent of them were graduates.[25]

Table 3.4 focuses on the proportion of contemporary party members in each of the parties who are university graduates and compares it with the proportion of those parties' voters who are also graduates. Once again, the overall score is also given: in 2017, some 51 per cent of party members had attended university (or its equivalent), compared to 26 per cent of voters. The scores for the parties reflect this marked difference but vary considerably. At one end of the spectrum, we have UKIP, which, as we have seen, has a relatively working-class and relatively old voter base and fewer middle-class and younger members than other parties; this almost certainly accounts for the fact that they are also the least well educated, only about a fifth of them having graduated from university; even so, this is proportionately more than the party's voters, only a tenth of whom appear to have been through higher education.

In the middle of the spectrum stand the Conservatives and the SNP, about two-fifths of whose members are graduates. In the Conservatives' case, this represents a big change since the party's members were first surveyed in the early 1990s and could, in time, produce a membership which is rather less deferential and no longer as prepared as it used to be to put up with having very little formal say on the party's policy positions – an issue to which we return later in the book.

At the other end of the spectrum sit Labour, the Liberal Democrats and the Greens, about six out of ten of whose members (or more) are graduates. Whether that is a good thing or a bad thing for Labour's electoral prospects may depend, as we discussed earlier in relation to social class, on whether it can nonetheless remain responsive to the demands and preferences of people who haven't accessed, and probably never will access, higher education – demands and preferences that, research shows, can often be very different from those of people who have.[26]

Employment sector

We also asked questions about which sector of the economy party members work in, and in this respect, as in many others, there is a very stark difference between the members of the Conservative and Labour parties. Tory members are far more likely to work in the private than in the public sector, while the reverse was true for their Labour counterparts – just as it was, incidentally, for members of the Green Party and the Liberal Democrats, when they were surveyed in the early and late 1990s,

TABLE 3.4 Educational profiles of party members and voters

	Conservative		Labour		Liberal Democrat		UKIP		Green		SNP		All parties	
	Mem	Vot	Mem	Vot	Mem	Vot	Mem	Vot	Mem	Vot	Mem	Vot	Mem	Vot
2015														
Grad.	39	26	57	28	56	40	24	15	57	43	43	27	46	28
M-V	13		29		16		9		14		16		18	
2017														
Grad.	42	21	57	29	65	39	22	10	67	29	42	28	51	26
M-V	21		28		26		12		38		14		25	

Note: All figures percentages of column categories. Mem = members; Vot = voters; Grad = graduates; M-V = gap between members' and voters' percentages supporting each party.

TABLE 3.5 Public- and private-sector occupational locations of party members

	Conservative		Labour		Liberal Democrat		UKIP		Green		SNP	
	2015	2017	2015	2017	2015	2017	2015	2017	2015	2017	2015	2017
Self-employed	25	26	15	20	20	21	33	30	21	22	20	17
Private	47	46	29	28	37	36	43	42	34	30	38	40
Nationalized	6	7	20	21	12	18	7	8	21	20	18	19
Other public	16	14	25	21	20	14	13	14	10	11	17	17
Charity	6	7	11	10	12	11	4	30	14	17	8	8

Note: All figures percentages of column categories. Comparison with voters is not possible since the sectoral variable does not appear on the relevant waves of the BES in 2015 and 2017.

respectively.[27] As Table 3.5 shows, things haven't changed much in this respect – relatively speaking anyway.

Public-sector employment, after shrinking under 18 years of Conservative government after 1979, rose a little under New Labour but then fell again sharply under the austerity policies introduced by the Tory–Liberal Democrat coalition after 2010. As a result, fewer party members across the board work in the public sector than they did when they were surveyed in the 1980s and 1990s. Nevertheless, members of left-wing parties are still more likely to work (or to have worked) in the public sector (and indeed in the charitable and voluntary sector) than their right-wing counterparts, with this tendency being particularly marked for Labour members, getting on for half of whom work (or have worked) in the public sector. Conversely, Conservative members are much more likely to be (or to have been) self-employed or employed in the private sector – as are UKIP members, who are significantly more likely than the members of any other party to be working (to have been working) for themselves. UKIP members are also three times more likely to be (or to have been) self-employed than the electorate as a whole.

Because there are more members of left-wing parties than right-wing parties – party members as a whole are slightly more likely to be working (or to have worked) in the public and the so-called third sector than most British people. Not for the first time, this raises questions about their representativeness – questions (again, not for the first time) which may be particularly troubling for the Labour Party. Given that its members are significantly more likely to work (or to have worked) in the public sector than the electorate as a whole, and are considerably less likely to work (or to have worked in the private sector), Labour's claim to represent the interests of working people – particularly those in the biggest (i.e., the private) sector of the economy – risks ringing a little hollow.[28] Of course, one could also make the point, that with the work experience of its membership skewed towards self-employment and the private sector, the accusation often levelled against the Conservative Party that it doesn't care as much as it should do about the public sector perhaps has some basis in fact.

Income

Public-sector employees are not necessarily paid less than those working in the private sector, especially at the lower end of the labour market, and there are plenty of well-remunerated professionals working outside the private sector. Still, it remains the case that the latter is where the really big money is. It comes as little surprise, then, that, as Figure 3.1 shows, it is members of the Conservative Party who are most likely to be among the highest earners, with nearly four in ten putting their annual income at over £30,000 (just over the median salary for a full-time employee) and one in 20 putting it at over £100,000 – a figure that is all the more striking considering how many Tories are of pensionable age. It also makes for a marked contrast with members of other parties: for instance, those on £30,000 or more make up just under and just over a third of Labour and Liberal Democrat members, respectively, but only a quarter of SNP and UKIP members and only a fifth of members of the Green Party (more than a quarter of whom have an income of less than £10,000 – possibly, who knows, because they have chosen to drop out of the proverbial rat race). In some ways just as fascinatingly (although we can only speculate as to why), UKIP and especially Conservative members are noticeably more reluctant than their more left-leaning counterparts to give a figure for their annual income.

Ethnicity

But although there is variation – often quite marked variation – between the parties when it comes to class, gender, age, education, and employment there is hardly any when it comes to something that intersects with, and perhaps even trumps, them: ethnicity. Previous surveys conducted in the late 1980s through to the late 1990s showed that both the Liberal Democrat and the Tory memberships were 99 per cent white and that Labour's membership was 96 per cent white.[29] Little has changed since then. The members of six of Britain's largest political parties, notwithstanding the growth of the country's ethnic minority community, are still overwhelmingly white overall – indeed, 96 per cent are white, when nowadays only around 80 per cent of the UK population identifies as such. The Greens have the lowest proportion of white members at 95 per cent, while the Tories have the highest at 97 per cent; each of the other parties records a figure of 96 per cent in our survey. In effect, this amounts to no variation at all across the parties given that every figure falls within the usual margin of error for survey data.

This probably comes as no surprise when it comes to UKIP or the Conservative Party, whose hard lines and rhetoric on migration and multiculturalism tend to reinforce the idea among BAME (black and minority ethnic) voters that they are not the parties for them.[30] But it is, perhaps more of surprise to see that Labour, which has a hugely disproportionate share (i.e., just over half) of the BAME vote and dominates the cities in which many minority communities live, has so few members who come from those communities – at least as a proportion of its total membership. In absolute terms, of course, Labour's sheer size advantage over its main rival means that it probably has around 25,000 non-white members compared to the Tories' 3,500. It is also true that, because ethnic minorities are less likely to turn out to vote, the parties'

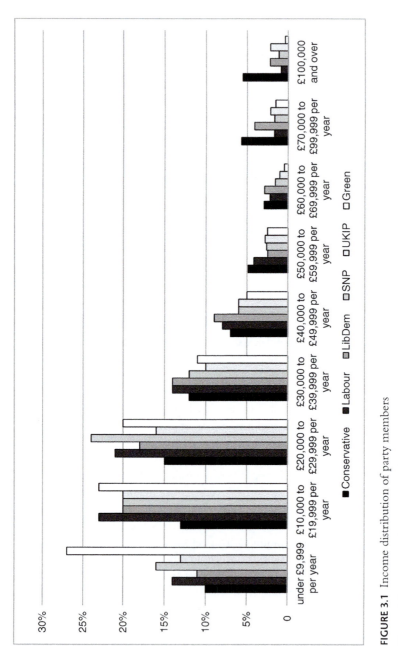

FIGURE 3.1 Income distribution of party members

Note: Each bar represents the percentage of the party membership falling into the relevant income category. Chart does not include those respondents who claimed not to know or declined to answer.

members are not quite as unrepresentative of their voters than they are of Britain as a whole: the biggest differences between parties' members and voters in terms of non-white support are for the Greens (3.6 percentage points) and Labour (3.4 points). That said, it is, of course, possible that we are dealing with another vicious cycle here: because ethnic minorities don't see themselves as represented in the system, they are less inclined to participate either as members or voters, and because of that, they are less likely to get selected as candidates and elected as MPs, and so on and so on.[31]

Location

Where we *do* see very obvious variation, both between and within parties, is in where their members live. We can get a sense of this by classifying exactly where they live in the parts of England known as government office regions (see Figure 3.2) and, so as to capture the rest of Great Britain, adding Scotland and Wales. Table 3.6

FIGURE 3.2 English regions

Source: https://publications.parliament.uk/pa/cm200607/cmselect/cmcomloc/352/35204.htm

Contains Parliamentary information licensed under the Open Parliament Licence v3.0

TABLE 3.6 Regional profiles of party members and voters

	Conservative		Labour		Liberal Democrat		SNP		UKIP		Green	
	Mem	Vot	Mem	Vot	Mem	Vot	Mem	Vot	Mem	Vot	Mem	Vot
2015												
North East	2	3	5	6	2	3	0	0	2	5	4	4
M-V	−1		−1		−1		0		−3		0	
North West	9	9	13	12	9	7	0	0	8	10	10	8
M-V	0		1		2		0		−2		2	
Yorks&Humber	6	7	9	10	7	7	1	0	7	9	10	10
M-V	−1		−1		0		1		−2		0	
East Midlands	6	8	7	7	4	4	0	0	7	8	6	6
M-V	−2		0		0		0		−1		0	
West Midlands	7	9	7	8	5	5	0	0	8	9	7	7
M-V	−2		−1		−1		0		−1		0	
East of England	12	11	7	7	11	9	1	0	13	12	12	8
M-V	1		0		2		1		1		4	
London	14	12	16	14	18	13	1	0	7	9	15	18
M-V	2		2		5		1		−2		−3	
South East	20	17	14	8	18	14	0	0	24	16	16	15
M-V	3		6		4		0		8		1	
South West	11	10	9	6	13	15	1	0	14	9	17	10
M-V	1		3		−2		1		5		7	
Wales	3	7	7	10	4	8	0	0	5	10	5	7
M-V	−4		−3		−4		0		−5		−2	
Scotland	10	7	7	13	9	15	96	100	3	3	0	7
M-V	3		−6		−6		−4		0		−7	
2017												
North East	3	4	5	5	1	3	0	0	3	6	3	2
M-V	−1		0		−2		0		−3		1	
North West	9	9	15	13	9	7	1	0	6	11	8	6
M-V	0		2		2		1		−5		2	
Yorks&Humber	6	8	10	11	8	6	0	0	8	9	9	6
M-V	−2		−1		2		0		−1		3	
East Midlands	7	8	8	7	6	5	0	0	8	8	7	8
M-V	−1		1		1		0		0		−1	
West Midlands	8	8	6	7	7	5	1	0	9	10	6	9
M-V	0		−1		2		1		−1		−3	
East of England	10	10	9	8	11	10	1	0	14	13	8	10
M-V	0		1		1		1		1		−2	
London	12	10	12	14	15	15	1	0	9	9	12	19
M-V	2		−2		0		1		0		−7	

	Conservative		Labour		Liberal Democrat		SNP		UKIP		Green	
	Mem	Vot	Mem	Vot	Mem	Vot	Mem	Vot	Mem	Vot	Mem	Vot
South-East	21	16	15	10	21	17	0	0	22	15	17	19
M–V	5		5		3		0		7		−2	
South-West	11	10	10	7	14	15	1	0	14	9	16	9
M–V	1		3		−1		1		5		7	
Wales	4	7	7	9	4	7	1	0	5	8	4	5
M–V	−3		−2		−3		1		−3		−1	
Scotland	10	10	5	9	5	10	94	100	3	3	13	8
M–V	0		−4		−5		−6		0		5	

Note: All figures percentages of column categories. Mem = members; Vot = voters; M–V = gap between members' and voters' percentages supporting each party.

gives the full picture for both 2015 and for 2017, showing both where party members and their voters live. What emerges is that parties don't always have lots of members where they have lots of voters.

For instance, the Tories are even more the party of southern England (i.e., Eastern England, London, South-East and South-West) with regard to their members than it is with regard to their voters. Labour clearly has lots of members in London, but the capital's share of Labour voters is actually stronger than its share of members, a disproportionate number of whom do live in the south but outside London in the South East and South West – areas where, outside the odd university town, Labour is very weak electorally. Interestingly, this is nothing new: previous research covering the late 1980s noted that the party's membership was 'skewed . . . towards the more Conservatively-inclined regions of the country'.[32] The Lib Dems have traditionally done quite well at the ballot box in the southwest and Wales, but they have fewer members there than one might expect, and like the two main parties, they have a bigger share of members than voters in the south-east. The results for the SNP are hardly surprising, although it is interesting to note that around 6 per cent of its members live in England and Wales. As for UKIP, like its larger rivals it, too, has a bigger share of members than voters in the south-east – and, in its case, the south-west, too. Still, UKIP's main areas of strength in terms of members would seem to be where it performs best electorally, namely, the east of England and the Midlands, although, interestingly, it has a smaller share of members than voters in another area where it also does quite well, namely, the north west of England. Finally, a greater proportion of Green Party members than voters live in the south-west and Wales, whereas the reverse is true when it comes to London and the south-east – areas where the Greens get a fair few votes but, relatively speaking, don't have that many members (which appears to represent something of a change to the situation back in the early 1990s).[33]

The question, of course, is whether any of this makes a difference not just to the outlook of the memberships of the different parties (and by extension the parties themselves) but also to their capacity to fight elections on the ground – something that research shows does matter.[34] Intuitively, and even in an era where telephone canvassing and social media campaigning can be done from anywhere in the country, that would seem to be the case. Anyone familiar with the Conservative Party will know that it has, for a long time, suffered because so many of its members belong to local associations in safe seats in the south rather than in marginal seats in other parts of the country.[35] Indeed, one of the reasons it ended up getting into trouble with the Electoral Commission (and not only the Electoral Commission) after the 2015 election was because of its desperation to get round the problem by bussing activists into marginal seats at the same time as trying to avoid their efforts being factored in to local campaign spending.[36] Labour's slightly more even spread might help it in that respect, but, from a purely electoral point of view, it would presumably swap some of the members it has in southern England, where it stands relatively little chance of overturning decades (even centuries) worth of Tory dominance, for more members in, say, the Midlands, which is so often a decisive battleground. As for the Liberal Democrats, the fact that they don't have as many members in the south-west as one might have thought probably doesn't bode well, at least in the short term, for their hopes of retaking the seats they lost to the Conservatives in 2015.

Inveterate joiners?

Something else we wanted to explore was whether party members are the kind of people who just enjoy signing up to things, either to express their support for their aims and values or to get the benefits of being a member, tangible or otherwise. Evidence from previous research suggests this is likely to be the case. For instance, in the British Participation Survey of 2011, respondents were asked if they had ever taken part in various pressure group activities, and party members were consistently more likely to have done so than non-members. Thus, 18 per cent of party members had held office in pressure group organizations, compared to just 2 per cent of non-members, while 32 per cent of members had taken part in pressure group campaigns, compared to 6 per cent of non-members, and 25 per cent of party members claimed to have held responsible positions in the voluntary sector or local community organizations compared to 7 per cent of non-members.[37] Similarly, 12.5 per cent of UK respondents to the World Values Survey of 2005 who described themselves as 'active party members' were also active members of other organizations, compared to just 0.4 per cent of those who were not members of political parties.[38] So, our survey asked our party members whether they were also members of a number of other non-party organizations. Admittedly, this is only a small sample of 14 such organizations, so it cannot be regarded as representative of the full range of organizations that people might join, but it is nevertheless indicative of patterns of activity among party members. A first glance at Table 3.7 suggests

TABLE 3.7 Organizational memberships of party members

	Conservative		Labour		Liberal Democrat		UKIP		Green		SNP	
	2015	2017	2015	2017	2015	2017	2015	2017	2015	2017	2015	2017
Trade union	5	5	39	32	12	12	6	7	19	21	16	15
National Trust	28	27	22	22	32	34	18	18	18	22	9	10
RSPB	9	6	10	10	9	9	6	6	12	14	5	6
Royal British Legion	7	5	2	1	2	2	9	7	1	2	2	1
Greenpeace	1	1	5	6	6	3	1	2	17	17	3	4
Freemasons	5	5	0	0	1	1	5	4	1	0	3	3
English Heritage	9	10	9	8	12	12	8	10	7	8	0	1
Women's Institute	2	2	1	1	1	1	1	1	1	1	1	1
Saga	7	6	3	2	6	3	6	3	2	1	3	2
Weightwatchers	1	2	1	1	1	1	1	1	1	1	1	1
Scout Association	2	1	1	0	2	2	1	0	1	1	1	1
St. John's Ambulance	1	1	0	0	1	1	1	1	0	1	1	0
Girlguiding	1	1	1	1	0	1	1	0	1	1	1	1
World Wildlife	2	1	3	2	3	3	3	3	4	4	2	2

Note: All figures percentages of column categories. 2015 n = 5,695; 2017 n = 5,219.

that a fair few party members are also members of the National Trust, English Heritage, and the Royal Society for the Protection of Birds (RSPB) – indeed, by our reckoning, they may be four or five times more likely to belong to them than most people.[39] Clearly, this may have a lot to do with how middle-aged and how middle-class many party members are: party members in the ABC1 group are twice as likely as their C2DE counterparts to be members of the National Trust, for instance, while two-thirds of party members who also belong to the National Trust are aged over 50. It is nonetheless suggestive of a bunch of people who like joining things, notwithstanding some differences between members of different parties.[40]

Most of those differences, in fact, are pretty predictable. Not many party members are also Freemasons, or at least prepared to admit that they are, but those belonging to the Tories and UKIP – both of which are traditionally business- (or at least small business–) friendly – are perhaps much more likely to don the leather apron and to learn the secret handshake than those belonging to the other parties. Likewise, given both their age profile and the fact that right-wing parties tend to be more supportive of military action in support of the national interest, it is not entirely surprising that Conservatives and UKIP members are more likely to belong to the British Legion than their left-of-centre counterparts. It is equally unsurprising to find that Greenpeace membership is far more popular among Green Party members than it is among members of the other parties, especially the two right-wing parties.

Most predictable of all, of course, is that members of the Labour Party are far more likely to belong to a trade union than are their counterparts in other parties – particularly (but, given their age profile and its record of conflict with organized workers, unsurprisingly) those who belong to the Conservative Party. The fact that at least a third of Labour members belong to a union means that they are significantly more inclined to join one than the average citizen of working age, under a quarter of whom are union members, with those working in the public sector far more likely to join than those working in the private sector. Perhaps worryingly for the unions – but not entirely surprisingly if one looks at union membership in the country as a whole – older Labour Party members are more likely to belong to a trade union than their younger counterparts, and over-65s make up around a quarter of trade union members amongst the party's membership. Middle-class Labour members are also more likely to be union members than their working-class counterparts. Most interesting of all, however, is the fact that two-thirds of Labour members, by *not* belonging to a union, could be deemed not to be adhering to the party's rules, which clearly state that, in order to be eligible for membership, each individual member must not only 'accept and conform to the constitution, programme, principles and policy of the Party' but 'if applicable, be a member of a trade union affiliated to the Trade Union Congress or considered by the NEC [National Executive Committee] as a bona fide trade union'.[41] Still, we mustn't run away with the idea that things have got worse recently: true, the survey of Labour members conducted in the late 1980s found that nearly two-thirds of them belonged to a trade union, but that had already dropped to just a third when they were surveyed a decade later in the late 1990s.[42]

Asking party members about which other organizations they belong to, of course, has its limitations: most obviously they could belong to a whole host of institutions, clubs and societies that we could never possibly hope to name, so our findings can only relate to those we suggested. We feel we are on surer ground when it comes to which newspapers they read, however (Table 3.8). Given how interested in politics they are likely to be, it is surprising to note that one in five party members doesn't bother reading one at all, although that still means they do so more than the electorate as a whole, a third of whom aren't fussed. Party members are also more likely than the electorate as a whole to read a broadsheet than a tabloid: for instance, half of party members read the *Telegraph* or the *Times* or the *Guardian* or the *Indy* or the *FT*, compared to just one in five of the public – and the latter are seven times as likely as the former to read the UK's best-selling paper, the *Sun*.

The differences between the members of the various parties are just as striking. SNP members are, predictably enough, much more likely to steer clear of the UK nationals (and their Scottish variants like the *Daily Record*) – and they, followed by UKIP and Green members, are most likely to read no paper at all. Least likely not to do so are Tory members, a full half of whom read the big-selling right-wing (Eurosceptic) titles, the *Telegraph* and the *Mail*. So do UKIP members, although

TABLE 3.8 Newspaper preferences of party members, 2017

	Conservative	Labour	Liberal Democrat	UKIP	Greens	SNP	All Party Members	Voters
Guardian	2	46	27	1	51	8	23	7
Herald/Scotsman	7	12	14	8	9	51	17	12
Telegraph	33	2	4	18	1	0	11	5
Mail	17	3	3	26	1	2	9	13
Times	21	5	11	5	2	2	8	4
Independent	2	8	17	2	11	3	7	2
Mirror	1	7	1	1	0	3	2	7
Sun	3	1	2	4	1	3	2	14
Express	2	1	0	11	0	0	2	2
FT	1	1	2	1	0	0	1	0
Star	0	0	0	0	0	0	0	1
None	11	15	19	22	24	28	19	31

Note: All figures are percentages of the column categories.

whereas Tories prefer the *Telegraph* to the *Mail*, they prefer the *Mail* to the *Telegraph*. They are also, incidentally, far more likely to read the zealously Eurosceptic and anti-immigration *Express*. On the left-hand side of the ledger, the *Guardian* is the clear market leader, being read by about half of all Labour Party and Green Party members. It also accounts for just over a quarter of Liberal Democrats, although members of the country's third party are also more likely than others to prefer the *Indy*, while one in ten reads the *Times* – the arguably less *parti-pris* 'paper of record' that is read by a fifth of all Tory members.

Conclusion

People who belong to political parties aren't *that* different – but they are different. They are, even if only on average and forgetting for the moment some significant differences between members of different parties, more likely to be well off and well educated. They are also more likely to be men than women, as well as much more likely to be white than from an ethnic minority community. And overall more party members live in the south of England and work in the public sector than one might expect. Party members seem more likely than most people to join some well-known, national, non-party organizations and to read newspapers, too. Exactly which newspaper they read, perhaps not surprisingly, often varies according to which party they belong to. The same, of course, is true of what they think about how society works and the direction they would like to see it head in. And that is the focus of our next chapter.

Notes

1 *Yes Minister*, Series 1, Episode 3, 'The economy drive', by Anthony Jay and Jonathan Lynn, adapted for radio, first broadcast 1 November 1983.
2 In the Hansard Society's annual *Audit of Political Engagement* some 11 per cent of respondents said they would be prepared to 'donate money or pay a membership fee to a political party'. Given that some of those people would rather just donate than become members, then, unless parties were prepared to give away membership for free, we can reasonably assume that nine out of ten people wouldn't dream of joining a party. See www.hansardsociety.org.uk/publications/reports/audit-of-political-engagement-16 for the full audit.
3 Pulzer, Peter (1967) *Political Representation and Elections in Britain* (London: George Allen & Unwin), p. 98.
4 See, for example, Evans, Geoffrey and Tilley, James (2017) *The New Politics of Class: The Political Exclusion of the British Working Class* (Oxford: Oxford University Press).
5 See, for example, Verba, Sidney, Nie, Norman and Kim, Jae-on Kim (1987) *Participation and Political Equality: A Seven-nation Comparison* (Chicago: University of Chicago Press).
6 See the following guide: www.ipsos.com/sites/default/files/publication/6800-03/MediaCT_thoughtpiece_Social_Grade_July09_V3_WEB.pdf.
7 On the differences in turnout between classes – something that has traditionally been assumed to disadvantage the left – see Heath, Oliver (2018) 'Policy alienation, social alienation and working-class abstention in Britain, 1964–2010', *British Journal of Political Science*, 48 (4), pp. 1053–1073.
8 Seyd, Patrick and Whiteley, Paul (1992) *Labour's Grass Roots: The Politics of Party Membership* (Oxford: Clarendon), p. 33; Whiteley, Paul, Seyd, Patrick and Richardson, Jeremy (1994) *True Blues: The Politics of Conservative Party Membership* (Oxford: Oxford University Press), p. 45; Whiteley, Paul, Seyd, Patrick and Billinghurst, Antony (2006) *Third Force Politics: Liberal Democrats at the Grassroots* (Oxford: Oxford University Press), p. 34. Rüdig, Wolfgang, Bennie, Lynn and Franklin, Mark (1991) *Green Party Members: A Profile* (Glasgow: Strathclyde University), p. 24, available online at https://ewds2.strath.ac.uk/Portals/75/Documents/GPMProfile1991.pdf
9 Seyd, Patrick and Whiteley, Paul (2002) *New Labour's Grassroots: The Transformation of the Labour Party Membership* (Houndsmills: Palgrave Macmillan), p. 35.
10 Rüdig, Bennie and Franklin, 1991.
11 Of course, this statement depends on exactly what one means by 'representative'. In this instance, we are using the term in the sense of demographically 'descriptive' rather than politically 'substantive' representation. See note 14 of this chapter. And for a full account of these concepts see Hannah Pitkin's classic work *The Concept of Representation* (Berkeley: University of California Press, 1967).
12 Allen, Peter (2018) *The Political Class: Why It Matters Who Our Politicians Are* (Oxford: Oxford University Press).
13 Hill, Eleanor (2018) 'It's not what you know, it's who you know: What are the implications of social networks in UK politics for electoral choice?', unpublished PhD thesis, University of Manchester.
14 See, for example, Phillips, Anne (1995) *The Politics of Presence* (Oxford: Clarendon Press).
15 Evans, Geoffrey and Tilley, James (2017) *The New Politics of Class: The Political Exclusion of the British Working Class* (Oxford: Oxford University Press).
16 Bale, Tim, Green-Pedersen, Christoffer, Krouwel, André, Luther, Kurt Richard and Sitter, Nick (2010) 'If you can't beat them, join them? Explaining social democratic responses to the challenge from the populist radical right in Western Europe', *Political Studies*, 58 (3), pp. 410–426. See also Consterdine, Erica (2018) *Labour's Immigration Policy: The Making of the Migration State* (London: Palgrave Macmillan) and Bale, Tim (2014) 'Putting it right? The Labour Party's big shift on immigration since 2010', *Political Quarterly*, 85 (3), pp. 296–303.

17 For more detail on trends in women's voting across several countries, see Abendschön, Simone and Steinmetz, Stephanie (2014) 'The gender gap in voting revisited: Women's party preferences in a European context', *Social Politics*, 21 (2), pp. 315–344.

18 Sanders, Anna, Annesley, Claire and Gains, Francesca (2019) 'What did the coalition government do for women? An analysis of gender equality policy agendas in the UK 2010–2015', *British Politics*, 14 (2), pp. 162–180.

19 Seyd, Patrick and Whiteley, Paul (1992) *Labour's Grass Roots* (Oxford: Clarendon), p. 39; Seyd, Patrick and Whiteley, Paul (2002) *New Labour's Grassroots* (Houndsmills: Palgrave Macmillan), p. 35; Whiteley, Paul, Seyd, Patrick and Richardson, Jeremy (1994) *True Blues* (Oxford: Oxford University Press), p. 43; Whiteley, Paul, Seyd, Patrick and Billinghurst, Antony (2006) *Third Force Politics* (Oxford: Oxford University Press), p. 24; Rüdig, Wolfgang, Bennie, Lynn and Franklin, Mark (1991) *Green Party Members: A Profile* (Glasgow: Strathclyde University), p. 14. The survey conducted by Childs and Webb put the gender split among Conservative Party members in 2009 at 60:40, which suggests that the imbalance has got a little more pronounced in the last decade. See Childs, Sarah and Webb, Paul (2012) *Sex, Gender and the Conservative Party: From Iron Lady to Kitten Heels* (Houndsmills: Palgrave Macmillan).

20 See www.fawcettsociety.org.uk/news/women-candidates-face-explicit-resistance-and-discrimination-within-political-parties Culhane, Leah and Olchawski, Jemima (2018) Strategies for Success (London: Fawcett Society).

21 Seyd, Patrick and Whiteley, Paul (1992) *Labour's Grass Roots* (Oxford: Clarendon), p. 32; Seyd, Patrick and Whiteley, Paul (2002) *New Labour's Grassroots* (Houndsmills: Palgrave Macmillan), p. 35; Whiteley, Paul, Seyd, Patrick and Richardson, Jeremy (1994) *True Blues* (Oxford: Oxford University Press), pp. 42–43; Whiteley, Paul, Seyd, Patrick and Billinghurst, Antony (2006) *Third Force Politics* (Oxford: Oxford University Press), p. 22; Rüdig, Wolfgang, Bennie, Lynn and Franklin, Mark (1991) *Green Party Members: A Profile* (Glasgow: Strathclyde University), p. 15.

22 Conservative activist, interview 13 November 2015.

23 The best source on differences between old and young is Phillips, Daniel, Curtice, John, Phillips, Miranda and Perry, Jane, eds. (2018) *British Social Attitudes: The 35th Report* (London: NatCen), available online at www.bsa.natcen.ac.uk/media/39284/bsa35_full-report.pdf.

24 Wattenberg, Martin P. (2015) *Is Voting for Young People?* (Abingdon: Routledge).

25 Seyd, Patrick and Whiteley, Paul (2002) *New Labour's Grassroots* (Houndsmills: Palgrave Macmillan), p. 35; Whiteley, Paul, Seyd, Patrick and Richardson, Jeremy (1994) *True Blues* (Oxford: Oxford University Press), p. 44; Whiteley, Paul, Seyd, Patrick and Billinghurst, Antony (2006) *Third Force Politics* (Oxford: Oxford University Press), p. 34; Rüdig, Wolfgang, Bennie, Lynn and Franklin, Mark (1991) *Green Party Members: A Profile* (Glasgow: Strathclyde University), pp. 18–19.

26 Runciman, David (2016) 'How the education gap is tearing politics apart', *The Guardian*, 5 October. See also Bovens, Mark and Wille, Anchrit (2017) *Diploma Democracy: The Rise of Political Meritocracy* (Oxford: Oxford University Press).

27 Seyd, Patrick and Whiteley, Paul (1992) *Labour's Grass Roots* (Oxford: Clarendon), p. 33; Seyd, Patrick and Whiteley, Paul (2002) *New Labour's Grassroots* (Houndsmills: Palgrave Macmillan), p. 37; Whiteley, Paul, Seyd, Patrick and Richardson, Jeremy (1994) *True Blues* (Oxford: Oxford University Press), p. 45; Whiteley, Paul, Seyd, Patrick and Billinghurst, Antony (2006) *Third Force Politics* (Oxford: Oxford University Press), p. 24; Rüdig, Wolfgang, Bennie, Lynn and Franklin, Mark (1991) *Green Party Members: A Profile* (Glasgow: Strathclyde University), p. 25.

28 There are a number of reasons why there might be a difference of political outlook between those working in the public and private sectors. Ideological predisposition could incline left-wing individuals to work in the public sector while right-wing individuals might well prefer a career in private enterprise, or working in one or other of these sectors might serve to socialize employees into a certain view of their interests – with public-sector workers feeling the need for higher taxes and public spending, but their private-sector

counterparts feeling the precise opposite (see Webb, Paul (2000) *The Modern British Party System* (London: Sage Publications), p. 57).

29 Seyd, Patrick and Whiteley, Paul (1992) *Labour's Grass Roots* (Oxford: Clarendon), p. 37; Whiteley, Paul, Seyd, Patrick and Richardson, Jeremy (1994) *True Blues: The Politics of Conservative Party Membership* (Oxford: Oxford University Press), p. 48; Whiteley, Paul, Seyd, Patrick and Billinghurst, Antony (2006) *Third Force Politics* (Oxford: Oxford University Press), p. 25.

30 See Ashcroft, Michael (2012) *Degrees of Separation: Ethnic Minority Voters and the Conservative Party* (London: Lord Ashcroft), available online at https://lordashcroftpolls.com/wp-content/uploads/2012/04/DEGREES-OF-SEPARATION.pdf. See also Katwala, Sunder and Ballinger, Steve (2017) *Mind the Gap: How the Ethnic Minority Vote Cost Theresa May Her Majority* (London: British Future), available online at www.britishfuture.org/wp-content/uploads/2017/09/Mind-the-gap-report-2017.pdf.

31 See Fisher, Stephen D., Heath, Anthony, Sanders, David and Sobolewska, Maria (2015) 'Candidate ethnicity and vote choice in Britain', *British Journal of Political Science*, 45 (4), pp. 883–905. See also Sanders, David, Fisher, Stephen D., Heath, Anthony and Sobolewska, Maria (2014) 'The democratic engagement of Britain's ethnic minorities', *Ethnic and Racial Studies*, 37 (1), pp. 120–139.

32 Seyd and Whiteley Seyd, Patrick and Whiteley, Paul (1992) *Labour's Grass Roots* (Oxford: Clarendon), p. 28.

33 Rüdig, Wolfgang, Bennie, Lynn and Franklin, Mark (1991) *Green Party Members: A Profile* (Glasgow: Strathclyde University), p. 16.

34 Fieldhouse, Edward, Fisher, Justin and Cutts, David (forthcoming) 'Popularity equilibrium: Testing a general theory of local campaign effectiveness', *Party Politics*.

35 Bale, Tim (2012) *The Conservatives Since 1945: The Drivers of Party Change* (Oxford: Oxford University Press), passim.

36 Howker, Ed and Basnett, Guy (2017) 'The inside story of the Tory election scandal', *The Guardian*, 23 March, available online at www.theguardian.com/news/2017/mar/23/conservative-election-scandal-victory-2015-expenses.

37 Evidence comes from British Participation Survey 2011; n=1355 for each of the relationships cited here. For further detail on this dataset see Webb, Paul (2013) 'Who is willing to participate? Dissatisfied democrats, stealth democrats and populists in the UK', *European Journal of Political Research*, 52 (6), pp. 747–776.

38 See www.worldvaluessurvey.org/WVSOnline.jsp.

39 We made the comparison by taking the latest membership figures of those organizations from their annual reports and then dividing them by the size of the relevant adult population.

40 The propensity for some people to join more than one civil society organization is well attested in the literature on political participation. See for instance Verba, Sidney, Schlozman, Kay and Brady, Henry E. (1995) *Voice and Equality: Civic Volunteerism in American Politics* (Cambridge, MA: Harvard University Press); and Dalton, Russell J. (2017) *The Participation Gap: Social Status and Political Inequality* (Oxford: Oxford University Press), Chapter 4.

41 *Labour Party Rule Book*, Clause 1 (6) 'Conditions of Membership'.

42 Seyd, Patrick and Whiteley, Paul (2002) *New Labour's Grassroots* (Houndsmills: Palgrave Macmillan), p. 35.

4

WHAT DO PARTY MEMBERS THINK?

We now have some notion of who the members of Britain's biggest political parties are, but what do they actually think? In this chapter we explore this by analyzing their views on classic left–right issues (like how income and wealth should be distributed and how much the state should be involved in the economy and welfare provision), as well as their views on the issues that distinguish social liberals from (small-*c*) social conservatives and, of course, their views on what seems to be the most divisive issue in contemporary British politics – Brexit.

Locating party members in one- and two-dimensional attitudinal space

We start by looking at where party members stand in simple left–right terms. Our survey posed the question, 'In politics people sometimes talk of left and right. Where would you place yourself on the following scale, where 0 represents the far left and 10 represents the far right?' Table 4.1 shows the average positions of the various groups of party members in 2015 and 2017. Overall, this suggests that British party members stand ever so slightly to the *left* of midway point (4.44 in 2015 and 4.14 in 2017), which is hardly surprising given our sample includes four parties that would generally be considered left-of-centre (Labour, Liberal Democrats, the Scottish National Party [SNP] and Greens) with a combined membership amounting to approximately 800,000, but only two parties to the right of centre (Conservatives and UK Independence Party [UKIP]), with a combined membership of little more than 200,000.

The subjective self-placements of the members follow this pattern in both years, with UKIP and Tory members comfortably furthest right and Green and Labour members furthest left. Liberal Democrat members are closest to the centre of the left–right scale, although they fall slightly to the left in both years. Both Labour and Liberal Democrat members appear to have shifted left over the two-year period, which might well reflect the nature of the considerable numbers of new members

TABLE 4.1 Self-location on left–right scale (0–10) by party membership, 2015 and 2017

Year	Conservative	Labour	Liberal Democrat	UKIP	Green	SNP	Total	Eta²
2015	7.8	2.4	4.1	7.3	1.9	3.0	4.4	0.712 (n = 5,594)
2017	7.6	2.1	3.9	7.4	2.0	3.1	4.1	0.667 (n = 5,154)

Note: All figures = mean scores on a scale where respondents are asked to locate themselves from 0 (far left) to 10 (far right). Eta² = measure of association between party and attitudinal scale. Between-party differences are significant at $p < .001$.

each party recruited during this time. Elsewhere, for instance, we have found that those who joined Labour after the general election of 2015 were generally more left-wing than existing members – partly, although by no means wholly, because around a third of them were 're-treads' who had left the party in the New Labour years and then rejoined after Jeremy Corbyn's ultimately successful leadership campaign persuaded them that they could 'get their party back'.[1]

Subjective self-placement on a general left–right scale is one thing, but there are other, more sophisticated ways we can measure people's attitudes. A more rigorous and nuanced method involves asking them two well-established sets of questions, one of which is intended to tap into their views on how state and society distributes and controls resources (the 'left–right' scale) and the other of which seeks to capture attitudes relating to tolerance, tradition and order (the 'liberty–authority' scale distinguishing the socially liberal from the socially conservative). These two sets of survey questions were first devised in the 1990s and have been regularly used in the British Election Study ever since.[2] We asked our party member respondents these questions in 2015 and 2017, and the results are broken down by party and reported in Table 4.2.

The respondents are presented with a series of statements and invited to say whether they agree, agree strongly, disagree, disagree strongly or neither agree nor disagree with each one. The table simplifies things by just reporting the percentages of each party whose members adopt either left-wing positions (i.e., by agreeing or agreeing strongly with the first five statements) or socially liberal positions (by disagreeing or disagreeing strongly with the last five statements). Moreover, we can summarize the overall position of respondents on each set of statements by creating simple additive scales for them (1 = left or liberal, 5 = right or socially conservative).

Focusing first on the mean scores for each set of party respondents, we see that the left–right additive scale essentially confirms the members' subjective perceptions of their ideological stances. The overall mean score of 2.18 in 2015 and 2.13 in 2017 locates the pooled sample a little to the left of the scale's midpoint of 3.00; it also shows that Conservative members are most right-wing (3.53 and 3.32), followed by UKIP members (2.44 and 2.47), while Labour (1.58 and 1.52) and the Greens (1.50 and 1.55) are furthest left. The Liberal Democrats (on 2.26 and 2.14) are located to the left of centre, although interestingly not that much further to the left of the midway point than UKIP members since, on the economy and welfare at least, the latter can hardly be described as devotees of neo-liberalism.

TABLE 4.2 Core left–right and liberty–authority indicators by party membership, 2015 and 2017

Statement	Conservative		Labour		Liberal Democrat		UKIP		Green		SNP		All Parties	
	2015	2017	2015	2017	2015	2017	2015	2017	2015	2017	2015	2017	2015	2017
Left–right indicators														
Government should redistribute from the better off	15.6	14.5	91.4	91.8	74.6	77.2	29.8	29.1	93.3	94.6	88.9	87.1	64.7 $V = 0.379$	68.1 $V = 0.383$
Big business takes advantage of ordinary people	27.5	40.7	92.4	97.4	74.7	79.3	74.0	72.9	96.2	98.3	93.7	93.3	74.8 $V = 0.347$	78.7 $V = 0.300$
Ordinary working people don't get fair shares	16.7	25.1	94.7	97.4	75.0	80.8	58.0	58.6	95.4	95.1	94.9	93.9	70.9 $V = 0.385$	75.4 $V = 0.350$
There is one law for the rich and one law for the poor	15.0	22.0	93.1	93.9	68.1	74.1	69.0	66.5	95.0	93.1	94.5	92.8	70.8 $V = 0.376$	72.7 $V = 0.343$
Management will always try to get the better of employees	24.2	33.7	81.4	76.2	54.3	54.6	62.5	62.6	78.8	63.2	79.0	77.5	62.5 $V = 0.272$	61.4 $V = 0.202$
Mean position on left–right scale (1 = left, 5 = right)	3.5	3.3	1.6	1.5	2.3	2.1	2.4	2.5	1.6	1.5	1.6	1.6	2.2 $eta^2 = 0.570$	2.1 $eta^2 = 0.501$

(Continued)

TABLE 4.2 (Continued)

Statement	Conservative		Labour		Liberal Democrat		UKIP		Green		SNP		All Parties	
	2015	2017	2015	2017	2015	2017	2015	2017	2015	2017	2015	2017	2015	2017
Liberty–authority indicators														
Young don't respect enough traditional British values	10.9	7.4	41.5	61.4	41.0	57.0	3.2	1.9	58.6	65.8	34.8	42.4	31.0 $V = 0.297$	52.0 $V = 0.334$
For some crimes, death is appropriate sentence	38.8	36.7	82.2	82.6	86.2	87.5	14.4	11.0	89.9	92.8	64.2	64.8	62.5 $V = 0.304$	67.8 $V = 0.303$
Schools should teach children to obey authority	4.8	5.6	30.5	46.3	28.7	34.2	6.4	5.8	50.3	52.4	27.1	31.6	23.9 $V = 0.266$	30.1 $V = 0.267$
Censorship is necessary to uphold moral standards	37.5	39.1	56.2	64.6	63.6	65.1	31.3	22.4	79.9	70.5	52.6	65.9	51.2 $V = 0.170$	55.9 $V = 0.170$
People who break the law should be given stiffer sentences	6.9	6.6	34.1	35.9	44.5	40.0	2.2	2.8	48.2	50.5	18.2	19.5	24.7 $V = 0.286$	27.7 $V = 0.282$
Mean position on liberty–authority scale (1 = socially liberal, 5 = socially conservative)	3.6	3.6	2.6	2.4	2.5	2.4	4.0	4.1	2.2	2.1	2.9	2.8	3.0 $eta^2 = 0.397$	2.8 $eta^2 = 0.416$

Note: Figures represent percentages of respondents agreeing or agreeing strongly with left-wing or socially liberal statements, unless otherwise indicated; V = Cramer's V measure of association between party and attitude; eta^2 = measure of association between party and attitudinal scale. All relationships significant at $p < .001$.

For the most part, there is considerable stability of opinion on the five left–right indicators from 2015 to 2017, although there are a few notable shifts. Most interesting, perhaps, are the increases in the percentage of Conservative members willing to concede that 'big business will always seek to take advantage of ordinary people', that 'ordinary workers don't get their fair share', that 'there is one law for the rich and another for the poor' and that 'management will always try to get the better of employees'. Admittedly, these movements are from low baselines, so in no case does a majority of Tory members accept these statements, but perhaps they do indicate a growing unease about the impact of nearly a decade of economic retrenchment and financial austerity or else the entry (indeed, the possible re-entry) of members who had previously been more attracted to UKIP. The Liberal Democrats' membership also shifted left somewhat after 2015, most obviously with respect to the 'fair shares' and 'one law for the rich' statements. The Greens remain a left-wing bunch overall, although there is a significant drop (from a high baseline) in the proportion willing to agree that 'management will always try to get the better of employees', perhaps reflecting an exodus of some of their most socialist-inclined followers to Labour after Jeremy Corbyn became leader – something we discuss in Chapter 8.

Turning to the indicators of social liberalism and (small-c) social conservatism, the most striking feature is the position of UKIP members as by far the most socially conservative, outdoing the Tories in this regard. Indeed, this shows that the conventional description of 'Kippers' as 'right-wing' only fully convinces in terms of this predilection for tradition, order and authority. As we have seen, their mean score on the left–right scale puts them to the left of centre, but on the liberty–authority scale their average is close to the latter pole (4.02 in 2015 and 4.10 in 2017). The other notable feature of the liberty–authority indicators is the movement of Labour members towards even greater social liberalism between 2015 and 2017, surely reflecting the impact of their new members. Here, we can see a quite remarkable increase in the percentage who oppose the view that 'Young people don't respect traditional British values enough' (from 41.5 per cent to 61.4 per cent) and almost equally striking rises in the numbers rejecting the claims that 'Schools should teach children to obey authority' (from 30.5 per cent to 46.3 per cent) and that 'Censorship of magazines and films is necessary to uphold moral standards' (from 56.2 per cent to 64.6 per cent). The Liberal Democrats too became a little more, well, liberal overall, largely on the basis of a jump in the number disavowing the argument that 'Young people don't respect traditional British values enough' (from 41 per cent to 57 per cent) – but neither they nor Labour members could quite match the most socially liberal of all parties – the Greens.

Views on immigration are also associated with social conservatism and liberalism. In 2015 and 2017, we asked respondents two relevant questions: 'Do you think that immigration undermines or enriches Britain's cultural life?' and 'Do you think that immigration is good or bad for the British economy?' Respondents were asked to locate themselves on scales running from 1 (representing the view that immigration was respectively bad for the economy or undermined cultural life) to 7 (that it was good for the economy or enriched cultural life). The mean positions for each group of party members are set out in Table 4.3. This largely confirms the pattern already observed: UKIP

TABLE 4.3 Attitudes towards immigration by party membership, 2015 and 2017

Statement	Conservative		Labour		Liberal Democrat		UKIP		Green		SNP		Total	
Immigration:	2015	2017	2015	2017	2015	2017	2015	2017	2015	2017	2015	2017	2015	2017
Is bad (1) or good (7) for the economy?	4.3	4.4	5.7	6.1	5.7	6.3	2.4	2.5	5.9	6.3	5.4	6.1	4.9	5.5
Undermines (1) or enriches (7) cultural life?	3.6	3.5	5.6	6.0	5.6	6.1	2.0	1.9	6.0	6.4	5.3	5.9	4.7	5.2

Note: All figures are averages scores on scales that run from 1 to 7. Differences between parties are all statistically significant at $p < .05$ or better.

members are clearly the least positive about the benefits of immigration (and even more pessimistic about its cultural than about its economic impacts), followed (admittedly some way behind) by Conservative members; at the other end of the scale, Greens are most positive, followed by Liberal Democrat, Labour and SNP members.

Which demographic and behavioural factors are associated with these core values? In Table 4.4, we report relationships between the party members' scores on the left–right and liberty–authority scales and various social background factors. In most cases, these bivariate relationships prove to be statistically significant and pretty straightforward to interpret.[3] Graduates are both more left-wing and more socially liberal than non-graduates, and this pattern also holds for public-sector employees compared to private-sector employees and for women compared to men. Similarly, on average, the more active members are during their parties' election campaigns, the more left-wing and socially liberal they are. In terms of social class, members from lower-grade occupations (C2DE) are consistently not only more left-wing but also more (small-c) socially conservative than those from higher occupational grades (ABC1). The evidence for age is a little less clear-cut than for the other variables, although there is a definite indication that older members generally tend to be more socially conservative. However, the connection between age and left–right position is far less emphatic: in the 2015 data there is a modest but significant relationship in that older members tend to be a little more right-wing on average, but in the 2017 data, there is no relationship at all.

TABLE 4.4 Demographic and behavioural correlates of core values

		Left–Right Scale		Liberty–Authority Scale	
		2015	*2017*	*2015*	*2017*
Education	Graduate	2.1	2.1	2.7	2.5
	Non-graduate	2.3	2.2	3.3	3.1
Class	ABC1	2.3	2.2	2.9	2.8
	C2DE	1.9	1.9	3.3	3.0
Sector	Private	2.3	2.2	2.9	2.9
	Public	2.0	2.0	2.7	2.6
Gender	Male	2.3	2.2	3.0	2.9
	Female	2.1	2.1	3.0	2.7
Age	Correlation	.08	.00	.29	.29
Activism	Correlation	−.09	−.16	−.13	−.18

Note: All cell entries are percentages, except those for age and activism, which are the Pearson's R correlation coefficients for the relationships between the age and the attitudinal scales and between the campaign activism index (0–9 activities undertaken during election campaign) and the attitudinal scales. All relationships are statistically significant at $p < .01$ or better, except for the correlation between age and left–right scale in 2017.

We can confirm or disconfirm these relationships by entering these terms into more complex multivariate models so that the strength of each relationship is tested net of all the others.[4] The detailed results are reported in Appendix 1. Doing this confirms what we already know in the sense of members' views varying according to which party they belong to, even when controlling for social background. We can also see, however, that, if we ignore party, then most of the social background factors do have an influence on attitudes. Indeed, in 2015, all these relationships are significant as far as the left–right scale is concerned: graduates, lower occupational class and public-sector employees, women and older and more active members are significantly more left-wing than their 'opposites'.[5] With respect to the liberty–authority scale, we can confirm that graduates, public-sector workers and younger and more active members are all significantly inclined to socially liberal positions, while gender and class do not appear to have a significant influence. However, in the 2017 data, class does become significant in as much as lower occupational grade workers are more (small-c) socially conservative.

Overall, these multivariate models largely serve to confirm the impression gained from the simple bivariate analysis: among party members, a university education, a middle-class occupation – especially if in the public sector – and being highly active in election campaigns tend to go hand in hand with socially liberal values. These attributes are also largely predictors of left-wing positions, except we must substitute lower for higher occupational class. Gender has much less clear-cut influence on members' core values. However, the party they belong to most definitely does.

Attitudinal clusters of party members

Of course, no political party is ideologically monolithic or homogeneous: all parties are to some extent coalitions of sometimes quite diverse individuals, and we can obtain a sense of this by turning to Figure 4.1 and Table 4.5. These show the results of a type of statistical investigation known as cluster analysis.[6] In our case, we can use the technique to identify groups of broadly like-minded party members in terms of their positions on the left–right and liberty–authority scales. These groups can be represented visually in two-dimensional space, with the left–right dimension arranged horizontally and the liberty–authority dimension cutting vertically across it, as in Figure 4.1. This space can be divided into four quadrants, so it is interesting to see if, by reducing our data to just four clusters, each quadrant has one of these clusters – and then to investigate how the various parties are distributed across the clusters.

The Figure reveals that we very nearly do find one cluster per quadrant. There is a socially conservative-right cluster and a socially conservative-left cluster, but there are two clusters in the socially liberal-left quadrant, although one of the latter is close to the cusp of the only quadrant that has no cluster – the socially liberal-right. That last cluster is so close to the midpoints of each scale (in terms of its central values) that it is neither clearly left or right or liberal or socially conservative,

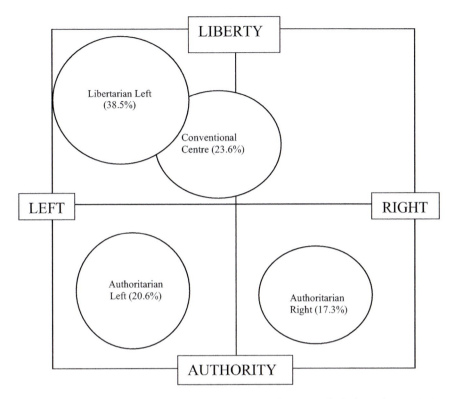

FIGURE 4.1 Clusters of British party members in two-dimensional ideological space, 2017

so it is perhaps best labelled the 'conventional centre' cluster. Working with the 2017 data, we see that the largest cluster is the socially liberal-left (38.5 per cent of respondents), followed by the conventional-centre (23.6 per cent), the socially conservative-left (20.6 per cent) and the socially conservative-right (17.3 per cent).

So how do these attitudinal clusters break down by party? Table 4.5 reveals the answer.[7] While no party's membership belongs entirely to just one cluster (confirming the internal diversity of each party), there are very definite patterns. The Tories are predominantly composed of people on the socially conservative-right (around 70 per cent of their members), with the remainder split between the conventional-centre and the socially conservative-left. The first of these brings to mind the moderate Tories who are not strongly Eurosceptic and are perhaps concerned about how far economic austerity should go because of their desire to protect public services. The latter might seem an oddity at first sight, however: left-wing Conservatives? However, the way to understand Conservatives falling into this cluster is as traditional 'One-Nation Tories', who are nationalistic and socially conservative (disliking gay marriage and what they regard as lax moral standards in modern life, for instance) but who believe in government spending on health and public services and who may resent the power of over-mighty corporations.

TABLE 4.5 Cluster analysis of British party members' ideological orientations, 2015 and 2017

Cluster	Conservative		Labour		Liberal Democrat		UKIP		Green		SNP		Total	
Year	2015	2017	2015	2017	2015	2017	2015	2017	2015	2017	2015	2017	2015	2017
Socially conservative right	70.9	69.7	0.8	0.0	3.8	3.9	29.3	30.9	0.4	0.7	1.6	2.4	20.0	17.3
Socially liberal left	0.5	0.4	65.8	67.4	37.9	36.4	1.5	1.0	82.7	74.4	53.8	50.1	39.9	38.5
Conventional centre	16.9	13.5	10.4	15.4	42.9	47.6	11.8	6.3	7.3	17.6	9.0	16.0	15.5	23.6
Socially conservative left	11.7	16.4	23.0	17.2	15.4	12.1	57.5	61.8	9.6	7.3	35.6	31.6	24.5	20.6
Total %	100	100	100	100	100	100	100	100	100	100	100	100	100	100

Note: Figures = percentages of respondents in each ideological cluster. Cramer's V = 0.521 (2015) and 0.510 (2017). N = 5,436 (2015) and 2,704 (2017).

Previous research has shown that such people are more likely to be working class and female than most Tory members.[8] A large number of UKIP supporters (around three-fifths) also fit this socially conservative, economically left-wing profile: as we have already seen, they are not particularly well-disposed to neo-liberal political economy, but are fierce defenders of traditional values and authority; their appeal to sections of the working class is well attested.[9] Most of the party's other members fall into the socially conservative-right cluster.

About two-thirds of Labour's members fall into the socially liberal-left cluster, with the remainder split roughly equally between the socially conservative left and conventional centre. The huge influx of new members since 2015 might have served to drive the overall position of the party's grassroots a little further left, but the overall balance of attitudinal types that it comprises does not appear to have changed all that much. As we saw in Table 4.2, the new members have probably made the party membership more socially liberal than more left-wing since it was already pretty left-wing to start with.

Unsurprisingly, perhaps, Britain's traditional 'centre party', the Liberal Democrats, are most likely to be located in the conventional centre, albeit with significant representation among the left-libertarians, and smaller numbers in the other two clusters. Proportionately, the Greens are the most left-libertarian of any party, with about three-quarters to four-fifths of their members so identified. Far smaller numbers can be found among the conventional centre and the socially conservative left. Finally, the bulk of Scottish Nationalist members fall into either the socially liberal- or the socially conservative-left category.

The touchstones of contemporary British politics: austerity and Brexit

We conclude this brief survey of party members' attitudinal profiles by examining their views on the two great issues that have dominated British politics over the last decade: austerity and Brexit. While the former provided the central fault line and narrative of UK politics from the time of the financial crisis in 2007–8 until the general election of 2015, the Tory manifesto promise at that election to hold a referendum on UK membership of the EU has meant that all other issues seem to have been effectively submerged by the overwhelming and polarizing impact of Brexit ever since. So, how do the country's party members line up on these great political questions?

Table 4.6 reports attitudes to austerity – essentially, the Tory–Liberal Democrat coalition government's drive to reduce the UK's deficit (and maybe even its debt) by cutting public expenditure. This question – 'Do you think that cuts to public spending have gone too far or not far enough?' – was posed in the 2015 and 2017 surveys and not only shows a definite pattern of views by party membership but also shows some marked shifts in opinion in a short space of time. Austerity was the major theme of the 2015 election campaign, and the members split along lines that largely reflect it. Tory members overwhelmingly believed in 2015 that spending

TABLE 4.6 British party members' views on austerity, 2015 and 2017

Cluster	Conservative		Labour		Liberal Democrat		UKIP		Green		SNP		Total	
Year	2015	2017	2015	2017	2015	2017	2015	2017	2015	2017	2015	2017	2015	2017
Not nearly/not far enough	56.2	28.3	1.2	1.3	9.2	1.7	45.2	31.0	0.7	0.8	2.6	2.1	19.9	8.7
About right	40.4	51.2	5.6	1.7	42.8	8.4	26.2	30.0	3.2	1.5	5.0	3.6	20.0	15.2
Too far/much too far	3.4	20.5	93.1	96.9	48.0	89.9	28.5	39.0	96.1	97.6	92.4	94.3	60.1	76.2
Total %	100	100	100	100	100	100	100	100	100	100	100	100	100	100

Note: Cell entries are mean scores for responses to the question, 'Do you think that cuts to public spending have generally gone too far or not far enough?' Cramer's $V = 0.424$ (2015) and 0.399 (2017); $n = 5,632$ (2015) and 2,841 (2017).

cuts were either 'about right' or had not yet gone far enough – a view consistent, some would say, with long-standing attitudes: when asked by researchers in the early 1990s whether government should cut government spending, some six out of ten Tory members back then agreed that it should.[10] In 2015, Labour, Green and SNP members overwhelmingly believed that cuts had gone too far – a finding which, in Labour's case, suggests that its membership feels even more strongly than it did on such matters back in the 1990s, when surveys found two-thirds to three-quarters of Labour members objecting to cutting government spending.[11] The other two parties were rather more internally divided on the question, with UKIP members being somewhat more inclined to feel that cuts had not yet gone far enough, while Liberal Democrats – never perhaps entirely comfortable with their party's role in participating in post-2010 financial austerity – rather more inclined to feel they had gone too far.

Intriguingly, by 2017 the members of all six parties had shifted against public spending cuts. In the case of Labour, the Greens and the SNP, these shifts were necessarily marginal given that their members were already so opposed to austerity. But the movements of opinion in the other three parties were marked, most notably in the case of the Liberal Democrats. By 2017, and with their party now out of office, nine out of every ten Liberal Democrat members had come to feel that spending cuts had gone too far – a collective expression of *mea culpa*, perhaps, from the members of a party no longer in coalition with the Conservatives, or else a function of the many new members the party had picked up in the two years since that coalition had ended? Among the Conservatives, the main shift was largely from thinking that cuts had not gone far enough (which dropped from 56 per cent to 28 per cent of members) to feeling that they were about right (which increased from 40 per cent to 51 per cent). However, there was still a notable jump (from 3 per cent to 20 per cent) in the number willing to concede that cuts had gone too far – many of them, perhaps, the traditional One-Nation Tories in the socially conservative-left quadrant who we mentioned earlier. Finally, support for further spending cuts dropped from 45 per cent to 31 per cent among UKIP members in 2017; by now, a plurality (39 per cent) felt that the cuts had gone too far.

But what of the equally vexed question of Brexit? As background, it is worth noting that there have long been party differences on Europe between the members of the parties. Surveys of Labour members in the 1990s, for instance, found that about seven out of ten of them disagreed that the party should resist further European integration and that nearly six out of ten were in favour of a single currency. Liberal Democrats were equally likely to disagree with the idea that European integration should be resisted and even more likely to support a single currency. When it came to their Conservative counterparts, who were surveyed in the early 1990s, some two-thirds agreed that Britain's national sovereignty was being lost to Europe and just over half (but, interestingly, *only* just over half) agreed that the party should be resisting any further European integration and a single currency.[12]

Table 4.7 reports a number of pertinent survey questions that were asked of our respondents in 2015 and 2017. Statistical analysis (in particular, the Cramer's *V* measure, which gauges the *strength* of any association between two variables) shows that by far the best predictor of members' views on the issue is the party they belong to. In 2015, when the promise to hold a referendum on UK membership of the EU had featured in the Conservative manifesto, at least eight out of ten Labour, Liberal Democrat, Green and SNP members said they would vote to remain come what may. UKIP members, not surprisingly, were equally emphatically of the opposite view: they would vote to leave regardless of any revised terms of UK membership that the Cameron government might be able to negotiate with the EU. The most ambiguous – perhaps surprisingly in hindsight – were the Conservatives. Approaching two-thirds of Tory members said that their decision would depend on the revised terms of EU membership that their then leader David Cameron had promised to 'bring back from Brussels' and set before the electorate in an in–out referendum.

Two years later, the party differences on Brexit had become even starker judging by the measures of association on the final three questions reported in Table 4.7. In response to the question of whether or not there should be a further referendum on the terms of the exit deal that Theresa May's government was able to agree with the EU, Labour, Liberal Democrat, Green and SNP members all agreed there should be – and in overwhelming numbers. By contrast, Tory and UKIP members were

TABLE 4.7 British party members' views on Brexit, 2015 and 2017

	Conservative	Labour	Liberal Democrat	UKIP	Green	SNP	Total	Cramer's V
2015								
How will you vote in referendum?								
Leave	15.6	4.7	2.1	86.3	2.1	4.7	17.6	.565
It depends	64.6	9.4	11.7	13.2	13.7	11.0	22.7	(n = 5,590)
Stay	19.8	85.9	86.3	0.5	84.2	84.3	59.7	
2017								
Do you think there should be a referendum on the final deal?								
Yes/more yes than no	13.7	81.9	92.1	3.3	92.2	90.3	67.1	.753
No/more no than yes	86.3	18.1	7.9	96.7	7.8	9.7	32.9	(n = 5,095)
Do you think, after Brexit, we should stay in the Single Market?								
Yes/more yes than no	26.9	92.1	97.3	4.9	96.7	96.6	75.0	.788
No/more no than yes	73.1	7.9	2.7	95.1	3.3	3.4	25.0	(n = 5,032)
Do you think, after Brexit, we should stay in the Customs Union?								
Yes/more yes than no	30.4	94.0	97.4	6.2	96.3	95.2	75.7	.771
No/more no than yes	69.6	6.0	2.6	93.8	3.7	4.8	24.3	(n = 4,887)
Do you think that, after Brexit, immigration from the EU should be subject to the same controls as immigration from outside the EU?								
Yes/more yes than no	85.0	37.4	26.9	94.7	20.0	31.5	47.2	.545
No/more no than yes	15.0	62.6	73.1	5.3	80.0	68.5	52.8	(n = 4,711)

Note: All figures are percentages.

equally, if not more, adamant that there should be no second referendum on the exit deal.

When asked if the UK should remain a member of the Single European Market and/or the Customs Union, the picture was essentially the same: more than 90 per cent of the left-of-centre parties' members said yes to both of these options, while a similar proportion of UKIP members rejected both. The Tory members were a little more ambivalent, with about a quarter to a third thinking that it would be a good idea to retain membership of one or the other (especially the Customs Union), but a comfortable majority were still against both. Although not quite as pronounced, the differences between the parties were also very apparent on the question of how to treat immigrants from the EU after Brexit: while Conservative and UKIP members saw no reason to treat EU migrants differently from non-EU migrants, clear majorities of members of the other parties obviously did (the implication being that such treatment would be in some way preferential for EU migrants).

By the end of 2018, as Theresa May struggled to get the deal she had agreed with the EU through Parliament, we commissioned a further survey that enabled us to probe more closely members' attitudes towards the deal and various other alternatives that were being floated at that time. This short survey was limited to members of the two largest parties, Labour and the Conservatives, and confirmed the crystallizing of divisions on Brexit along party lines. Table 4.8 reports the results of this research.

TABLE 4.8 Labour and Conservative members' and voters' views on Brexit, December 2018

	Members		Voters	
	Conservative	Labour	Conservative	Labour
Brexit is the most important issue facing country	75	61	70	53
Government is doing well at negotiating Brexit	29	4	30	7
Strongly support or tend to support Theresa May's proposed deal	38	9	40	11
The proposed deal respects the 2016 referendum result	42	38	39	25
Theresa May has got a good deal for Britain	15	3	10	3
Labour would probably get a better deal	2	58	1	29

(Continued)

TABLE 4.8 (Continued)

	Members		Voters	
	Conservative	Labour	Conservative	Labour
If Theresa May's proposed deal is rejected by Parliament:				
Theresa May should resign as prime minister	44	68	29	57
Would support a new referendum on the deal	14	79	25	58
Would choose remain as 1st preference in a new referendum	15	88	23	63
Would choose proposed deal as 1st preference in new referendum	23	3	24	8
Would choose leaving with no deal as 1st preference in new referendum	57	5	43	15
Leaving the EU without a deal would cause severe short-term disruption and shortages	18	82	17	52
Leaving the EU without a deal will be positive for the UK economy in the medium to long term	64	5	40	11
In hindsight, the UK was right to vote to leave the EU in 2016	79	8	67	22
The 'backstop' makes sense and should be part of deal	11	38	15	22
Would you feel delighted, pleased or relieved if, eventually:				
The UK ended up leaving the EU without any deal?	63	5	37	12
The UK ended leaving on the terms negotiated by the government?	36	10	31	8
The UK ended up leaving the EU but remaining in Single Market and Customs Union?	22	52	25	35
The UK had a new referendum and voted to remain in the EU after all?	16	82	22	61

Note: Members sample: Conservative *n* = 1,215, Labour *n* = 1,034; Voters sample: Conservative *n* = 558, Labour *n* = 527. All relationships are statistically significant at *p* < .001.

These tables confirm the growing impression that the UK's relationship with Europe has become the central dividing (and, indeed, polarizing) line in British politics today. Its power to separate one citizen from another seems to be unparalleled, and the parties appear to have adapted to this by becoming decisively pro- or anti-Brexit. At any rate, this appears to be the case with respect to the parties' grassroots, even if one couldn't necessarily say the same of all their MPs and even their leaders. Table 4.8 shows that the major parties' memberships were most clearly divided on how positive or damaging for the country the effects of leaving without a deal would be, on how they would react to a no-deal Brexit, on whether there should be a new referendum on Brexit, on whether they would choose to remain in the EU or leave without a deal in such an event, and on whether, with the benefit of hindsight, the UK was right to have voted to leave in 2016.

Statistical analysis suggests a strong relationship between the answers given by a member and the party they belong to.[13] In every case, Labour members were far more inclined to favour anti-Brexit options than were their Conservative counterparts. Thus, the former were far *less* likely to think the UK made the right decision in voting to leave the EU in the 2016 referendum (only 8 per cent agreeing that this was so, compared to 79 per cent of Conservatives) but were far *more* likely to think that quitting the EU without a deal would cause severe short-term disruption and shortages (82 per cent to 18 per cent) and far *less* likely to believe that it would bring medium- to long-term economic benefit (5 per cent to 64 per cent). Labour members were also hugely more likely than Tories to want another referendum to be held on Brexit (79 per cent to 14 per cent) and to feel 'delighted, pleased or relieved' if, in the event that such a referendum were held, the UK were to decide to remain in the EU (by 82 per cent to 16 per cent), while Tories were much more favourably disposed to a no-deal Brexit (by 64 per cent to 5 per cent). Not surprisingly, then, Labour members were massively in favour of choosing to Remain as their first preference (88 per cent to 15 per cent), while Tory members' top preference would be a no-deal exit (57 per cent to 5 per cent).

The differences between the two sets of party members were less pronounced on the other questions we asked them on Brexit but were generally significant nonetheless. Conservatives were more likely than Labour members to support the deal that Theresa May had negotiated with the EU (38 per cent to 9 per cent) and to choose this deal as their first preference in any new referendum (36 per cent to 10 per cent); they were also far less inclined to think a Labour government could get a better deal out of the EU (2 per cent to 58 per cent) or that Theresa May should resign as party leader and prime minister if Parliament voted down her deal (44 per cent to 68 per cent). On other questions, there were party differences, even though Conservative members could be said to be less than enthusiastic about the government's performance on Brexit: only 29 per cent of them agreed that it was doing well at negotiating with the EU (but this compared to just 4 per cent of Labour members who felt as much), and only 15 per cent of Tory members actually felt that it had managed to achieve a good deal (compared to a predictably minuscule 3 per cent of Labour members). There was little difference between the parties in terms of whether or not they felt the deal respected the 2016 referendum result (42 per cent to 38 per cent). But on one basic question clear majorities of both sets of party members were in agreement: Brexit was undoubtedly the most important single political issue facing the country (75 per cent to 61 per cent).

This is not the place to rehearse the various arguments about the causes of Euroscepticism or the merits and demerits of British membership of the EU, but there can be no doubt that it has become the defining UK-wide political issue of our time. It has plainly dominated the political agenda since the 2015 general election and has so polarized public opinion that it carries with it considerable potential to realign electoral support across political parties in the UK. But whether or not it does so depends on the strategic shifts of the party leaderships. Can they adapt to offer citizens clear and unambiguous choices on Europe, or will they allow their parties to be fractured by this issue?

The results of our surveys strongly suggest that the party members, at least, have sorted themselves out quite neatly in pro- and anti- (or at least hard and soft) Brexit groups; the most strongly pro- and hard Brexit party memberships are to be found in the right-wing parties, the Conservatives and UKIP, while the anti- and soft Brexit memberships are all left of centre (Labour, Liberal Democrat, Green and SNP). Moreover, Table 4.8 suggests that this is largely true, albeit less emphatically, of the major parties' voters as well.

In general, those who voted Conservative in 2017 are more likely to adopt pro-Brexit than anti-Brexit positions – but not as likely as the party's members. The exact opposite is true of Labour voters; they generally display anti-Brexit attitudes, though not in the same proportions as the party's members. However, at the time these surveys were conducted, there was a sense that, although there was some evidence of polarization, the parties' elites – in other words, their MPs – had not succeeded in arranging themselves into quite such cohesive pro- and anti-Brexit groups.[14] To this extent, they seemed to lag behind their own memberships – at least in the case of the two major parties.

The vexed process of ratifying in Parliament the withdrawal deal that Theresa May negotiated over the winter of 2018–19 proved horribly complicated, with blocking majorities quickly emerging not just against the deal itself but initially, at least, also against possible alternatives (a new general election, a second referendum, a 'Norway Plus' deal involving continued UK membership of the Single Market and Customs Union or a no-deal Brexit). With defeat in the Commons looming the prime minister felt compelled to postpone the fateful vote itself that had been scheduled for December 2018 and attempt to wring further concessions from the EU and wider support in Parliament. Meanwhile, it became increasingly apparent that Jeremy Corbyn, for all his avowals of grassroots democracy, was highly reluctant to adopt the unambiguously anti-Brexit position favoured by the overwhelming majority of his own members. His long-held doubts about the EU were widely known, and he caused considerable consternation among members and many fellow MPs when he gave an interview to the *Guardian* in December 2018 in which he asserted that Brexit would go ahead even if Labour won a new general election in 2019.[15]

The danger to each of the major parties posed by Brexit is clearly illustrated by one other finding of our survey of December 2018. When asked 'Has the party policy on Brexit since 2016 caused you to consider leaving the party?' some 56 per cent of *both* Labour and Conservative rank-and-file members who opposed the stance that their party had taken on Brexit (i.e., 29 per cent in Labour's case and 31 per cent in the Conservatives') indicated that it had done so. There is evidence that voting in the general election of 2017 was strongly influenced by electors' feelings about Brexit, with the Conservatives attracting pro-Brexit voters and Labour becoming a refuge for remainers who still hoped the country could be kept in the EU.[16] Plainly, what followed left large sections of both parliamentary and extraparliamentary parties disillusioned by the more ambivalent positions adopted by their leaders. If those leaders, whoever they are, ultimately prove unable to manoeuvre their parties into positions that fully satisfy their supporters on the Brexit issue, then this disillusion may well spread to voters, as well as members, creating space that parties strongly identified with either leave or remain may well rush in to fill.

Conclusion

In this chapter we have seen how the various party memberships line up in two-dimensional ideological space. Conservatives are the most right-wing in terms of classic questions of state versus market allocation of resources, inequality and economic austerity, while members of the other parties – including UKIP – are generally left of centre (or, indeed, quite far to the left in the case of Labour and the Greens). UKIP members are much more socially conservative than the members of any other party, including the Tories, while the Greens are the most socially liberal. Notwithstanding the general differences between parties in these terms, we have also seen how different party memberships spread across distinctive attitudinal clusters in this space; to this extent, all parties are still coalitions of different voices. Party members have highly polarized (albeit in the case of UKIP and Tory members slightly shifting) attitudes to austerity. But this is equally, if not even more, the case when it comes to Brexit. The latter has largely been assimilated into right-wing and left-wing party boxes – but more clearly at the grassroots than at Westminster. This holds out the intriguing (and, for the major parties, highly worrying) prospect of a future realignment of support, both among rank-and-file members and voters – a realignment that, potentially at least, could blow apart the existing British party system.

Notes

1 Whiteley, Paul, Poletti, Monica, Webb, Paul and Bale, Tim (2019) 'Oh, Jeremy Corbyn! Why did Labour Party membership soar after the 2015 general election?', *British Journal of Politics & International Relations*, 21 (1), pp. 80–98.
2 Heath, Anthony, Evans, Geoffrey and Martin, Jean (1993) 'The measurement of core beliefs and values: The development of balanced socialist/laissez faire and libertarian/authoritarian scales', *British Journal of Political Science*, 24, pp. 115–158.

3 A *bivariate* correlation implies a relationship between any two variables: for instance, as X increases, so does Y. If a correlation reaches *statistical significance*, that does not necessarily mean that the relationship between the two variables is important, but it does mean that we can be fairly certain that it isn't merely down to chance. For example, the fact that men have larger brains than women does not tell us anything worth knowing, but it is clearly *statistically* significant.

4 Multivariate analysis involves observing and analysing the relationship between a dependent variable and multiple independent variables that might impact on it. See Appendix 1 for more details.

5 In the smaller 2017 sample, gender, sector and age effects lose their significance, however.

6 Cluster analysis enables us to identify homogeneous groups (or clusters) of MPs by measuring their Euclidian distances from each other on the two attitudinal scales. This may sound like an obscure formulation, but in essence, the idea is quite simple. The goal of cluster analysis is to identify homogeneous groups or clusters of cases (in this case, party members). It generally achieves this by using algorithms based on (squared) Euclidian distances of cases from one another across a range of variables. In hierarchical clustering, there are as many clusters as there are cases at the outset of the analysis. At the first stage of analysis, the two cases which are nearest to each other in terms of Euclidian distance are then merged into a single cluster. At the following stage, the next nearest case is then added to this cluster, or two other cases which are nearer to each other are then joined together to form a new cluster. This proceeds until all cases have been merged into a single cluster, although it is almost certain that this final 'unified' formation will actually be very heterogeneous and, therefore, substantively meaningless. Once a cluster has been formed, it cannot be split apart at a later stage of analysis; it can only be merged with other cases or clusters. It is the task of the researcher to interpret cluster analysis results in the light of substantive knowledge and theory; in particular, this blend of quantitative and substantive knowledge is critical in informing the decision about the number of clusters a model should have. See Webb, Paul (1997) 'Attitudinal clustering within British parliamentary elites: Patterns of intra-party and cross-party alignment', *West European Politics*, 20, pp. 89–110.

7 Note that the coordinates of each cluster in the two-dimensional ideological space are as follows:

		Left–Right position	Liberty–Authority position	
Socially conservative right:	2015	3.71	3.84	(20.0% of sample)
	2017	3.61	3.78	(17.3% of sample)
Socially liberal left:	2015	1.46	2.16	(39.9% of sample)
	2017	2.86	2.51	(15.5% of sample)
Conventional centre:	2015	2.86	2.51	(15.5% of sample)
	2017	2.54	2.38	(23.6% of sample)
Socially conservative left:	2015	1.71	3.97	(24.5% of sample)
	2017	1.78	3.88	(20.6% of sample)

8 Webb, Paul and Childs, Sarah (2011) 'Wets and dries resurgent? Intra-party alignments among contemporary Conservative Party members', *Parliamentary Affairs*, 64 (3), pp. 383–402.

9 Ford, Robert and Goodwin, Matthew (2014) *Revolt on the Right: Explaining Support for the Radical Right in Britain* (Abingdon: Routledge).

10 Whiteley, Paul, Seyd, Patrick and Richardson, Jeremy (1994) *True Blues* (Oxford: Oxford University Press), p. 59.

11 Seyd, Patrick and Whiteley, Paul (2002) *New Labour's Grassroots: The Transformation of the Labour Party Membership* (Houndsmills: Palgrave Macmillan), p. 58.

12 Seyd, Patrick and Whiteley, Paul (2002) *New Labour's Grassroots* (Houndsmills: Palgrave Macmillan), p. 70; Whiteley, Paul, Seyd, Patrick and Richardson, Jeremy (1994) *True Blues* (Oxford: Oxford University Press), p. 70; Whiteley, Paul, Seyd, Patrick and Billinghurst, Antony (2006) *Third Force Politics* (Oxford: Oxford University Press), p. 27.

13 For each of these questions, the statistical measure of association, Cramer's *V*, is uncommonly high at around .6 or .7.

14 On the differences between Labour and Conservative MPs on Brexit, see https://ukandeu.ac.uk/wp-content/uploads/2019/01/MPs-survey-write-up-1.pdf.

15 Stewart, Heather (2018) 'Corbyn: Brexit would go ahead even if Labour won snap election', *The Guardian*, 21 December.

16 Fieldhouse, Ed and Prosser, Chris (2018) 'General election 2017: Brexit dominated voters' thoughts', *BBC News Website*, 1 August, available online at www.bbc.co.uk/news/uk-politics-40630242.

5

THE SUPPLY SIDE

Why do people join parties?

> People join because they really do care about the direction of the country and they decide they want to do something about it, or they want to get involved in politics . . . and they want to be local candidates, or they just want to do their bit. But they're a very select band, I agree.[1]

Party membership is not expensive: virtually all parties allow members to pay monthly and their annual fees (even for those who don't qualify for reduced rates because they are, say, students or retirees or unwaged or members of the armed forces) are by no means prohibitive.[2] Yet party membership is very much a minority sport: very few citizens are generally inclined to become party members, and as we noted in Chapter 2, until very recently the numbers doing so were in persistent decline. Since the 1950s, the percentage of registered electors joining up dropped pretty consistently, bar the occasional uptick. Around 9 per cent of voters were individual party members in 1964, but only 1 per cent were by 2015. Yet, as we have seen, some of the country's parties have recently enjoyed impressive surges in membership, even if it remains the case that only about 2 per cent of the UK's 46 million registered voters are currently party members. So, what might lie behind this pattern? To answer the question, we need to understand the factors that influence an individual's decision to become a party member in the first place.

How do people join parties?

Before examining the motives behind the decision to join a political party, we start by briefly considering *how* people join. In Table 5.1, we report on whether party members claim to have taken the initiative to join up themselves, or whether they were approached by a party – and whether their initial point of reference was the

TABLE 5.1 Thinking back to the time you first joined the party, did you approach the party or did someone from the party approach you?

	Conservative		Labour		Liberal Democrat		UKIP		Green		SNP	
	2015	2017	2015	2017	2015	2017	2015	2017	2015	2017	2015	2017
I approached the local party	45	35	39	24	39	25	28	31	27	25	30	29
The local party approached me	18	8	7	2	15	6	5	6	2	2	2	3
The national party approached me	5	4	3	2	3	4	5	5	2	3	1	2
I approached the national party	24	48	47	69	40	63	57	51	65	66	65	64
Don't remember	7	4	4	3	4	3	4	6	4	4	2	2
Number	1192	476	1180	309	730	722	784	210	845	459	963	604

Note: All figures are percentages, totalling 100 per cent by column. Rounding errors may mean that not all columns add up to exactly 100 per cent.

national or local party. From this it is abundantly clear that people generally take it on themselves to approach the party; they do not wait to be asked. Furthermore, with the sole exception of our Conservative sample in 2015, they are generally more likely to approach the national party organization than their local constituency party when seeking membership. This is especially apparent in the case of those parties that have enjoyed membership surges in recent years – Labour and the Liberal Democrats after 2015 and UKIP, the Greens and the SNP prior to 2015. However, if people are approached about becoming members, then it is somewhat more likely to happen via the local party rather than the national party – which makes sense since such personal encouragement will often require face-to-face contact.

In Table 5.2, we can delve further into the process by which people join up. This confirms paths to membership that are consistent with the relatively large number who join by approaching the national party organizations – that is, after watching Party Political Broadcasts or Party Election Broadcasts (PPBs/PEBs) or checking the party websites. The latter route appears to be especially important for the smaller parties, with somewhere between a quarter and a half of SNP, Green and UKIP members claiming to have joined after going on their websites. Unsurprisingly, given that relatively few join up after being approached by the party, the various ways in which this might be done – via email, Facebook or even canvasser contact – do not feature especially prominently. What is interesting, however, is the extent to which personal contact matters. About 15 to 20 per cent of members across the parties say that they took the decision to join a party after speaking with friends or family.[3] As we will see, the influence of social norms is not necessarily the most important of motivations to join parties, but it is far from insignificant. Moreover, being part of a social network connected with a political party can be critically important when it comes to the question of whether members actively engage in working for their parties or not, as we shall see in Chapter 6.

So, why do people join political parties?

The most widely cited political science approach to explaining the decision to join a political party is the General Incentives Model, associated with the seminal work of the British pioneers in the study of party members, Patrick Seyd and Paul Whiteley.[4] Indeed, one might almost refer to it as conventional wisdom or orthodoxy, and it has certainly spawned a host of adaptations to other settings by scholars around the world.[5] It was inspired by American social scientists, Peter B. Clark and James Q. Wilson, whose research distinguished between three types of incentives – purposive, material and solidary.[6] *Purposive* incentives are connected with the stated goals of an organization: people are frequently motivated to join parties by these core organizational purposes. By contrast, *material* incentives reflect the desire to achieve tangible personal material rewards – perhaps in the form of career benefits – for participation. *Solidary* incentives relate to the satisfaction derived from the process of participation, including sociability and camaraderie.

TABLE 5.2 Organizational memberships of party members

	Conservative		Labour		Liberal Democrat		UKIP		Green		SNP	
	2015	2017	2015	2017	2015	2017	2015	2017	2015	2017	2015	2017
Talking to a canvasser on the doorstep	6	4	3	1	8	3	3	3	1	1	4	2
Talking to friends	20	12	19	17	19	11	15	13	21	15	20	21
Talking to family	18	12	18	16	11	11	10	11	12	14	17	15
Talking to colleagues	4	4	9	6	5	2	12	4	10	2	13	5
Watching a PPB/PEB	12	11	10	11	13	12	31	30	12	17	20	14
Checking the party website	18	19	15	21	19	26	49	44	58	42	31	24
Getting an email from the party	10	11	6	5	4	5	11	10	7	5	5	3
Getting contacted by the party via Facebook	2	3	2	4	2	4	3	3	4	5	3	2
Seeing a Tweet from the party	2	3	2	6	3	4	3	4	9	6	5	4

Note: All figures percentages of column categories. 2015 total n = 5,694; 2017 total n = 5,219.

Seyd and Whiteley built on Clark and Wilson's work by developing an approach

> grounded in the assumption that participation occurs in response to differ-
> ent kinds of incentives . . . but it goes beyond a narrowly cast economic
> analysis of incentives to include emotional attachments to the party, moral
> concerns, and social norms, variables which lie outside the standard cost-
> benefit approach to decision-making.[7]

To summarize, the GIM approach incorporates a combination of the following
reasons for joining a party:

- The individual's perception of the probability that participation in group activity through the party will achieve a desired collective outcome; in other words,
  the respondent's sense of *group efficacy*
- The individual's desired *collective policy outcome*, such as the introduction of a
  particular policy
- The individual's assessment of the *selective outcome benefits* of activism, that is,
  material or career benefits
- The individual's assessment of the *selective process benefits* of activism, that is, the
  intrinsic pleasure derived from involvement in political action
- The individual's *altruistic* motivations for activism
- The individual's perception of *social norm* incentives for activism, that is, the
  desire to conform with the behaviour and expectations of personal contacts
- The individual's *expressive or affective* motivations for activism, such as the
  strength of commitment to or identification with a given party or leader
- The individual's perception of the *costs* of activism; properly speaking, this is a
  *dis*incentive.
- The individual's belief that individual acts can influence and have a real impact
  on political decisions, that is, the respondent' sense of *personal efficacy*
- The individual's *ideological* motivations for activism

Although the research that demonstrated that this incentives-based approach worked
well in explaining why people joined Britain's three biggest parties was conducted
by Seyd and Whiteley and their colleagues back in the 1990s, there is no obvious
prima facie reason to suppose that the reasons they join nowadays will be any different.
Table 5.3 therefore reports the responses of the members we surveyed to a similar
series of questions designed to gauge motives for joining, all of which take the general
form 'How important were the following reasons for you joining the party?' with
possible answers ranging from 0 (not important at all) to 10 (extremely important).

As revealed by the table, collective policy, expressive and altruistic motivations
generally elicited the highest levels of agreement from respondents, with social
norm and selective outcome incentives attracting least agreement.[8] Variation by
party on the different indicators is limited, but the standard deviations (which
show how far away from the average each measurement is) located at the bottom
of each column suggest that party members differ most in terms of social norms

TABLE 5.3 General incentives for membership, by party, 2015

	Collective policy incentives		Expressive incentives		Selective outcome incentives		Selective process incentives	Social norm incentives	Altruistic incentives
	To support the party's general policies or a specific policy that mattered greatly	To oppose the policies of a rival party, or the power of a social or economic group	An attachment to the party's principles	Belief in the party's leadership	For career reasons	In order to become an elected politician	To engage in activities in which I would be mixing with other like-minded individuals	Because of the influence of family, friends or colleagues	To support the democratic process
Conservative	8.78	7.90	8.97	8.21	2.74	3.16	5.89	3.38	8.21
Labour	8.74	8.53	9.18	6.83	2.13	2.52	5.83	3.61	8.39
Liberal Democrat	8.77	6.63	9.26	6.87	2.00	2.85	5.49	3.03	8.50
UKIP	9.89	7.43	9.25	9.23	1.91	2.51	5.37	2.30	8.84
Green	9.55	7.78	9.39	6.67	1.56	1.91	4.83	2.42	8.41
SNP	9.83	7.62	9.39	9.65	1.85	1.94	5.94	2.85	9.21
Overall mean	9.22	7.74	9.22	7.91	2.08	2.51	5.61	3.00	8.57
Standard Deviations	2.20	3.14	2.17	2.87	2.49	2.85	3.40	2.89	2.65

Note: Cell entries are mean scores for responses to the question, 'How important were the following reasons for you joining the party?' with possible answers ranging from 0 (not important at all) to 10 (extremely important). $N = 5,696$.

and collective negative motivations: Labour and Conservative members are notably more likely than Green Party or UKIP members to admit joining because of the influence of their peers, while Labour members are far more likely than Liberal Democrats to claim to have joined in order to oppose the policies of rival parties. Interestingly, the assumption often made in Liberal Democrat circles that, given the party's lack of any obvious association with a particular sectional interest, their members are more heavily into policy than are members of other parties – one reason why its policy-making process is so democratic – does not, in fact, appear to be the case.[9]

These findings are interesting, but they do not, in and of themselves, tell us why some people with partisan inclinations decide to become members, while others (indeed, the overwhelming majority) do not. Surveys of party members, which, by definition, exclude non-members, only provide limited insight. True, members generally score highly in terms of, say, collective policy or ideological incentives – but how do we know that non-members might not *also* feel strongly about matters of policy or ideology? Our way around this is to combine simultaneously conducted surveys of members and supporters (i.e., voters who strongly identify with a party but do not go so far as to formally join it) so that we achieve variation on the key question we wish to explain – to join or not to join? Doing this gives us a combined 2015 data set that includes 12,079 respondents who identified strongly with one of the six political parties in our study, of whom 5,700 were party members while 6,379 were not. And it allows us, for the first time, to model party membership properly in a statistical sense. Why do some people who are strongly supportive of particular parties choose to belong to them while others who are similarly supportive (and whom we will call *party supporters*) prefer not to?

In addition to examining the impact of the incentives highlighted by previous research, we can also look at whether joining is influenced by the kind of socio-demographic characteristics we looked at in Chapter 3, which, along with ideology and personal efficacy (i.e., your sense that what you do can actually make a difference), are well-known predictors of political participation. If we recall that 'resources' such as education and/or particular careers can provide people with the chance to develop the organizational and communication skills that are relevant to political participation, it seems reasonable to assume that this is also the case when it comes to party membership. These resources are central to what is known as the 'Civic Voluntarism Model', so in taking into account demographics *and* personal political efficacy, we are in effect recognizing that elements of both incentives and civic voluntarism theory might help us understand why someone might join a political party.

If the general incentives and civic voluntarism approaches are indeed useful in understanding an individual's decision to join a political party, then we would expect our data to show that people are significantly more likely to be members than mere supporters if (a) they score highly on each of the variables we use to measures the various incentives referred to above (ideology, collective policy, selective outcomes and processes, expressive/affective, social norms) and (b) they have a significantly higher sense of personal or group efficacy. But (c) we would expect them to have a significantly *lower* perception of the costs of party membership. And (d) we would also expect those who are better educated and have a higher social status to be more likely to join because these are precisely the kind of 'resources' that facilitate political participation. Previous research also tends to show that younger people and women are generally less inclined to participate, so we would expect (e) older respondents (up to a very advanced age at least) and men to be more likely to become party members.[10]

Table 5.4 shows how members and supporters compare and contrast in terms of these demographic and general incentives factors. And it shows that

TABLE 5.4 Social and political characteristics of British political party members and supporters, 2015

Attribute	Supporters	Members	N	Significance
Mean age	52	51	12,069	*
Male (%)	48.0	65.0	12,072	***
Graduates (%)	32.1	46.2	11,780	***
ABC1 (%)	59.1	77.6	11,914	***
Mean left–right				
Left parties	1.99	1.75	7,660	***
Conservative Party	5.08	6.34	2,264	***
UKIP	2.62	3.59	1,790	***
Mean left–right extremism				
Left parties	−0.09	0.08	7,660	***
Conservative Party	−0.62	0.64	2,264	***
UKIP	−0.41	0.56	1,790	***
Mean liberty–authority				
Left parties	5.40	3.93	7,317	***
Conservative Party	7.39	6.58	2,232	***
UKIP	7.97	7.54	1,790	***
All parties	6.22	4.99	11,339	***
Personal efficacy	4.18	6.28	11,758	***
Group efficacy	5.13	7.33	10,855	***
Expressive incentives	6.34	8.28	12,053	***
Altruism	5.80	7.07	11,649	***
Selective process	5.76	7.15	11,076	***
Selective outcome	5.11	6.54	11,130	***
Social norms	29.60	48.20	12,071	***
Cost of activism	6.87	6.44	11,001	***

Note: All figures are mean scores on 0–10 scales, unless otherwise stated. For details of variables, see Appendix 1.

* $p < .05$; ** $p < .01$; *** $p < .001$.

the differences between members and supporters are significant for all variables, demographic and attitudinal, although the mean age difference (51 for party members to 52 for party supporters) seems far too small to warrant serious consideration as an important explanation of why people might or might not join parties. The members are notably more male, middle class and better educated than supporters, however, suggesting that socio-demographic resources are indeed an important factor.

Party members are also less moderate ideologically than party supporters. If we look at the basic left–right index scores in Table 5.4, we see that left-of-centre parties, such as Labour, the Greens, Liberal Democrats and SNP members are more left-wing than 'mere' supporters, whereas they are more right-wing in right-of-centre parties like the Conservatives and UKIP. However, when we turn to the liberty–authority dimension discussed in earlier chapters, we find that members are more socially liberal than supporters in both left- *and* right-wing parties. We cannot be certain why this is the case, but it could be because social liberalism is consistent with placing greater emphasis on democratic engagement as a civic right and as a means of maximizing liberty while enhancing political knowledge and personal development, meaning that people with socially liberal instincts are generally more likely to want to participate politically than their more socially conservative counterparts.[11]

Furthermore, as general incentives theory would suggest, members significantly outscore supporters on each of the incentives reported – personal and group efficacy, expressive ideals, altruistic concerns for the well-being of the political system and on the selective outcome and process incentives of membership. That is, members have a far more prominent expressive belief in the ability of particular parties, as well as in the ability of party members, to bring about political change (i.e., group efficacy). They are also much more likely to rationalize their membership in terms of a high-minded desire to contribute to the healthy functioning of democracy (an altruistic motivation). At the same time, however, members are also more likely to think that being a party member is a good way to meet like-minded people (a selective process incentive) as well as a way to potentially fulfil an ambition to become a politician (a selective outcome incentive). Moreover, members are more likely to be influenced by social norms as they are also part of a wider network of civil society organizations. By interacting regularly with others in these organizational settings they go through processes of socialization which bring with them the learning of shared values and group norms. On the other hand, it is supporters, rather than members, who perceive the cost of party activism (in terms of the time they presume it takes up) to be high.

These simple descriptive statistics clearly suggest the continuing validity of the General Incentives approach to explaining party membership. Moreover, elsewhere we have tested that approach more rigorously through more complex multivariate modelling and confirmed that it performs well: holding all other factors constant, each of the demographic resources and incentives has a statistically significant bearing on an individual's decision to become a party member and in the expected way.[12] In short, the factors that clearly distinguish members from supporters, and may go furthest in explaining why they bother to join, are

- being male, better educated and coming from higher up the social hierarchy (in other words having more resources),
- being socially liberal and ideologically more radical (for parties on the left),
- having a strong sense of personal and collective political efficacy,
- believing strongly in a particular party and (more altruistically, perhaps) in the wider importance of political participation,
- valuing selective process and outcome benefits (in other words, taking pleasure from getting involved and anticipating that it will bring material or career advantages),
- being involved in other civil society organizations (as suggested in Chapter 3) and
- *not* being put off by the presumed time commitment that membership implies.

All this amounts to a clear confirmation of the continuing relevance, in the twenty-first century, of the general incentives explanation for why people join political parties.

Interestingly, more detailed analysis also reveals how party *supporters* believe that party *members* must somehow derive intrinsic pleasure from involvement in party life, that they anticipate career or material benefits and that they must be embedded in a social network that draws them into the party.[13] Actual members, however, are far less likely to say that this is the case – especially with respect to selective outcomes or social norms. This points to different understandings or *narratives* of what party membership actually entails: while supporters imagine – perhaps somewhat cynically – that opposing rivals' policies, meeting like-minded people and the hope of material advancement are key factors in the decision to join, party members think that they are motivated by rather high-minded attachments to party principles, policies and leaders, as well as by a desire to support the democratic process and the national interest.

Of course, whether this means that members really *are* more altruistic and principled than supporters, or whether they are merely in denial about (or simply unaware of having considered) the potential material or career benefits they hope (or hoped) to gain from party membership, is ultimately impossible to tell. Since '[c]onscious deliberation and rumination is . . . the rationalization of multiple unconscious processes that recruit reasons to justify and explain beliefs, attitudes and actions', we need to be careful.[14] And clearly it can be difficult to accurately parse and categorize mixed motives, be they one's own or someone else's. For instance, one politician we interviewed told us that one of his initial reasons for getting involved locally was his realization that 'this bunch of charlies: they don't know what they're doing on the council. Even I could do better than that!'[15] Does that count as career-driven or personal efficacy or both – or something else altogether? We should also note that there may be gender differences in this and other respects. For instance, a Conservative MP told us, when talking about younger people who joined her party,

> Half think they want to be politicians. . . . One of the challenges is to actually motivate girls to think in those terms as well. . . . Females on the whole don't tend to think of themselves as the next prime minister. An awful lot of the younger lads think of themselves as the next prime minister.[16]

Even so, these findings do seem to provide a strong clue as to the gap in perception that distinguishes members from supporters. In other words, if supporters do not believe they themselves are driven by the same motives as party members, and/ or if they find those motives somehow off-putting, they are probably less likely to become members themselves. This might have practical implications. By respectfully and sensitively challenging supporters' narratives about members – perhaps by encouraging activists to talk more about the realities of membership wherever possible – political parties may ultimately be able to convert more supporters into members. These are the sort of questions we explore in more detail in Chapter 9.

Why the long-term decline in party membership – and why the recent resurgence?

We now have a good idea of the factors that compel certain individuals to become members of political parties. Can this help us understand the two aggregate-level trends in party membership that we outlined in Chapter 2, namely, the seemingly inexorable decline of membership from the 1950s to 2010 and then the surprising reversal (temporary or otherwise) of this secular trend for most (although not all) of the major British parties since then?

It is useful to think about these questions not only in terms of General Incentives theory but also in terms of the supply and demand approach we touched on in Chapter 2. Thinking about the supply side encourages us to think about why citizens of advanced industrial democracies such as the UK may not be as inclined to join parties as previous generations. Thinking about the demand side prompts us to explore why parties might no longer wish to invest time and effort in recruiting mass memberships.

If we take supply first, class dealignment (the process by which people come to identify less than they used to with a particular social class) and partisan dealignment (the process by which they come to identify less than they used to with a particular party) may well have 'reduced the supply of loyalists from which parties can recruit their members'.[17] Whereas Great Britain was largely understood as a country with a simple 'two-party, two-class' system of politics until the 1970s, the picture is now far more complex. Fewer people see political parties as a natural expression of their class identity (working class = Labour, middle class = Conservative) for reasons that have been well rehearsed by commentators, and this helps explain why they are much less likely to feel a close affinity to a particular party. Whereas some

44 per cent of British Election Study respondents claimed to have a 'very strong' partisan identity in the 1960s, this was down to no more than 18 per cent at the 2015 and 2017 elections. It is hardly surprising, then, that far fewer of them would therefore wish to actually join a party. In general incentives terms, we are seeing an erosion of expressive incentives and, given that expressive social and political identities are often the result of socialization by families and the wider social networks in which people operate, a weakening of social norms.

Another related supply-side explanation suggests that people nowadays prefer to join single-issue pressure groups rather than political parties.[18] In fact, this argument is perfectly consistent with the rise of partisan dealignment: as political parties struggle to coherently aggregate the growing diversity of group interests, many citizens no longer see the point of strong partisan affinities and instead prefer to act through organizations that focus on issues and agendas of particular concern to them. Certainly, there is evidence to indicate that more British citizens are prepared to participate in single-issue group activity than to join a political party, and that membership of interest groups has not only increased over time but also at the very same time (namely, from the middle to the end of the twentieth century) as party membership has declined.[19] In terms of general incentives theory, this preference for single-issue participation over involvement in parties that aggregate (i.e., pull together) a range of demands and interests speaks to an erosion of parties' capacity to provide effective collective policy incentives.

Closely related to this is the possibility that ideological incentives for party membership have weakened, perhaps because of (what was anyway) a widespread perception that ideological and policy differences between the major party alternatives had narrowed. To the extent that people struggle to see significant differences between the major party alternatives, they are less likely to feel it is necessary to mobilize as party members. That said, it is too simplistic to think that party membership figures neatly follow patterns of major party ideological polarization and convergence, growing, say, when Labour and the Tories are poles apart on policy, and shrinking when they are substantively closer. Using data from the Comparative Manifesto Project, which collects data on parties' election platforms from all over Europe, we can gauge the location of the major parties in left–right ideological terms since 1945.[20] And when we do that, it is clear that the gap between them fluctuates over time, even as their memberships decline in essentially secular (i.e., non-cyclical) fashion. When postwar membership was at its zenith in the 1950s, the ideological gap between Labour and the Conservatives was arguably at its lowest. As we know, party memberships continued to fall steadily thereafter, notwithstanding a prolonged period of two-party polarization from 1974 to 1992, peaking in 1983 when a Thatcherite (but, at that time, still pro-European) Conservative Party faced off against a Labour Party offering widespread nationalization, unilateral nuclear disarmament and withdrawal from the European Economic Community (EEC).

Finally, it is also possible that party membership has fallen as the value of the non-political benefits provided by parties has diminished. For instance, party membership has always been a form of social as well as political activity, and all the main parties traditionally recruited at least some of their members from their associated social clubs (the Conservative clubs, Liberal clubs and various workingmen's and trades and labour clubs affiliated to Labour), which provided relatively cheap and congenial sources of entertainment and leisure for people, whether or not they had much of an interest in politics *per se*. However, it is quite possible that the attractiveness of such benefits has declined considerably with the expansion of alternative (and non-partisan) sources of entertainment and leisure. Certainly, the number of such clubs has fallen considerably over the years: for instance, the Club and Institute Union, covering both Labour and Liberal clubs, affiliated more than 4,000 different bodies in the early 1970s but currently affiliates approximately 1,600.[21] By contrast, shrinkage in the number of organizations affiliated to the Association of Conservative Clubs has been far more modest (from a zenith of 1,300 during the interwar era to 1,100 today).[22] On the other hand, the erosion of Conservative youth organization has been a major component of the declining social function of parties in Britain. The once legendary 'marriage bureau' for the sons and daughters of the middle class comprised as many as 170,000 Young Conservatives in 1951 but fewer than 8,000 by the 1990s.[23] In terms of incentives theory, the weakening of these social and leisure functions of party membership speaks to the erosion of selective process incentives for joining.

So much for supply-side explanations for the long-term decline of party membership in Britain. What about the demand side of the equation? Is it possible that the parties themselves have simply neglected the task of recruiting members? Chapter 9 looks at what parties want from members in more detail, but it is certainly possible that electorally motivated leaders might conclude that life would be easier without (many) members. It might, for instance, cut down on damaging intra-party arguments. It might also save time and money spent on activities such as recruiting members, hiring facilities and organizing meetings and conferences for them, writing and printing and distributing literature for them, as well as talking to, arguing with, persuading, cajoling and disciplining their more recalcitrant elements, all of which dissipates leadership energy and organizational resources. Might it not be better simply to concentrate valuable resources on more effective forms of direct communication with the electorate, especially in the era of social media? And, of course, state funding might mean that there is little financial incentive for parties to put much effort into drumming up more members.

The latter example actually provides the first indication that we can, in fact, all but dismiss demand-side explanations for membership decline. For one thing, public funding for UK political parties is relatively limited. Although state subsidies have grown over the years since they were first introduced in the 1970s, they remain low in comparison with those on offer in other parliamentary democracies; indeed, in accounting for just 11 per cent of national party income, they are easily the lowest around.[24] Moreover, it is far from clear that party leaderships have given up on recruiting members for fear that they might be too ideologically radical, as per what political scientists sometimes refer to (somewhat ironically perhaps) as 'May's law of curvilinear disparity' – the idea (first formalized not by the UK's second female prime minister but by American academic John D. May back in 1973) that a party's members are more ideological than either its voters or its MPs and leaders.[25] If anything, the preferred strategy has been either to grant grassroots members more participatory rights in a bid to dilute the influence of radical activists (Labour leader Neil Kinnock's approach in the 1980s) or, more recently, to ally with members in a bid to overcome the internal opposition from recalcitrant parliamentary colleagues (Jeremy Corbyn's approach since 2015).[26] Either way, the major argument against any kind of demand-side explanation is simply that there is no good evidence to suggest that British parties *have* reduced their demand for members. Indeed, as we will see in Chapter 9, parties still seem to believe that the membership constitutes a valuable resource in a number of ways.

The explanation, then, for the decline in party membership in the UK that took place between the mid-1950s and the early 2000s must lie primarily with supply-side factors.[27] In essence, party membership declined because fewer citizens were prepared to make the commitment to join and remain involved in party life rather than because the parties gave up trying to recruit them. As we have seen, the most likely supply-side reasons are the declining value of non-political selective benefits which are bestowed by party membership (such as leisure and cultural activities), and the erosion of expressive incentives in the form of social group identities linked to partisan affinities (i.e., their importance as markers of social class). But this then leaves us confronting a further conundrum. Why has party membership unexpectedly (and in one or two cases spectacularly) bounced back in recent years?

Explaining the recent reversal of the long-term decline of party memberships in Britain

The exact reasons for the recent resurgence of party membership in the UK may vary from party to party, but the case that probably merits most attention – not least because, unlike the SNP, whose membership has also risen rapidly in the last few years, it campaigns right across Great Britain – is that of the Labour Party. Just why did it succeed in mobilizing so many new supporters after the summer of 2015? This is an issue that we have explored in more detail elsewhere but which we can summarize easily here.[28] A combination of data from the British Election Study and our own surveys supports a number of complementary explanations.

The first of these is derived from what has been termed 'relative deprivation theory' – the idea that people join movements advocating for change in order to acquire something (such as status, financial security, life chances) which others possess but which they believe they are somehow entitled to as well. We found that those who joined the Labour Party for the first time after the 2015 election were more likely to feel a sense of relative deprivation than those who were already members or who were re-joining the party. First-time joiners were less educated, less likely to work in high-status occupations and had incomes well below those of existing or returning members. In other words, the 'objective' conditions for creating a sense of relative deprivation were more apparent among the new members than they were among members in general. More than this, some 37 per cent of the first-time joiners reported that the lack of money was fairly or very likely to be a problem in the future, compared with just 16 per cent of returning members and 19 per cent of existing members – a very striking difference. In addition, graduates who joined the Labour Party for the first time after the 2015 election were more likely to feel a sense of relative deprivation than graduates who were already members or who were re-joining the party. Only about a fifth of the existing graduate and returning graduate members thought that they would have difficulty making ends meet in the future, compared with a third of the first-time graduate joiners – people we label the 'educated left-behind'.

But ideology mattered too, especially for those who re-joined the party in 2015 after a long period away from it. A sense of relative deprivation could only impel people to join Labour if they sensed that the party had a message of hope for them, and Jeremy Corbyn was essential to this message. Many of those who rushed to join the party once he was a candidate and, after he won the leadership race, were ambivalent, at best, about capitalism and drawn to the socialist prescriptions of this veteran left-winger. In particular, we found that individuals who were 'returning members' – that is, people who had previously been Labour members but left in protest against what they saw as the neo-liberalism and the war-mongering of Tony Blair and Gordon Brown – were significantly more left-wing and hostile to capitalism than were existing members or first-time joiners in 2015.

If radical left-wing ideology was a particularly strong draw for returning members, many of the new 'first-time' joiners were motivated by a further consideration, namely, disillusionment with 'politics as usual'. Corbyn offered a new style of politics based on a more democratic Labour Party, in which members would supposedly have a greater say in policy-making. This had a particular appeal for those who previously steered clear of politics because of a distinct feeling that most politicians did not care about them: some 30 per cent of first-time members strongly agreed with the statement that 'politicians don't care what people like me think', compared to only 19 per cent of returning members and just 13 per cent of existing members. In short, a degree of cynicism about the way that politics appears to be conducted also played a part in them joining.

When looking at the phenomenal rise in membership in Corbyn's Labour Party, then, we are looking at a pattern in which, to use the terminology of the general incentives approach, ideological, expressive and collective policy incentives seem to feature most prominently. But we are also looking, of course, at an event – a leadership contest – which, if it is seen as a high-stakes occasion by enough potential members, can, almost in and of itself, encourage an influx of members. The contest to replace Theresa May as leader of the Conservative Party stands out in this regard, too. Deep divisions over Brexit meant that it could be easily portrayed as a battle for the soul of both the party and even the nation. Moreover, since it was signalled months, even years, in advance, then those wishing to take part (and, just as crucially, to be eligible to do take part) had ample opportunity and motive to join in anticipation of it taking place. Whether or not they were former UKIP supporters, as some alleged, is hardly irrelevant, of course.[29] But the episode is a useful reminder that, while incentives matter when it comes to joining, so, too, do triggers.

The experience of the SNP is another reminder of this.[30] We know that its tremendous surge in membership coincided with the referendum on Scotland's independence from the UK in 2014; although the 'yes' side did not ultimately win the vote, support for independence grew from a typical opinion poll level of about 30 to 35 per cent to 45 per cent. The process of campaigning on the issue most fundamental to the SNP's *raison d'être* – and at a time when the party had shown itself to be a safe pair of hands in running the devolved administration north of the border – succeeded in mobilizing an extraordinarily positive feeling for many voters in Scotland. It spoke to the patriotism and sense of national pride that many of them naturally felt, and transformed itself into a willingness to express this through campaigning for, and then membership of, the SNP. The surge the party enjoyed, then, can be understood both in terms of a collective policy objective (national independence) and an expressive incentive (a badge of patriotic identity).

In a similar way, UKIP – another party whose members have recently attracted the interest of other researchers – enjoyed both electoral and membership gains during the run-up to the referendum on UK membership of the EU in 2016.[31] Again, one can see this development as driven, in part, by a collective policy incentive (Brexit) and, in part, by an expressive motivation (a signifier of national identity). In UKIP's case, however, the apparent achievement of the collective policy objective (British withdrawal from the EU) in 2016 seems to have removed a key incentive to join or remain a member at a stroke (see Chapter 9). But the case of UKIP is also a very good illustration of the fact that trends in membership recruitment and retention should not be understood solely in terms of the actions of one party acting alone. Of course, UKIP did itself a huge favour when it chose Nigel Farage as its leader – a canny populist determined to fuse together Euroscepticism and rising anti-immigration sentiment. But David Cameron's initial desire not to follow his three immediate predecessors as Tory leaders in, as he himself put it, 'banging on about Europe' may well have helped trigger support for (and a flow of members into) UKIP after 2005 – something that only increased when he later felt obliged to do exactly that, eventually conceding a referendum on the UK's EU membership, the continuation of which he clearly hoped to persuade the public to back. However, by accepting the outcome of the referendum and embracing a 'Hard Brexit', his successor, Theresa May, managed to siphon off a significant number of voters (and, some moderate Tories later alleged, members) from UKIP to the Tories.[32] Her apparent failure, however, to deliver the kind of Brexit those voters and members wanted raised the possibility that some of them would return to UKIP. Ironically, however, the chances of them doing that suddenly seemed much reduced with the formation (by, of all people, Nigel Farage) of the Brexit Party.

Inter-party dynamics almost certainly have had much to do with the Green Party of England and Wales's membership trend in the same period, too. Membership of the party (which had a higher profile anyway after its first MP was elected to the Commons in 2010) took off after the then leader, Natalie Bennett, initially appeared to have been excluded from plans for a party leaders' debate in the 2015 general election campaign.[33] In just seven months, between October 2014 and May 2015, the Green Party's membership increased from fewer than 20,000 to more than 60,000 – very possibly because sympathizers felt sufficiently aggrieved at what they saw as an affront to democracy to demonstrate their solidarity with the Greens by joining the party.[34] It is likely that the party also benefitted from Ed Miliband's Labour Party's ambivalent response to Tory austerity and, even more important, a collapse in support for Liberal Democrats in 2015. In many respects, the Greens and Liberal Democrats occupy similar socially liberal and cosmopolitan political terrain, but the latter suffered in 2015 from the perception that they had betrayed their principles and supporters by sharing power nationally with a Conservative Party pursuing austerity. Thus, it is no surprise to discover that fully 23 per cent of our sample of party members who had voted for the Liberal Democrats in 2010 shifted to support the Greens in 2015. Not, of course, that this influx from other parties and none was always met with unalloyed joy among some older (in both senses of the word) Green members: one of the party's staffers noted that the difference between the two groups was not just visible – the new members 'look different, they feel different, they haven't all got long hair and beards' – but attitudinal. Accordingly, some of the older members, many of whom lived and breathed alternative lifestyles and, in some cases, had 'a deep suspicion of success', worried that the new members, who may have been left-wing, socially liberal and environmentally conscious but were more at ease in the modern world, would, in their desire to get things done rather than debate every decision and even in their willingness to see party merchandise sold at its annual conference, change the Greens' identity and direction – and not for the better.[35]

The Liberal Democrats are in some respects the most intriguing example of post-2015 membership growth. Having suffered the most dismal electoral reverse in their history at the general election of May 2015, when they lost 15 percentage points in vote share and an incredible 49 of their 57 seats, an odd thing happened: thousands of people rushed to join the party. In the first month after the election, the membership had grown by 15,000 (over one-third of the pre-election total), and all in all, it swelled from 44,000 in 2014 to nearly 100,000 over the course of the ensuing two years. But did this signify a general revival in the party's electoral and political fortunes? Emphatically not, at least until very recently. In June 2017, the Liberal Democrats made scant progress, gaining just four seats (going from 8 to 12 MPs) in the Commons but adding nothing to their share of the national vote. And yet, as we saw in Chapter 2, those who had swollen the ranks of the party's membership stuck around. Why was this the case?

The first thing to say is that the Liberal Democrats' experience, although particularly stark (both in terms of the scale of their parliamentary losses and the pick-up they then experienced in membership) is not unique: Labour's spectacular membership revival certainly owed a lot to the 'Corbyn effect', but it actually began *before* Jeremy Corbyn was on ballot – in the immediate aftermath in 2015 of the loss of an election that many sympathizers had expected Labour to win. This 'loser's bonus' (the flood of new members into a party almost immediately after it performs poorly at a general election) would seem to be an expressive reaction against the disappointment of recent defeat – that is, an act of solidarity (possibly involving a sense of guilt for not getting stuck in before or during the election) in support of the values that the vanquished party is seen to stand for. One new recruit to the Liberal Democrats in May 2015 said,

> There was a personal, emotional response – Clegg's resignation speech struck a chord with me, and I felt the Lib Dems had been the victims of an electoral system which doesn't support smaller parties. But I also suddenly felt very strongly that the Lib Dems stood for the centre-ground of politics, and they need to reclaim it.[36]

Once again, then, we find that expressive and ideological incentives are powerful motives for joining, even in the face of sometimes acute electoral disappointment. That said, as we go on to note in Chapter 9, parties themselves may play a big part in ensuring that those who are so motivated follow through and actually sign up as a member.

Conclusion

In this chapter we looked at why some individuals feel moved to join political parties, as well as patterns of change in the numbers doing so. Seen through the lens of the General Incentives and Civic Voluntarism approaches developed by social scientists, our data suggest that expressive, ideological and collective policy incentives matter most among the various motives that incline people towards party membership, while personal resources such as education and social class also play a role. The long-term secular decline of party membership in the post-war era can be attributed to a number of factors, prominent among which is an erosion of the expressive incentive to join as the major parties have become less clearly identifiable as vehicles of class interest and ideology. At the same time, a growing preference for single-issue participation suggests the weakening of parties' capacity to provide effective collective policy incentives, while selective process incentives based on cultural and social activities connected with party life have also very probably dwindled.

We can dismiss the notion that membership decline follows ideological convergence between the major parties of left and right in any simple sense. However, it is interesting to note the rare counter-examples of membership growth during the decades-long decline since the 1950s. Two instances stand out, both involving the Labour Party. The first was the 'New Labour bounce', which followed the emergence of Tony Blair as party leader in the mid-1990s when, between 1992 and 1997, the party's membership jumped from 280,000 to 405,000. The second is the even more remarkable explosion in membership numbers since Jeremy Corbyn first announced his candidacy for (and then won) the party leadership in 2015.

The first of these moments most certainly did not coincide with any ideological polarization in British politics, although the more recent rise of Corbynism might. But the thing that really links the two instances is leadership: very different kinds of citizens, politically speaking, were inspired to join the Labour Party by the prospect of national leadership by these very distinctive politicians. Each was certainly widely seen to embody a definite set of values and can be associated with particular policy preferences. Yet, as we have noted, ideological trends and membership trends simply do not co-vary closely over time. It therefore seems more sensible to conclude that, while the loss of expressive group and selective process incentives might broadly explain the long-term decline in party membership in the UK, sudden reversals in this trend are best accounted for by the impact of particular leaders and, perhaps, the key policy proposals with which they are especially associated. Contingency matters: as an elected member of Labour's NEC – and no great fan of Jeremy Corbyn, mind – told us at the end of 2018, '[i]f David Miliband had been elected in 2010 and any other candidate had been elected in 2015, membership would now be below 200,000 and falling'.[37]

However, while ideological, expressive and policy incentives may provide particularly strong reasons for joining political parties, they do not necessarily provide the best explanation of what members actually do for their parties and how active they are once inside 'the club'. The nature and extent of members' political activity on behalf their parties are the crucial themes that we move on to address in the next chapter.

Notes

1 Conservative MP, interview 15 March 2016.
2 In early 2019 the standard annual rates were as follows: Labour £52; Conservatives £25; Liberal Democrats £72 recommended (£12 minimum); SNP £72 default (£12 minimum); UKIP £48; and Greens £36.
3 Cross-national research on young party members found that, of the 500 or so interviewed in six countries, only just over one in ten said that the trigger for them joining had been friends or family, but over half mentioned that a family member was connected with a political party. See Bruter, Michael and Harrison, Sarah (2009) *The Future of Our Democracies: Young Party Members in Europe* (Basingstoke: Palgrave), pp. 42, 57.
4 See Seyd, Patrick and Whiteley, Paul (1992) *Labour's Grassroots: The Politics of Party Membership* (Oxford: Clarendon Press); Whiteley, Paul, Seyd, Patrick and Richardson, Jeremy (1994) *True Blues: The Politics of Conservative Party Membership* (Oxford: Oxford University Press); and Whiteley, Paul, Seyd, Patrick and Billinghurst, A. (2006) *Third Force Politics: Liberal Democrats at the Grassroots* (Oxford: Oxford University Press).
5 Many of these other studies are mentioned in Chapter 2, the most up to date of which are featured in van Haute, Emilie and Gauja, Anika, eds. (2015) *Party Members and Activists* (Abingdon: Routledge). For a full-length study in English but not about the UK, see, Gallagher, Michael and Marsh, Michael (2002) *Days of Blue Loyalty: The Politics of Membership in the Fine Gael Party* (Dublin: PSAI Press).
6 Clark, Peter B. and Wilson, James Q. (1961) 'Incentive systems: A theory of organization', *Administrative Science Quarterly*, 6, pp. 129–166.
7 Whiteley, Paul, Seyd, Patrick and Richardson, Jeremy (1994) *True Blues: The Politics of Conservative Party Membership* (Oxford: Oxford University Press), p. 109.
8 Note that the results for our 2017 sample are very similar to those reported in Table 5.3: we report the 2015 results here because the sample is somewhat larger.

9　Liberal Democrat staffer, interview 25 February 2015.

10　We have discussed this at greater length in another publication. Readers who would like to see the full multivariate model can find it in Poletti, Monica, Webb, Paul and Bale, Tim (2019) 'Why do only some people who support parties actually join them? Evidence from Britain', *West European Politics*, 42 (1), pp. 156–172. However, we will summarize the main findings here.

11　Howarth, D. (2007) 'What is social liberalism?', in Duncan Brack, Richard Grayson and David Howarth (eds.) *Reinventing the State: Social Liberalism for the 21st Century* (London: Politicos).

12　See Poletti, Monica, Webb, Paul and Bale, Tim (2019) 'Why do only some people who support parties actually join them? Evidence from Britain', *West European Politics*, 42 (1), Table 5.4.

13　See Poletti, Monica, Webb, Paul and Bale, Tim (2019) 'Why do only some people who support parties actually join them? Evidence from Britain', *West European Politics*, 42 (1), Table 3.

14　Lodge, Milton and Taber, Charles S. (2013) *The Rationalizing Voter* (New York: Cambridge University Press), p. 22.

15　Green politician, interview 5 April 2016.

16　Conservative MP, interview 15 March 2016. Note that, in March 2018, we presented our findings on women members (which included the fact that fewer women than men cited the desire for a political career as a reason for joining a party) to a seminar at the Social Market foundation to kick off a fascinating discussion on the subject by four prominent female MPs from the Conservatives, Labour, the SNP, and the Liberal Democrats – a discussion we summarized here: www.democraticaudit.com/2018/03/22/same-difference-female-and-male-members-of-britains-political-parties/.

17　Scarrow, Susan (1996) *Parties and Their Members* (Oxford: Oxford University Press), p. 8.

18　See Richardson, Jeremy J. (1995) 'The market for political activism: Interest groups as challenge to political parties', *West European Politics*, 18 (1), pp. 116–139.

19　For instance, Kees Aarts reports that the proportion of Britons involved in social organizations increased from 48 to 61 between 1959 and 1990 (1995: 232). Similarly, Peter Hall has calculated that 'the average number of associational memberships among the adult population grew by 44 between 1959 and 1990, rising most rapidly in the 1960s but subsiding only slightly thereafter'. Meanwhile, Patrick Dunleavy has calculated that between 1970 and 2006 the number of professional, general interest and campaigning groups in the UK more than doubled, from 1056 to 2146, with eight out of ten of these groups recruiting individual members. See Aarts, Kees (1995) 'Intermediate organizations and interest representation', in H. D. Klingemann and D. Fuchs (eds.) *Citizens and the State* (Oxford: Oxford University Press); Hall, Peter (1999) 'Social capital in Britain', *British Journal of Political Science*, 29, pp. 417–461; Dunleavy, Patrick (2018) 'Chapter 3.2: The interest group process', in Dunleavy et al. (eds.) *The UK's Changing Democracy* (London: LSE Press), available online at https://doi.org/10.31389/book1.g.

20　More on the manifesto project can be found at https://manifesto-project.wzb.eu/. For the UK, see Allen, Nicholas and Bara, Judith (2017) 'Public foreplay or programmes for government? The content of the 2015 party manifestos', *Parliamentary Affairs*, 70 (1), pp. 1–21.

21　Webb, Paul (2000) *The Modern British Party System* (London: Sage Publications), p. 222, available online at www.wmciu.org.uk/.

22　https://en.wikipedia.org/wiki/Association_of_Conservative_Clubs.

23　See Holroyd-Doveton, John (1996) *Young Conservatives: A History of the Young Conservative Movement* (Durham: Pentland Press).

24　Van Biezen, Ingrid and Kopecky, Petr (2017) 'The paradox of party funding: The limited impact of state subsidies on party membership', in Susan Scarrow, Paul Webb and Thomas Poguntke (eds.) *Organizing Political Parties: Representation, Participation and Power* (Oxford: Oxford University Press), p. 87.

25　See Norris, Pippa (1995) 'May's law of curvilinear disparity revisited', *Party Politics*, 1 (1), pp. 29–47, which found (as have many studies in other countries) that, contrary to the theory, it was actually MPs and leaders (i.e., 'party elites') who were most ideological.

26 See Watts, Jake and Bale, Tim (2019) 'Populism as an intra-party phenomenon: The British Labour Party under Jeremy Corbyn', *British Journal of Politics and International Relations*, 21 (1), pp. 99–115.

27 It should be said that in an ideal world, we would want to create a statistical model incorporating both supply- and demand-side factors which could pinpoint the most significant causes of membership decline, but this strategy is rendered impractical by the unavailability of reliable time-series data for a number of the relevant variables: in particular, there are too few data points in the party membership time series (the dependent variable). Nevertheless, we believe that careful consideration of other evidence enables us to draw the conclusions reached in this chapter.

28 For further details, see Whiteley, Paul, Poletti, Monica, Webb, Paul and Bale, Tim (2019) 'Oh Jeremy Corbyn! Why did Labour Party membership soar after the 2015 general election?', *British Journal of Politics and International Relations*, 21 (1), pp. 80–98.

29 See Newton Dunn, Tom (2019) 'BLUKIP Senior Tories fear thousands of Brexit activists are infiltrating the Conservative Party to have a say on who the next PM will be', *Sun*, 15 April, available online at www.thesun.co.uk/news/politics/8870950/.

30 Lynn Bennie (Aberdeen University), James Mitchell (Edinburgh University) and Rob Johns (Essex University) are working on an ESRC-funded project entitled *Recruited by Referendum: Party Membership Energised.*

31 See Clarke, Harold D., Goodwin, Matthew J. and Whiteley, Paul (2017) *Brexit: Why Britain Voted to Leave the European Union* (Cambridge: Cambridge University Press).

32 See Bale, Tim (2018) 'Who leads and who follows? The symbiotic relationship between UKIP and the Conservatives – and populism and Euroscepticism', *Politics*, 38 (3), pp. 263–277. See also Gilligan, Andrew (2019) 'Caught between deselection and infiltration', *Sunday Times*, 24 February and Wallace, Mark (2019) 'Blukip! Purple momentum! But . . . the big problem with Tory entryism claims is that there's no evidence that they're true', *ConservativeHome*, 22 February, available online at www.conservativehome.com/thetorydiary/2019/02/blukip-purple-momentum-but-the-big-problem-with-tory-entryism-claims-is-that-theres-no-evidence-theyre-true.html. And see Webb, Paul and Bale, Tim (2014) 'Why do Tories defect to UKIP? Conservative Party members and the temptations of the populist radical right', *Political Studies*, 62 (4), pp. 961–970; Webb, Paul, Bale, Tim and Poletti, Monica (2017) '"All mouth and no trousers?" How many Conservative Party members voted for UKIP in 2015 – And why did they do so?', *Politics*, 37 (4), pp. 432–444.

33 Mason, Rowena (2015) 'Green membership surge takes party past Lib Dems and UKIP', *The Guardian*, 15 January, available online at www.theguardian.com/politics/2015/jan/15/green-party-membership-surge-leaders-debates.

34 See Poletti, Monica and Dennison, James (2016) 'The Green surge and how it changed the membership of the party', *LSE Politics & Policy Blog*, 3 March, available online at https://blogs.lse.ac.uk/politicsandpolicy/the-green-surge-and-how-it-changed-the-membership-of-the-party.

35 Green staffer, interview 5 June 2016. See also Green politician, interview 4 June 2016.

36 Barford, Vanessa (2015) 'Why do people join losing political parties?', *BBC News Website*, 16 May, available online at www.bbc.co.uk/news/uk-politics-32739591.

37 Labour activist, interview 10 September 2018.

6

WHAT DO MEMBERS DO FOR THEIR PARTIES – AND WHY?

As to whether they get involved or not, I think that depends more on practical than philosophical factors. Is the party active on the ground where they are? If they go along to a meeting, is it interesting? Are the people cliquey or do they take the trouble to talk to you? Are there things to get involved in? Are there *easy* things to get involved in? Unless people have a positive experience, people can often just turn up to one thing and go. Whilst I think that the motivation for signing up and joining can be quite a high-minded, idealistic, philosophical decision, as to whether people actually get involved, I think that's based far more on very practical and social factors.[1]

Introduction

As we will go on to show in Chapter 9, parties can see plenty of reasons for continuing to need individual citizens to join and support them. But if British parties' demand for members remains undiminished, how far do those members actually live up to the expectations and hopes of their leaders? Once they have joined, how active are party members, and what do they do? And what explains why some members do lots while others do relatively little – or even nothing at all beyond, that is, renewing their subscription each year?

Do members do what parties might expect of them?

Members perform a range of functions and therefore provide a number of benefits for their parties.[2] Even a party interested primarily in electoral success may need to demonstrate that it has a vibrant appeal and a healthy level of internal activity in order to establish its basic legitimacy with the electorate. In other words, impressive membership statistics are in themselves an electoral asset: members therefore provide what we might call *legitimacy benefits*. Second, they provide a more or less reliable core of loyal voters: these are direct *electoral benefits*.[3] More important, perhaps, members ideally act as 'ambassadors' or opinion leaders for the party in the local community and so multiply its electoral support, thereby providing what we might term *outreach benefits*. Moreover, and notwithstanding the changes in modern campaign communications, parties undoubtedly still rely on local members to do a great deal of necessary voluntary work during an election campaign (namely, *labour benefits*), and constituency campaigns can have a significant impact on election results at this level, especially in close-fought marginal constituency contests.[4]

But these aren't the only benefits members confer. Particularly in parties with pretensions to internal democracy, they could be a potentially valuable source of policy ideas (though this innovation benefit might also restrict the leadership's capacity for control and autonomous action, of course, thus transforming itself into a 'cost'). Relatedly, although modern electorally motivated parties rely heavily on professional opinion research, members can also act as a source of information about public concerns (*linkage benefits*). Moreover, a party's membership is critically important as a source of its candidates for public office (*personnel benefits*) the provision of which is a vital function of political parties in liberal democratic regimes and is central to the way in which parties penetrate and control the state. Finally, members can be a source of *financial benefit*: indeed, the financial significance of party memberships in the UK has, if anything, been of growing importance in recent years in the case of those parties, such as Labour, which have enjoyed substantial membership growth.

Nearly all the benefits (with the possible exception of finance) that we've discussed earlier are amplified if members are active rather than passive. But how active are they? The seminal research conducted in the 1990s uncovered all sorts of interesting answers to that question.[5] Most obviously, Labour members were far more likely to be active than Conservative members: broadly speaking, between one-third and two-thirds of Labour members claimed to take part in various activities on a frequent basis, compared to just over a quarter of Conservatives, with Liberal Democrat members somewhere between the two.[6] This meant that the two major parties probably had similar numbers of activists even at a time when the Conservatives nominally had far more individual members. And if these same differences exist today, then, Labour's huge membership surge since 2015 may even have furnished it with an even bigger advantage than many assume.

The explanation for these behavioural differences in the 1990s (and perhaps beyond) may well have been due to the rather different political outlooks of the two sets of party members. Parry and his colleagues argued that participation is both more highly valued and more commonly undertaken by those who are left-wing.[7] This coincides neatly with the fact that the Conservative Party was, until the early 2000s, an openly hierarchical organization that placed little emphasis on political participation *per se*: the chief role of the membership was to help select candidates and then ensure that they were returned to office; the political elite was expected to get on with the job of governing, subject to the constraints of remaining in touch with the vaguely defined 'mood' of the grassroots and, indeed, the public at large.[8]

By contrast, participation as a valued end in itself is emphasized more in the parties which have long had formal pretensions to internal democracy. It is hardly surprising, then, that Labour's individual members have always been significantly more inclined to extend their political activism beyond the narrow confines of election campaigning. As Parry and his colleagues put it, '[t]he Tory campaigners get out the vote. The Labour . . . activists pursue their goals across the participatory landscape'.[9]

Both major parties, however, must have been concerned at the 'de-energization' of local party memberships reported by academics in the 1990s – a net surplus of members reporting themselves to be 'less active' over those reporting themselves to be 'more active' than five years previously, with a net 23 per cent of Labour members surveyed 'de-energized', compared to 17 per cent of Tories.[10] Later research by them on Labour members also showed 'a striking reduction in the number of hours of work done for the party by the average member' between 1990 (when half of them said they spent no time on party activity in the average month) and 1999 (when the figure had risen to two-thirds).[11] But do these patterns and trends picked up 20 or more years ago still ring true today – even in the face of sudden membership growth for Labour and some of the smaller parties?

The first thing we can do is to see how much time members spent campaigning in the general election campaigns of 2015 and 2017 (or, at least, how much time they claim to have spent campaigning). Table 6.1 reports this. We can observe a slight overall decline in the levels of activity between the two elections. The simplest way of identifying this is to focus on the final column (the totals for the whole sample, regardless of party) and, in particular, the two most extreme categories. While there was an increase from 28.9 per cent to 36.2 per cent in the proportion admitting they spent no time at all on the campaign, there was a corresponding fall at the other end of the spectrum in the proportion claiming to have devoted more than 40 hours of their time to campaign work (from 14.1 per cent to 10.4 per cent). This is not surprising really: given the relatively short period of time between the two contests, a degree of 'election fatigue' might be expected.

The second point is that most members actually do little or nothing for their parties during campaigns. In 2015, 51.4 per cent did less than five hours work during the five-week campaign, and 61.3 per cent did less than 10 hours; two years later, the corresponding figures (for a longer seven-week campaign) were 59.9 per cent and 70.1 per cent, respectively. While the number of members recorded in each category goes down steadily as the time spent campaigning goes up to 40 hours, it is interesting to note that there is a small bump at the very highest level; while only 3.6 per cent and 3.1 per cent of all party members did between 30 and 40 hours campaigning in 2015 and 2017. As already noted, 14.1 and 10.4 per cent, respectively, did more than 40 hours, hinting at the existence of a small group of super-dedicated people.

Finally, it appears that the Greens and UKIP had the most difficulty in getting their members to campaign for them, while the SNP and Liberal Democrats generally fared best in both years. In 2015, 62.6 per cent of Green members did less than 10 hours work for the party, and in 2017 the figure was 70.7 per cent. For UKIP, the figures were 51.2 per cent and 60.6 per cent, respectively. By contrast, the figures for the

TABLE 6.1 Over the 5/7 weeks of the election campaign this year, how much time did you devote to your party's activities?

Time campaigning	Year	Conservative	Labour	Liberal Democrat	UKIP	Green	SNP	All parties
None	2015	29.3	27.4	29.2	30.4	35.4	23.2	28.9
	2017	43.9	33.0	30.9	39.8	43.7	31.0	36.2
Up to 5 hours	2015	21.6	23.1	18.6	20.8	27.2	23.3	22.5
	2017	19.7	26.9	23.7	20.8	27.0	23.6	23.7
6–10 hours	2015	9.6	11.4	7.8	9.7	10.2	10.0	9.9
	2017	7.9	10.3	13.5	8.0	10.4	9.6	10.2
11–20 hours	2015	6.9	9.5	7.8	8.7	7.6	9.1	8.3
	2017	6.7	7.3	7.7	8.7	5.3	9.9	7.6
21–30 hours	2015	6.4	7.0	7.9	6.4	4.7	8.3	6.8
	2017	4.8	4.3	4.5	3.2	2.1	4.7	4.2
31–40 hours	2015	3.5	3.4	4.1	4.3	3.0	3.6	3.6
	2017	2.8	3.0	4.0	3.2	3.3	2.6	3.1
Over 40 hours	2015	17.4	13.8	19.5	13.1	6.5	13.8	14.1
	2017	10.4	10.4	13.2	10.1	3.9	11.7	10.4
Don't know	2015	5.3	4.4	5.1	6.6	5.4	8.6	5.8
	2017	3.9	4.8	2.5	6.2	4.4	6.9	4.6
Total	Both years	100	100	100	100	100	100	100
N	2015	1,193	1,180	730	785	845	963	5,696
	2017	1,003	1,023	1,083	437	666	1,011	5,223

Note: All figures percentages, unless otherwise stated. Cramer's V (2015) = 0.072 ($p < .001$); Cramer's V (2017) = 0.081 ($p < .001$).

SNP were 46.5 per cent in 2015 and 54.6 per cent in 2017. At the other end of the scale, the Greens only managed to get 6.5 per cent of members to devote more than 40 hours campaign time to the party in 2015 and 3.9 per cent in 2017, while the Liberal Democrats benefitted from nearly a fifth of their members doing that many hours in 2015 and 13.2 per cent doing so in 2017. When one also takes into account the fact that the Greens and (especially) UKIP lost members between the two elections, while the Liberal Democrats and the SNP gained members, this suggests that the overall level of campaign activity of the latter two would have been boosted considerably, while that of the former two would have been significantly eroded. Incidentally, the table as a whole provides no consistent confirmation of the idea – expressed by more than one of the politicians and staffers we interviewed – that being involved in a winning campaign increases activism: the fact, for example, that the Tories pulled off a surprise victory in 2015 and that the Liberal Democrats were trounced does not seem

TABLE 6.2 NOT including the weeks of the official election campaign itself, would you say that you were . . .?

		Conservative	Labour	Liberal Democrat	UKIP	Green	SNP	All parties
About the same	2015	39.6	33.1	31.0	27.1	11.8	17.1	27.5
	2017	23.6	13.4	16.8	34.0	26.8	32.4	24.2
Less active than five	2015	17.7	19.2	28.1	7.1	3.9	3.9	13.5
years ago	2017	10.4	0.9	6.2	17.5	7.4	8.0	8.0
More active than five	2015	25.9	29.7	23.7	31.5	32.8	41.4	30.8
years ago	2017	22.4	41.6	29.4	16.5	20.4	26.0	25.9
Not sure	2015	4.1	3.4	1.6	3.4	1.3	2.4	2.8
	2017	3.2	1.3	1.4	4.7	2.1	3.8	2.6
Not in the party five	2015	12.7	14.5	15.6	30.8	50.2	35.0	25.3
years ago	2017	40.4	42.9	46.2	27.4	43.2	29.8	39.3
Net balance of more	**2015**	**8.2**	**10.5**	**−4.4**	**24.4**	**28.9**	**37.5**	**17.3**
active − less active	**2017**	**12.0**	**40.7**	**23.2**	**−1.0**	**13.0**	**18.0**	**17.9**
N		1,193	1,180	730	785	845	963	5,696

Note: all figures are percentages.

to have made any difference (at least at the national level) to how much effort their respective memberships put in to the 'snap' election held two years later.[12]

Notwithstanding this evidence of lower campaign activity in 2017 than in 2015, it is interesting (if somewhat paradoxical) to note that fewer members consider themselves to have become less active in recent years. Given that this appears to have happened in the context of membership growth for several of the parties, this calls for a radical reconsideration of the 'spiral of demobilization' perspective that was apparent a generation ago. In both 2015 and 2017, there was a net surplus of members of all parties claiming to have become more active over those claiming to have become less active during the past five years, standing at just over 17 percentage points (Table 6.2). Only two of the parties recorded a net deficit in the course of these two surveys – the Liberal Democrats in 2015 and UKIP in 2017. For the most part, each party seems to have enjoyed considerable net increases in claimed activity levels – the SNP by some 37.5 points in 2015 and Labour by an astonishing 40.7 points in 2017. This pattern clearly points to a decided increase in the number of people who consider themselves active party members in Britain.

What about the nature of the election campaign activities undertaken by party members? Table 6.3 describes these. We have split campaign acts into three broad categories from low through medium to high intensity, with three activities falling into each of these categories, as follows:

- Low intensity (liking something party-related on Facebook, tweeting or re-tweeting a party-related message on Twitter, displaying a poster on behalf of a candidate)

- Medium intensity (delivering leaflets to residential accommodation on behalf of candidates, attending election hustings or other related meetings, driving voters to polls)
- High intensity (canvassing, running local party committees, standing as candidates)[13]

The rationale for this tripartite classification is as follows: low-intensity acts do not require party members to walk out of their front door, or have any direct contact with others: each of these acts can be performed while remaining comfortably at

TABLE 6.3 Which of the following things did you do for the party during the election campaign?

Activity	Year	Conservative	Labour	Liberal Democrat	UKIP	Green	SNP	All parties
'Liked' something by party/	2015	39.6	51.1	47.4	44.2	67.6	72.7	53.4
candidate on Facebook	2017	39.2	63.9	63.2	34.8	63.6	70.7	57.4
Tweeted/re-tweeted party	2015	26.0	36.9	31.1	22.9	45.7	48.6	35.2
messages	2017	24.3	38.9	40.1	18.8	39.8	43.7	35.7
Displayed election poster in	2015	29.6	51.2	37.8	42.9	45.1	67.7	45.7
window	2017	21.6	56.2	48.2	33.6	39.7	59.0	44.4
Delivered leaflets	2015	43.5	42.5	45.9	38.3	28.8	35.4	39.4
	2017	30.5	31.6	44.0	27.7	22.9	30.4	32.3
Attended public meeting or	2015	31.3	31.4	28.2	40.5	27.3	49.0	34.6
hustings	2017	19.8	25.1	23.1	30.0	19.5	34.7	25.2
Drove voters to polling	2015	6.4	7.2	4.9	5.7	2.6	7.5	5.9
stations	2017	2.3	4.6	2.7	4.8	2.0	5.5	3.6
Canvassed face-to-face or	2015	36.5	35.7	32.6	26.1	19.1	28.2	30.4
by phone	2017	21.3	26.8	22.6	16.2	14.0	20.0	21.0
Helped run party	2015	12.5	8.4	13.0	5.7	2.4	5.3	8.1
committee room	2017	7.0	4.0	5.5	4.8	2.4	4.3	4.8
Stood as candidate	2015	9.1	7.0	15.1	13.0	10.2	0.2	8.6
(councillor or MP)	2017	2.2	0.8	3.6	4.8	3.3	1.0	2.3
Other	2015	16.3	14.2	20.8	14.1	12.8	16.6	15.7
	2017	10.2	13.8	16.2	6.2	10.7	9.7	11.8
None	2015	23.0	12.9	18.4	20.8	15.3	7.8	16.3
	2017	24.7	8.9	10.8	25.6	17.0	8.3	14.6
Campaign Activism Index –	2015	2.35	2.71	2.56	2.39	2.49	3.15	2.61
Mean	2017	1.68	2.52	2.53	1.76	2.07	2.69	2.27
Number	2015	1,193	1,180	730	785	845	963	5,696
	2017	1,002	1,024	1,082	437	665	1,009	5,219

Note: All activities figures are percentages. Campaign activism index is based on an additive scale that runs from 0 (no activity during the election campaign) to 9 (maximal activity during the campaign, excluding "other"). All relationships between party and type of campaign activity reported in this table are significant at $p < .001$.

home; basic social media activity might require some investment of time, although nothing out of the ordinary compared to other citizens who are not even party members. Medium-intensity acts require that individual party members step out of the comfort zone of home and interact (although maybe only passively – which is to say, without actually engaging in face-to-face political discussion) with others. Being physically present in the effort to disseminate party publicity, support a candidate and mobilize the vote requires a greater commitment of time and effort than any of the low-intensity acts. High-intensity acts require still greater efforts of time and commitment and carry with them a higher level of political and organizational responsibility than low- or medium-intensity acts: to run party committees or stand as a candidate, even in a local election, is to share in the responsibility for strategic and/or logistical thinking; to canvass voter support is to share in the responsibility for implementing such plans and to risk – albeit often inadvertently and far less frequently than many nervous first-time canvassers fear will be the case – being drawn into political discussion as a party spokesperson.[14]

Unsurprisingly (especially perhaps to anyone who has ever tried to gird them into action!) we see party members are more inclined to get involved in lower-intensity than higher-intensity activity. In 2015, the average number of members claiming to have done one of more of the low-intensity activities was 44.8 per cent, while it was 26.6 per cent for medium-intensity activities and just 15.7 per cent for high-intensity activities. The corresponding figures for 2017 were 45.8 per cent, 20.4 per cent and 9.4 per cent, respectively.[15] The campaign activism index reported at the bottom of Table 6.3 is simply the mean number of acts that each set of party members undertook in each year, and was just 2.61 (out of a possible 9 activities) in 2015 and 2.27 in 2017 (again confirming the slight drop-off in activism across the two elections). The party rank-order of activism was very similar in each year, with SNP members generally being most active, followed by Labour, Liberal Democrats (although the order of these two was reversed in 2017), Greens and UKIP, while the Conservatives trailed in last.

Individual party members are not the only people who campaign on behalf of parties, of course – especially in the era of 'multi-speed membership parties' we have already mentioned – an era in which different types of adherents and followers play roles of varying natures and intensities and traditional party members are no longer necessarily the only significant campaigners.[16] First, as we saw in the last chapter, there are those who feel generally sympathetic towards specific parties without ever actually formally joining, although some of them might be the kind of 'registered supporters' that Labour created in 2013. Second, in the particular case of the Labour Party, there is a long tradition of calling upon the voluntary efforts of members of trade unions affiliated to the party, only some of whom will be individual members of the party, too.

We are able to gain some insight into the contribution made to parties' campaign activities by non-member supporters and affiliated union members because we surveyed these two groups at the same time as the party members themselves in 2015. How do they all compare?

TABLE 6.4 Which of the following things did you do for the party during the 2015 election campaign? Comparing members with supporters and trade unionists

Activity	Members	Supporters	Trade unionists
'Liked' something by party/ candidate on Facebook	53.4	21.0	15.8
Tweeted/re-tweeted something by party	35.2	8.6	8.7
Displayed election poster in window	45.7	9.5	9.9
Delivered leaflets	39.4	2.6	4.1
Attended public meeting or hustings	34.6	6.6	7.6
Canvassed face-to-face or by phone	30.4	2.4	4.2
Campaign Activism Index	2.39	0.51	0.50

Note: Campaign activism index is based on an additive scale that runs from 0 (no activity during the election campaign) to 6 (maximal activity during the campaign). All activities figures are percentages. Members: $n = 5,696$; supporters: $n = 6,337$; trade unionists: $n = 1,098$.

In Table 6.4, we report the rate at which the three groups of respondents undertook various types of campaign activity.[17] It is readily apparent from Table 6.4 that party members are far more likely to have campaigned for their party than either non-member supporters or trade union members; this is so with respect to each and every type of campaign activity that we asked all three groups about. But, although party members might easily outweigh supporters and union members at the individual level, this might not mean that one or other of the latter is equally important at the aggregate level. Given that there were far more voters in the electorate who could be regarded as non-member supporters by virtue of their status as self-proclaimed 'very strong' partisan identifiers (8.8 million) and far more members of affiliated unions (approximately 3 million in 2015) than there were individual party members (600,000), it is quite possible that the overall quantity of campaign work done at the aggregate-level changes the relative importance of these three groups. Indeed, we have demonstrated as much elsewhere in respect of supporters and party members.[18] Here we develop that analysis by adding trade union members to the picture.

In Table 6.5 we estimate the aggregate number of different types of campaign work contributed by members, supporters and union members in 2015. We start by recognizing that by no means all members of unions affiliated to the Labour Party will necessarily be Labour supporters; in fact, in 2015 only 45 per cent of them were.[19] The numbers of supporters and union members that can be attributed to each of the six parties are estimated using the procedure explained in the notes to Table 6.4, and then this number is multiplied by the campaign activism score for each party category – the members, the supporters and the unionists – in turn. This produces an estimate of the minimum number of campaign activities that each group performed on behalf of their preferred parties.

TABLE 6.5 Estimates of mean number of campaign activities by party members, non-member supporters and affiliated union members, 2015

	Conservative	Labour	Liberal Democrat	UKIP	Green	SNP	All parties
1. Estimates of national totals, 2015							
Members	150,000	198,000	51,000	42,000	61,000	110,000	602,000
Supporters	3,061,993	3,883,464	446,623	636,577	165,192	659,054	8,852,903
Unionists	528,000	1,335,000	279,000	453,000	231,000	171,000	3,000,000
2. Campaign activism index (0–6)							
Members	2.06	2.49	2.23	2.15	2.33	3.02	2.39
Supporters	0.24	0.48	0.41	0.37	0.79	0.80	0.51
Unionists	0.20	0.62	0.28	0.35	0.79	0.71	0.50
3. Mean total number of campaign activities							
Members	309,000	493,020	113,730	90,300	142,130	332,200	1,438,780
Supporters	734,878	1,864,063	183,115	235,533	130,502	527,243	4,514,981
Unionists	105,600	827,700	78,120	158,550	182,490	121,410	1,500,000

Note: 'Members' = number of political party members at time of May 2015 general elections or as near as possible thereof. 'Supporters' = projected numbers of non-members who are 'very strong' partisan identifiers for each party, based on British Election Survey 2015 Internet Panel (post-election), Wave 6.0; the number of party members is then subtracted from this figure in order to avoid double counting, given that most party members are also highly likely to designate themselves 'very strong' partisan identifiers. 'Unionists' = members of Labour-affiliated trade unions. Very strong partisans are excluded from this last category in order to minimize the risk of including (and therefore double counting) individuals who are already part of the members' and supporters' categories. The number of trade union members attributed to each party is estimated on the basis of who they reported having voted for in 2015. In the second part of the table, the campaign activism index is calculated as the mean number of campaign activities undertaken out of a maximum possible of 6, by party. In the third part of the table, each figure is the mean number of campaign activities reported by each group (as indicated by the campaign activism index in part 2 of the table), multiplied by the estimated number of people in each group (as reported in part 1 of the table). The figures may therefore be interpreted as the minimum overall number of campaign activities conducted by each group.

Not surprisingly, Labour benefitted most from the voluntary efforts of affiliated union members and (less obviously) from the input of their non-member supporters in 2015. But each of the parties enjoyed at least some benefit from the campaigning of supporters and union members as well. Overall (looking at the total column of the table), it is evident that supporters, in particular, contribute a huge amount to election campaigning, thus substantiating the multi-speed membership model of contemporary party life. But there is an important caveat: while supporters and trade unionists might do a good deal of campaigning work in the aggregate, party members remain critically important to the most demanding forms of activity. Indeed, Table 6.5 excludes some of these because, by their very nature, non-members either cannot do these or are most unlikely to do so. Individual party members are central to organizing and running local campaigns, to offering themselves as candidates for elective office and to canvassing electoral support. Indeed, the relative gap between members and non-member supporters grows the more intensive the form of activity becomes.[20]

This brings us to another point: party members are of course central to the task of maintaining a party organization at the local level between elections. While non-members might be drawn into helping the cause during an election campaign, they are unlikely to play much of a role outside of these moments of intense political activity. Members, on the other hand, play an ongoing role in sustaining party life year-round, week in, week out. What do they do at such times for their parties? Table 6.6 tells us something about this.

Of the seven non-electoral campaign activities that members might undertake, signing petitions supported by their parties is the most common in both 2015 and 2017, followed by attending party meetings (2015) and donating financially over and above their annual subscriptions (2017), then taking part in candidate-selection processes or leadership elections and helping to run social functions or events. The least common activities are participating in policy-making processes and standing for office within the party organization.

Overall, there was little variation between Labour, the Conservatives and the Liberal Democrats in terms of the number of these activities their members engaged in (see Activism Index scores towards the bottom of Table 6.6), while SNP and UKIP members lagged further behind and Greens apparently did least. We also note quite striking drops in the number of activities reported from 2015 to 2017. For Labour and the Liberal Democrats in particular, this might partly be driven by the sheer increase in their membership numbers: even if the absolute number of people making donations, attending meetings and so on changes little, those people will inevitably form a smaller proportion of a much bigger overall membership. However, it might also reflect the fact that many of these new members are relatively inactive after joining and paying their subscriptions – something that is often said (not necessarily fairly) by more experienced members of the Labour Party about those who joined it to support Jeremy Corbyn.[21] In any case, it is evident that all of the parties, including those that did not enjoy substantial membership growth across the two-year period, are associated with considerably lower activism scale scores in 2017. This is consistent with the pattern of election campaign activity that we found and suggests party members became generally less active overall during the period, even though there were significantly more of them. Possibly this reflects a degree of fatigue on the part of people who might have experienced a prolonged cycle of major electoral events – not only the general election campaigns of 2015 and 2017 but also the Brexit referendum campaign in 2016 and, for Scottish party members, the Independence referendum of 2014 and the devolved elections in 2016 (the latter applying to members in Wales as well). In addition, most parties will be involved in local elections of one kind or another most years. Ultimately, however, this is speculation which we are unable to substantiate definitively with our data. What the latter does allow us to do, however,

TABLE 6.6 Which of the following things have you done for your party in recent years?

Activity	Year	Conservative	Labour	Liberal Democrat	UKIP	Green	SNP	All parties
Donated money (over & above subscription)	2015	23.1	31.4	32.1	24.7	13.0	24.9	25.0
	2017	11.3	11.6	21.8	28.9	14.7	30.7	20.3
Signed a petition supported by the party	2015	19.7	46.4	34.4	36.2	52.3	37.2	37.2
	2017	15.0	41.8	42.7	36.5	52.5	47.1	39.5
Attended a party meeting	2015	31.6	29.7	35.3	31.5	14.6	26.0	28.2
	2017	12.2	6.9	15.1	26.5	13.4	24.8	16.6
Helped a party social function	2015	21.1	14.7	21.6	12.9	6.4	13.7	15.3
	2017	7.1	2.6	7.1	12.7	4.5	14.8	8.4
Stood for office within the party organization	2015	13.7	10.9	18.9	10.2	3.8	5.1	10.4
	2017	4.8	1.7	4.2	6.2	2.3	7.3	4.6
Taken part in selection of candidate/leader	2015	18.7	29.2	29.0	12.7	7.6	20.0	19.9
	2017	7.2	9.5	9.5	18.0	9.6	19.1	11.8
Taken part in policy-formulation process	2015	8.4	9.3	14.2	4.5	4.4	7.6	8.1
	2017	4.1	2.6	5.1	7.1	4.5	9.3	5.7
Activism Index – Mean	2015	1.82	1.87	1.86	1.33	1.02	1.34	1.44
	2017	0.33	0.17	0.76	0.66	0.72	0.96	0.59
Number	2015	1,193	1,180	730	785	845	963	5,696
	2017	1,002	1,024	1,082	437	665	1,009	5,219

Note: All activities figures are percentages of respondents answering 'frequently' to these questions. Activism index is based on an additive scale that runs from 0 (no activity) to 7 (maximal activity). All relationships between party and type of activity reported in this table are significant at $p < .001$.

is to look at what influences party members to get active in the first place, and it is to this that we turn next.

What drives some party members to be more active than others?

In seeking to understand what distinguishes those members who undertake the activities that parties rely on to make their election campaigns effective from those who are more inclined to sit back and do little or nothing, we can, first, take a look at whether there are links between activism and characteristics like class, age, gender and so on. Do more active members tend, for instance, to be middle-class, well-educated, older men?

The answer, judging from Table 6.7, which looks at the range of activities carried out by members, would appear to be not really. There is no significant correlation

TABLE 6.7 Social and demographic characteristics and activism

	2015		2017	
	Score	*Number*	*Score*	*Number*
Social grade				
ABC1	2.64	5,695	2.27	5,079
C2DE	2.60		2.29	
Household income				
Under £25k pa	2.75	5,696	2.28	5,219
£25–50k pa	2.81		2.30	
£50–100k pa	2.78		2.34	
More than £100k pa	2.73		2.20	
Gender				
Male	2.60	5,695	**2.21**	5,219
Female	2.63		**2.36**	
Age				
18–34	**2.70**	5,664	**2.32**	5,219
35–54	**2.83**		**2.40**	
55+	**2.44**		**2.18**	
Education				
Graduate	2.67	5,695	**2.38**	5,219
Non-graduate	2.57		**2.16**	
Ideology				
Left–Right	−.087	5,436	−.164	2,704
Liberty–Authority	−.127	5,474	−.178	2,740

Note: Figures = mean scores on the campaign activism index (0–9), except for the Left–Right and Liberty–Authority entries, which are correlation coefficients for the relationships between these ideological scales (0–10) and the activism scale. Figures in bold are all significant at $p < .05$ or better.

between activity, on one hand, and either class (strictly speaking, social grade) or household income. Nor does it look as if men are more active than women or vice versa, although women perhaps tended to do a little more for their parties in 2017 than did men. As to education, the jury is out: graduates were more likely to be active than non-graduates in 2017, but not significantly more so in 2015. There does appear, however, to be a more consistent link with age in that middle-aged members (those aged 35–54) appear to do more for their parties than do younger and older members (aged 18–34 and over 55, respectively) – which is interesting in view of the fact that we might expect them to be busier with work and family commitments. Ideology seems to matter, too: irrespective of party, the more left-wing and/or socially liberal members are the more likely they are to be active.

We can now turn once again to the General Incentives Model that we introduced in Chapter 2 and focused on in Chapter 5, and ask, 'Are higher levels of activism associated with particular incentives?' For instance, are people who are especially motivated by expressive or ideological incentives more likely to be activists once they have signed up for party membership? This approach, which grows naturally out of the question of why people join in the first place, is certainly useful but is not enough in and of itself. As we have shown in more detail elsewhere, though, it can be elaborated and enhanced by taking into account a number of other factors as well.[22]

For instance, taking an individual party member's score on the campaign activism index as our dependent variable (i.e., the thing that we are seeking to explain in a statistical sense), we have been able to show that ideological incentives are important in a number of ways. Party members generally tend to have higher campaign activism scores when they hold definite views (whether they are leavers or remainers doesn't matter) on UK membership of the EU, but they are less active when they were unsure about what has become a (if not the) central question of British politics in recent years. It is also generally true that members are more likely to be active if they hold socially liberal rather than socially conservative values, and if they are sympathetic to post-materialist causes like the quality of democracy or protection of the environment. Crucial, too, is the degree of overall ideological congruence between members and their national party leaderships in left–right terms; when asked to locate themselves and their parties on scales where 0 represented the far left and 10 represented the far right, the smaller the gap between where they put themselves and where they put their party, the more members campaigned – all of which seems to make sense intuitively.

In other words, we can say with some confidence that the ideological drivers that compel many people to join parties in the first place also influence how hard they work for their parties once they are members. We also know that local context plays a part. Most obviously, the more marginal a constituency contest is (i.e., the smaller the winning margin in the previous general election), the more likely it is that party members will make the effort to campaign. Again, the reason for this is fairly intuitive: the tighter the race, the more likely it is that the efforts of campaign teams in the locality will make a decisive difference to the overall outcome. But we can further elaborate on the impact of local contexts. In a second detailed piece of research, we explored this issue in more depth and investigated the possibility that local contextual factors might matter more for some forms of campaign activity than for others.[23] We found that they did.

Specifically, we distinguished 'online' forms of campaign activity (putting out messages in support of party or candidate on Facebook or Twitter) from more traditional 'offline' activities (leafletting, attending hustings, canvassing and so on). We also broadened the scope of 'local constituency contact' so that it stretched beyond electoral marginality, asking members a series of questions about how they viewed their local constituency parties. Did they generally feel close to other local members in terms of left–right ideological values? Did they feel local party meetings were 'united', 'friendly' and 'interesting'? And were they originally recruited to become members directly by contact with the local party? At the same time, we probed members' perceptions of the national party: Did they feel close to the national party in left–right terms? Did they feel that the party leadership generally respected the membership? And were they recruited through direct contact with the national party rather than via the local constituency organization?

We found that general incentives motivations for joining parties in the first place are all significantly associated with higher scores on both types of activity but that factors associated with local constituency context play a particular part in boosting *offline* forms of activity, while factors associated with the national political context are more significant for *online* campaigning. In short, the General Incentives Model should remain central to our understanding of offline participation, while factors associated with the national parties improve our understanding of participation by party members both offline and online. But taking into account local factors helps considerably if we want to explain *offline* activism: if an individual is recruited locally rather than nationally, then becomes embedded within their local party's social network, forms a positive impression of the way it conducts its business and feels comfortable with its general ideological outlook, he or she will be significantly more likely to campaign for it at election time – all the more so if this all happens to occur in a marginal constituency (especially if he or she is a member of one of Britain's two main parties, Labour or the Conservatives). This certainly fits with what we were told anecdotally by some of those politicians and staffers we interviewed for this study. One Tory MP we interviewed insisted that '[t]here's a lot of social bonds. . . . You can't replace those completely by modern digital methods'.[24] One of her Labour counterparts went even further: in addition to those who are active because they are (or want to be) local councillors, he noted,

> We have a lot of people whose whole social life and social interaction revolves around . . . coming to our Labour club and meeting people. . . . It literally becomes their family. And so people find a welcome and a family. And it's combined with something to believe in and something to work towards . . . And there's a certain amount of ceremony involved. . . . In many ways, it's like a sort of community or faith-based organization with politics thrown in.[25]

So far we have concentrated on explaining the *breadth* of campaign activities: How well do the explanatory factors described explain the *number* of (offline or online) activities that members engage in during election campaigns? But there are other equally interesting ways of thinking about campaign activism that promise further insights. In particular, we might go beyond simply examining the number of activities that members undertake to investigate *how much time* they devote to campaigning, and *how demanding* such activities are. Each of these serves to better measure the *intensity* of their campaign participation. To do that we can group the various incentives set out in Seyd and Whiteley's General Incentives Model into three main categories – material, solidary and purposive – recalling Clark and Wilson's seminal work on incentives theory we mentioned in Chapter 5.[26] Seyd and Whiteley note that 'mixing with other like-minded individuals and harbouring ambitions for a political career are both powerful motives for participating in high-cost types of activities. Not surprisingly, they play a much less significant role in explaining low-intensity participation'.[27] In other words, they suggest that two types of incentive are especially powerful predictors of high-intensity activity (selective outcome and process incentives) while, by implication, a third type (ideological incentives) is more important for low-intensity action.[28]

We would expect most party members to share their party's broad values: after all, it is hard to imagine anyone who did not do so joining a party in the first place. In Clark and Wilson's terms, these ideological motivations are *purposive* incentives. But purposive incentives alone are unlikely to be sufficient to inspire people to commit significant amounts of time and effort to election campaign activity. Those who become party members as an expression of their political identity but who, beyond this, have no aspiration to pursue a political career or to immerse themselves in a social network based around the local party, are unlikely to turn into highly committed activists. They may be happy to wear their political adherence as a badge of identity but not to pay the opportunity costs of heavy campaign commitment. By contrast, the selective outcome ambition of a political career represents an obvious motivation for becoming highly active in party activity; in Clark and Wilson's terms, this amounts to a *material incentive* and makes intuitive sense since it is difficult (unless one is especially lucky) to get adopted as a candidate for elective office without first having demonstrated a high level of commitment through one's willingness to campaign on behalf of other candidates.[29] Equally, when one is embedded in a social network of personal contacts in the local community, in which there are strong norms of engagement in both social and political activity, this is likely to lead to high levels of campaign activity. Those who see party membership as more than a passive expression of political identity do so 'not only as a means for the cooperative pursuit of interests, but also specifically in order to fulfil the need for a network of friends and acquaintances with whom one can enjoy a shared life'.[30] Once a person becomes immersed in a network of personal contacts with shared purposive goals, group norms of participation and mutual support effectively snowball: 'the more people interact with one another within a social context, the more norms of participation will be transmitted and the more people will be recruited into political activity'.[31] These are the *solidary incentives* that Clark and Wilson spoke of.

In order to test this empirically, we can return to the distinction between low-, medium- and high-intensity campaign activities that we introduced earlier. We would expect to find that purposive incentives are significant drivers of low-intensity activity but that higher-intensity activity requires the extra motivation provided by material and/or solidary incentives – the sense that it might boost one's chances of becoming a candidate, for instance, and/or the feeling of friendship generated by being part of a group. We therefore construct additive scales – measures designed to tap each of the three different types as set out earlier in this chapter. Depending on how many of each type of activity a member has done during a campaign (the 2015 election in this case), they could score 0, 1, 2 or 3 on each of these campaign-intensity scales.

Before examining the connection between incentives and campaign intensity, however, we first look at their relationship with the time devoted to the 2015 election campaign. Table 6.8 presents the association between this and the various general incentive questions pertaining to purposive, material and solidary incentives in our data set. There are two with which we tap *purposive* incentives for joining the party (collective policy motivations and support for party principles), while the selective outcome indicator (i.e., the desire to become an elected politician) measures the *material* motivation, and the selective process indicator (i.e., the desire to mix with like-minded individuals) gauges the *solidary* impulse.

In virtually all cases a pattern is evident: those members who are highly motivated by these incentives prove less likely to do nothing at all in the campaign than do those who are not so highly motivated, and they are more likely to put in more hours in each category of activity. Moreover, the difference between the highly motivated and less motivated respondents is greater for selective outcome (i.e., the material incentive) and (especially) selective process factors (i.e., the solidary incentive) than it is for either of the purposive factors. As an illustration of this, we can focus on the most active of the groups – those claiming to work for more than 40 hours on their party's campaign. For collective policy incentives, the gap between the high- and low-incentive members is just 2.9 (15.4 – 13.5), and 5.3 (17.7 – 12.4) for party principle incentives. However, when we examine the selective outcome (i.e., material) incentive, the gap rises to 10.1 (21.3 – 11.2) and for selective process (solidary) incentives it is fully 12.3 (22.1 – 9.8). Comparison of the statistical measure Cramer's V (which tests how strongly two variables are associated) at the bottom of each column confirms that the relationship between material or solidary incentives and hours worked is much stronger than that between either of the purposive incentives and hours worked. In short, when it comes to getting active, a party member's desire to become an elected politician and/or whether they are embedded in local social networks matters far more than whether they agree with their party's officially stated objectives.

Next, we seek further evidence of the importance of solidaristic social networks for campaign activity. Table 6.9 presents the associations between various forms of

TABLE 6.8 Hours worked on election campaign and purposive, material and solidary incentives

% having worked on campaign:	Purposive					Material		Solidary	
	Collective policy incentives			Party principles		Selective outcome		Selective process	
	Low	Med	High	Low	High	Low	High	Low	High
None	35.9	30.7	25.0	35.1	26.3	36.3	21.3	40.4	17.4
Up to 5 hours	23.7	23.2	25.2	24.3	23.6	25.0	22.2	25.5	21.9
From 6–10 hours	9.5	11.1	10.9	10.0	11.0	10.3	10.9	9.8	11.5
From 11–20 hours	7.7	9.0	9.7	8.9	8.7	8.5	9.3	6.8	11.5
From 21–30 hours	5.9	7.0	8.9	6.2	8.2	5.6	9.8	5.1	10.1
From 31–40 hours	3.8	3.8	4.0	3.2	4.5	3.0	5.2	2.7	5.4
More than 40 hours	13.5	15.2	16.4	12.4	17.7	11.2	21.3	9.8	22.1
Cramer's *V*		0.071			0.118		0.206		0.297

Note: All figures are percentages. $p < .001$, $N = 5,360$ for all relationships.

TABLE 6.9 Hours worked on election campaign and contacts with party social networks

	Face-to-face		Phone		Email	
	Frequent/ occasional	Rare/not at all	Frequent/ occasional	Rare/not at all	Frequent/ occasional	Rare/not at all
None	12.8	58.9	13.7	42.4	28.5	61.7
Up to 5 hours	21.7	27.5	18.1	27.9	23.9	24.2
From 6–10	13.2	6.3	11.1	10.1	10.9	4.5
From 11–20	12.5	2.9	10.9	7.4	9.2	3.7
From 21–30	10.4	2.2	10.9	4.7	7.5	3.4
From 31–40	5.8	0.8	6.6	1.9	4.0	1.4
More than 40	23.6	1.4	28.7	5.6	16.0	1.1
Cramer's V	0.564		0.436		0.196	

Note: All figures are percentages. $p < .001$, $N = 5,360$ for all relationships.

social network contact that members have with their parties and hours devoted to campaign activity. What is immediately apparent from the Cramer's *V* measures is that face-to-face and phone contacts seem to be better predictors of campaign activism than email contacts. Again, this can be illustrated by focusing on the most active category of respondents – those doing more than 40 hours of campaigning. In all cases those reporting frequent or occasional contacts are significantly more likely to campaign than those reporting rare or no contact at all, but the gap is notably larger with respect to face-to-face (22.2 points) or phone (23.1 points) contacts than it is for email (14.9 points) contacts. This would seem entirely consistent with the theory that the more embedded in a local party social network a party member is, the more active they will be in an election campaign: if one is in frequent or occasional face-to-face or phone contact with other members, then one is necessarily engaged in close networking since these are, by their very nature, personal forms of communication; by contrast, contact via email *may* tap into a real (rather than virtual) social network but could just as easily be about the passive receipt of circular messages put out by the national or local party that could be ignored.

In Table 6.10 we turn to the second of our dependent variables, measuring the intensity of forms of campaign activity (low, medium and high). The table reports the association between these and the various general incentive questions pertaining to purposive, material and solidary incentives. The table is detailed, but there are two key points which stand out. First, the Cramer's V measures confirm that solidary (i.e., selective process) and material (selective outcome) incentives are stronger drivers of activism than are any of the purposive incentives. The only exception to this is that material incentives are not strong with respect to low-intensity activity; indeed, belief in party principles (a purposive incentive) enjoys a stronger relationship with the low-intensity dependent variable than with the desire to be an elected politician (a material incentive). This is all consistent with

TABLE 6.10 Intensity of election campaign activities and purposive, material and solidary incentives

		Purposive					Material		Solidary	
		Collective policy incentives			Party principles		Selective outcome		Selective process	
		Low	Med	High	Low	High	Low	High	Low	High
Low-intensity activity scale	0	34.3	27.3	22.2	33.1	22.9	30.0	24.9	33.1	21.1
	1	26.8	27.1	27.6	27.4	26.9	27.2	27.0	27.4	26.8
	2	24.2	28.4	29.5	25.1	29.7	26.6	28.7	25.3	30.2
	3	14.7	17.3	20.7	14.5	20.5	16.3	19.4	14.2	21.9
Cramer's V			0.081			0.128	0.062		0.152	
Medium-intensity activity scale	0	52.4	46.7	45.2	51.3	44.8	53.6	39.0	58.7	33.7
	1	26.4	28.2	26.6	27.2	27.2	26.0	29.2	24.7	30.6
	2	18.7	22.0	23.9	18.9	24.2	17.8	27.6	14.5	31.0
	3	2.4	3.0	4.3	2.6	3.8	2.6	4.2	2.1	4.7
Cramer's V			0.054			0.081	0.153		0.266	
High-intensity activity scale	0	69.1	65.2	64.1	69.4	62.7	73.6	53.9	75.6	53.3
	1	20.8	23.3	24.8	20.8	25.1	20.4	27.2	17.3	30.6
	2	7.6	9.5	8.5	7.9	9.4	5.3	14.2	5.8	12.4
	3	2.5	2.0	2.5	1.9	2.7	0.8	4.7	1.3	3.7
Cramer's V			0.037			0.072	0.237		0.236	

Note: $p < .001$ for all relationships. $N = 5,693$. All figures are percentages.

the expectation that the more intensive the form of campaign activism, the greater the relative explanatory power of material and solidary incentives. Second, more-over, the gap in explanatory power between solidary and material incentives, on one hand, and purposive incentives, on the other, grows with the level of campaign intensity.[32] This is not surprising. Those members who joined largely because of their support for general party principles and objectives but who lack either the motivation of political career ambition or integration into a local party social net-work are not unwilling to participate in low-cost activities like displaying posters or engaging on social media. However, when it comes to the more time-con-suming and psychologically demanding commitments involved in medium- and high-intensity campaigning, those same members are noticeably less keen to step up. The greater the demands of campaign activity, the more important material and solidary motivations become.

Finally, Table 6.11 presents the associations between various forms of social net-work contact that members have with their parties and levels of campaign intensity. The most striking finding here is that the impact of face-to-face and phone contact is notably greater than email contact for medium- and high-intensity forms of campaigning, while this is not the case for low-intensity campaigning.[33] In general terms, this seems to confirm once again that the more that members are integrated into a solidary network of personal ties with other local party members, the more

TABLE 6.11 Intensity of election campaign activities and contacts with party social networks

		Face-to-Face		Phone		Email	
		Frequent/ occasional	Rare/not at all	Frequent/ occasional	Rare/not at all	Frequent/ occasional	Rare/not at all
Low-intensity activities	0	20.4	40.0	21.7	32.3	26.1	54.3
	1	27.8	26.1	27.5	26.9	27.3	26.0
	2	29.1	24.8	28.8	26.4	28.2	15.8
	3	22.8	9.1	22.0	14.4	18.4	3.9
Cramer's V		0.246		0.135		0.170	
Medium-intensity activities	0	26.3	82.0	27.3	62.2	46.1	75.3
	1	35.2	14.7	31.0	24.5	27.8	19.0
	2	33.4	3.1	35.3	12.2	22.7	5.5
	3	5.1	0.2	6.4	1.1	3.4	0.3
Cramer's V		0.556		0.382		0.154	
High-intensity activities	0	50.3	90.8	45.3	80.2	64.4	89.1
	1	32.1	8.8	32.3	16.6	23.9	9.9
	2	13.9	0.4	17.0	2.9	9.2	1.0
	3	3.7	0.1	5.3	0.2	2.5	0.0
Cramer's V		0.424		0.391		0.133	

Note: All relationships significant at $p < .001$. $N = 5{,}693$. All figures are percentages.

likely they are to engage in higher intensity campaign activity. That network doesn't have to be that big – certainly to start out with. One Conservative MP recalled being told when they were first selected as a candidate, 'There'll be ten people who will win the election for you.'[34] And one staffer from one of the smaller parties told us, 'a gang' of five or six people at local level is sometimes all it takes to form a nucleus: 'All it needs is a core group of very organized people who are really agreed on what they want to do and they just go off and bloody do it and drag everyone else with them.'[35] This can, of course, ultimately prove counterproductive: an organizer from one of the bigger parties told us,

> It is hard when you need stuff doing to prevent one group – who will at least do that work for you – getting hold of positions of power and just hanging onto them forever. . . . And what happens then is that they attract more [people like them] because people come along and find fellow souls and stay, and people who have a different view think, 'I have nothing in common with these people' and then move away.[36]

It is also worth bearing in mind that the strength and vitality of such networks may nevertheless ultimately depend, especially in the long term, on more than the spontaneous efforts of members alone. As one of the activists (and a Labour NEC member) we interviewed was surely right to remind us, people employed by the party at a local level can play an important role in this respect: 'When you've got someone paid in place who has the time and capacity to organize things, that makes a big difference.'[37] MPs and candidates (especially if they are themselves determined door knockers) can encourage activity too – and if they represent a party in which things can sometimes get a little fraught, they may have a direct interest in doing so. As one Labour MP in a marginal seat noted, getting his local members out on the doorstep not only forced some of the newer, more ideologically driven among them to listen to the often very different concerns of 'real voters', it was also a far more productive use of everyone's time:

> It's not rocket science. For me it's about . . . instilling a campaigning culture. Because, actually, the more you campaign, the less you sit around in meetings arguing with each other and talking about Trident or whatever.[38]

That said, MPs themselves may well overstate how much they themselves are a spur to activism. One Conservative organizer told us,

> Most people join a political party because they believe in that party's agenda. I think a bad MP or an MP that doesn't engage can be a negative but . . . an MP seldom adds value. . . . I've never met huge numbers of activists who are tramping the street because of the MP. . . . I think MPs are often disappointed when they find out that . . . isn't [the case]![39]

Overall, then, the data provide strong evidence in support of our arguments about the connection between the intensity of activism and the incentives for membership. The greater a member's desire to become an elected politician, and/or the more he or she is embedded in a local party's social network, the more active he or she will be in an election campaign, and the more likely he or she will be to undertake high-intensity forms of activity. Overall, material and solidary incentives appear to be stronger drivers of campaign activism, and especially of high-intensity activism, than purposive incentives.[40]

Conclusion

Most members do not actually do that much for their parties during election campaigns, even if around a third of them devoted at least ten hours of voluntary work to their parties in 2015 and 2017. While non-member supporters and affiliated union members also contribute significantly to party campaigns, it is party members who play the most vital roles and take on the most intensive and demanding forms of activity. This applies not only to election campaigns themselves but also to the business of maintaining local constituency organizations between elections, when crucial tasks such as selecting candidates for elective office have to be completed. While the General Incentives theory provides a useful basis for understanding the factors that influence members to be active, we also need to take into account local constituency contexts, particularly when it comes to explaining traditional, 'offline' methods of participation. Finally, we have seen that while ideological and purposive incentives can account for low-intensity participation, selective outcome benefits (such as career ambitions) and social network effects are crucial motivations for engagement in higher-intensity activities. Of course, as we have already noted, members' willingness to get involved can sometimes be influenced by their impressions – favourable or otherwise – of their local party. But members can also have strong views on how, more generally, their party works and, indeed, should work. It is to these views that we now turn.

Notes

1 Green politician, interview 4 June 2016.
2 Scarrow, Susan E. (1996) *Parties and Their Members: Organizing for Victory in Britain and Germany* (Oxford: Oxford University Press), Chapter 2 and Scarrow, Susan E. (1994) 'The paradox of enrolment: Assessing the costs and benefits of party memberships', *European Journal of Political Research*, 25, pp. 41–60.
3 Not all party members are absolutely guaranteed to vote for their parties; for a variety of reasons related to strategic voting, and short-term ideological or leadership evaluations, they may sometimes opt for other parties. See De Vet, Benjamin, Poletti, Monica and Wauters, Bram (forthcoming) 'The party (un)faithful: Explaining party members' defecting voting behaviour in different contexts (Belgium and Britain)', *Party Politics*,
4 See, for example, the following: Denver, David and Hands, Gordon (1992) 'Constituency campaigning', *Parliamentary Affairs*, 45, pp. 528–544; Whiteley, Paul and Seyd, Patrick (1992) 'The Labour vote and local activism: The local constituency campaigns', *Parliamentary Affairs*, 45, pp. 582–595; Pattie, Charles J., Whiteley, Paul, Johnston, Ron and Seyd,

Patrick (1994) 'Measuring local campaign effects: Labour Party constituency campaigning at the 1987 general election', *Political Studies*, 42, pp. 469–479; Pattie, Charles J., Johnston, Ron and Fieldhouse, Edward (1995) 'Winning the local vote: The effectiveness of constituency campaign spending in Great Britain, 1983–1992', *American Political Science Review*, 89, pp. 969–986; and Fisher, Justin and Denver, David (2009) 'Evaluating the electoral effects of traditional and modern modes of constituency campaigning in Britain 1992–2005', *Parliamentary Affairs*, 62, pp. 196–210.

5 Parry, Geraint and Moyser, George (1990) 'A map of political participation in Britain', *Government & Opposition*, 25, pp. 147–169; Seyd, Patrick and Whiteley, Paul (1992) *Labour's Grassroots: The Politics of Party Membership* (Oxford: Clarendon Press); Whiteley, Paul, Seyd, Patrick and Richardson, Jeremy (1994) *True Blues: The Politics of Conservative Party Membership* (Oxford: Oxford University Press); Whiteley, Paul, Seyd, Patrick and Billinghurst, Antony (2006) *Third Force Politics: Liberal Democrats at the Grassroots* (Oxford: Oxford University Press).

6 Seyd, Patrick and Whiteley, Paul (1992) *Labour's Grassroots: The Politics of Party Membership* (Oxford: Clarendon Press), p. 95; Whiteley, Paul, Seyd, Patrick and Richardson, Jeremy (1994) *True Blues: The Politics of Conservative Party Membership* (Oxford: Oxford University Press), p. 74; Whiteley, Paul, Seyd, Patrick and Billinghurst, Antony (2006) *Third Force Politics: Liberal Democrats at the Grassroots* (Oxford: Oxford University Press), p. 72.

7 Parry, Geraint, Moyser, George and Day, Neil (1992) *Political Participation and Democracy in Britain* (Cambridge: Cambridge University Press), p. 194.

8 See Kelly, Richard N. (1989) *Conservative Party Conferences: The Hidden System* (Manchester: Manchester University Press).

9 Parry, Geraint, Moyser, George and Day, Neil (1992) *Political Participation and Democracy in Britain* (Cambridge: Cambridge University Press), p. 236.

10 Whiteley, Paul, Seyd, Patrick and Richardson, Jeremy (1994) *True Blues: The Politics of Conservative Party Membership* (Oxford: Oxford University Press), p. 69. See also Whiteley, Paul and Seyd, Patrick (1998) 'The dynamics of party activism in Britain: A spiral of demobilization?', *British Journal of Political Science*, 28 (1), pp. 113–137.

11 Whiteley, Paul and Seyd, Patrick (2002) *High-Intensity Participation: The Dynamics of Party Activism in Britain* (Ann Arbor: University of Michigan Press), p. 99.

12 For example, Conservative MP, interview 1 February 2016 and Conservative Peer, 15 August 2016. It may be the case, of course, that a dataset capable of making fine-grained distinctions between members living in constituencies that were won and constituencies that were lost might reveal this effect. It may also be the case that volunteering on a winning campaign (either at the local or the national level) early on, one's membership might make the difference between becoming an active and becoming a passive member.

13 Note that in 2015 local government elections were held on the same day as the parliamentary election, which explains the relatively high number of party members who claimed to have stood as candidates for elective office: many of them will have been local election candidates rather than national parliamentary candidates.

14 As one veteran MP we interviewed noted, '[c]anvassing is regarded as something of a social event, and people do actually enjoy it. But it's getting people to canvass for the first time [that's difficult]. They think people are going to ask them about the first eight points of the party's economic programme . . .', Labour MP, interview 13 April 2016. This concern can be gotten round, another veteran campaigner noted, by (a) sharing a few funny stories (normally 'about people greeting you in the nude') and (b) emphasising they won't be on their own: 'Some people are utterly immovable but the vast majority of people, if they are reassured, will go out with other people.' Conservative Peer, interview 15 August 2016.

15 The descriptive data information reported in Table 6.3 might seem to suggest that driving voters to polling stations would be better placed in the high-intensity category of activity, while canvassing should be located in the medium-intensity category. However, we do not find this convincing given that canvassing is a logical precursor of driving people to polling stations. Canvassing is a crucial campaign activity that many

members prefer to avoid if possible, perhaps because it seems to hold out the prospect of potential hostility from householders. See Ward, Alexander and Goodfellow, Mollie (2015) 'General election 2015: Five canvassers share their experiences from the frontline', *Independent*, 11 April and Wheeler, Brian (2010) 'What is the point of canvassing?', *BBC News Website*, 9 April, available online at http://news.bbc.co.uk/1/hi/uk_politics/election_2010/8605756.stm.

16 Scarrow, Susan E. (2015) *Beyond Party Members: Changing Approaches to Partisan Mobilization* (Oxford: Oxford University Press).

17 Note that we have excluded three of the activities mentioned in Table 6.3 – either because they are activities that require party membership (running a party committee or standing as a candidate) or because they were not part of all three surveys (driving people to the polls, which was not asked of trade union members). Thus, we only report those aspects of campaigning for which direct comparison is possible.

18 Webb, Paul, Poletti, Monica and Bale, Tim (2017) 'So, who really does the donkey work in "multi-speed membership parties"? Comparing the election campaign activity of party members and party supporters', *Electoral Studies*, 46, pp. 64–74.

19 The breakdown of parties voted for by trade union members in the 2015 general election was as follows: Conservative – 17.6 per cent, Labour – 44.5 per cent, Liberal Democrat, – 9.3 per cent, UKIP – 15.1 per cent, Greens – 7.7 per cent and SNP – 5.7 per cent. To minimize the risk of double-counting an individual who may also fall into the party member or party supporter category, this calculation excludes 'very strong' partisan identifiers ($n = 1,098$).

20 Webb, Paul, Poletti, Monica and Bale, Tim (2017) 'So, who really does the donkey work in "multi-speed membership parties"? Comparing the election campaign activity of party members and party supporters', *Electoral Studies*, 46, p. 69.

21 One veteran Labour activist, and no particular fan of Mr Corbyn, acknowledged this was a widespread perception but noted that Momentum 'get quite a lot of people out for some things and [as for] the existing members, quite a lot of *them* would rather sit in a nice warm room arguing rather than go out and confront a voter'. Labour activist, interview 10 September 2018. See also Poletti, Monica, Bale, Tim and Webb, Paul (2016) 'Explaining the pro-Corbyn surge in Labour's membership', *LSE Politics & Policy Blog*, 16 November, available online at https://blogs.lse.ac.uk/politicsandpolicy/explaining-the-pro-corbyn-surge-in-labours-membership/.

22 See Bale, Tim, Webb, Paul and Poletti, Monica (2018) 'Participating locally and nationally: Explaining the offline and online activism of British party members', *Political Studies*, published online 18 September 2018; and Webb, Paul, Bale, Tim and Poletti, Monica (forthcoming) 'Social networkers and careerists: Explaining high-intensity activism among British party members', *International Political Science Review*.

23 See Bale, Tim, Webb, Paul and Poletti, Monica (2018) 'Participating locally and nationally: Explaining the offline and online activism of British party members', *Political Studies*, published online 18 September 2018.

24 Conservative MP, interview 15 March 2016.

25 Labour MP, interview 9 March 2016.

26 Clark, Peter B. and Wilson, James Q. (1961) 'Incentive systems: A theory of organization', *Administrative Science Quarterly*, 6, pp. 129–166.

27 Whiteley, Paul and Seyd, Patrick (2002) *High-Intensity Participation: The Dynamics of Party Activism in Britain* (Ann Arbor: University of Michigan Press), p. 87.

28 Whiteley, Paul and Seyd, Patrick (2002) *High-Intensity Participation: The Dynamics of Party Activism in Britain* (Ann Arbor: University of Michigan Press), p. 112.

29 It also makes sense, incidentally for those with thoughts of a political career to attend party meetings – and not simply to be seen to be participating but because they have a vocabulary and a set of procedural rules that have to be learned if one wants to persuade and progress: as one MP we talked to put it, '[u]nderstanding how constituency parties work is very important if you want to become an MP. . . . If you haven't been along to

loads of party meetings, you don't know how it works'. Labour MP, interview 20 April 2016.

30 Moyser, George and Parry, Geraint (1997) 'Voluntary associations and democratic participation in Britain', in Jan van Deth (ed.) *Private Groups and Public Life: Social Participation, Voluntary Associations and Political Involvement in Representative Democracies* (London: Routledge), pp. 24–46.

31 Mutz, Diana (2002) 'The consequences of cross-cutting networks for political participation', *American Journal of Political Science*, 46, p. 839.

32 The mean Cramer's V for the relationships between the two purposive incentives and low-intensity activity is 0.105, while it is only slightly higher at 0.107 for the relationships between material/solidary incentives and low-intensity activity. This overall difference of 0.002 grows to .142 (.210 − .068) for medium-intensity activities and to .182 (.237 − .055) for high-intensity activities.

33 If we refer to Cramer's V, we see that the measure of association for face-to-face contact climbs from .246 in respect of low-intensity activity to .556 for medium-intensity activity and .424 for high-intensity activity. For phone contact, the corresponding progression in the strength of the relationship is from .135 to .382 and .391, respectively. By contrast, Cramer's V suggests that the impact of email contact actually *diminishes* as the intensity of activity grows.

34 Conservative MP, 12 April 2016.

35 Green staffer, interview 5 June 2016.

36 Conservative organizer, interview 27 July 2016.

37 Labour activist, interview 7 April 2016.

38 Labour MP, interview 9 March 2016.

39 Conservative organizer, interview 27 July 2016.

40 A more detailed account of this argument is provided and tested with rigorous multivariate modelling in Webb, Paul, Bale, Tim and Poletti, Monica (2019) 'Social networkers and careerists: Explaining high-intensity activism among British party members', *International Political Science Review*.

7

WHAT DO MEMBERS THINK OF THEIR PARTIES AND HOW THEY OPERATE?

> The membership will put up with a lot from the leadership as long as it thinks the leadership is listening to it and treating it with respect.[1]

In this chapter, we explore members' views on how their parties are run – and how they should be run. Do they feel that their parties are sufficiently democratic, especially when it comes to selecting candidates for office, choosing leaders, and making policy? Do they feel respected by their leaders? Do they want more say in decision-making? What are their attitudes to recent reforms, including the opening up of their parties in some cases to 'registered supporters'? Before we can answer these questions, however, we need to set out the rights and privileges afforded to members by each of the parties we focus on, not least because in this, as in so many other things, they vary considerably.

Rights and privileges

The Green Party of England and Wales

Green parties throughout the world are renowned for their bottom-up, grassroots democracy – the idea that power flows upward from local parties and their members as opposed to downward from the leadership and party HQ. It therefore comes as no surprise that (as long as they are full members and not 'local associate members' who can get involved but have no voting rights) Green members have a big say in how their party is run and the direction it takes. Green leaders (there are normally two of them, one male, one female) are (re-)elected every two years by the membership in a postal ballot. And, although anyone wanting to stand needs to have been a member for three years, they only require 20 of their fellow members to nominate them in order to enter the contest. On the flipside, should they win that contest (either as a single or a co-leader), they need to bear in mind that it only takes 10 per cent of the membership to petition for their recall to trigger another leadership contest. Parliamentary candidates are also subject to deselection if just 20 per cent of the local party which originally chose them demands a simple majority vote. Indeed, getting selected in the first place is potentially fairly demanding should there be a contest, since selections are conducted via a system not just involving the single transferable vote (STV – which tends to require those standing to appeal to a wide range of members) but also containing a provision for negative voting – in other words, for anyone dissatisfied with the choice before them to demand that nominations be re-opened.[2] The latter, incidentally, automatically occurs in the event that no female candidate is nominated.

The combination of STV and the provision for negative voting also operates in the annual ballot to choose members of the party's executive. Internal party posts, be they local, regional or national may initially be relatively easy to secure – after all, as one Green politician reminded us, '[i]n a small party there aren't huge numbers of people around to volunteer to do stuff so you can find yourself taking on quite responsible roles fairly rapidly'.[3] However, they are also subject to term limits. Ordinary members, subject to their having belonged to the party for a year or more, as well as to certain rules on confidentiality, also have the right to observe the meetings of any of the parties' elected bodies. In addition, any member has the right to attend and vote at the party's annual conference, which has the final say on policy proposals, the latter being approved (or rejected) by a simple majority should it not prove possible to arrive at a consensus after consultation. Conference can also vote by a simple majority to trigger an all-member ballot on changing (by a two-thirds majority) the 'philosophical basis' of the party; it can also change its constitution (also by a two-thirds majority) – a document that already stands out, incidentally, for its commitment to holding a conference that 'encourages participation and empowers members to make decisions for the Party'.

The Liberal Democrats

The Liberal Democrats are almost as, if not more, enthusiastic about grassroots influence and involvement as the Greens, with members famous for their eagerness to discuss policy. The party's Federal Conference is formally sovereign, with any party member able to attend getting to vote (either by a show of hands or, if called for, a counted vote) to approve or reject (or refer back) policy proposals put to it by the party's Federal Policy Committee (FPC), its local parties, other bodies, or the members. The conference agenda is not, of course, a free-for-all, being decided by a Federal Conference Committee, albeit one that has a majority of elected members and which makes an effort to get around various regional conferences to get a sense of what members (or at least activists) want to talk about. Nor, in practice, does the FPC operate simply at the beck and call of the membership, particularly when it comes to producing the manifesto. The FPC is usually chaired by the party leader, but 15 of its 29 members are directly elected (by STV) by the membership, and it has a duty to (and in practice does) consult on policy as it is being developed throughout the year, as well as at sessions held during the conference. The latter also gives the membership (by a two-thirds majority of those present and voting) the chance to amend the party's constitution and (by a simple majority) to trigger a ballot of all members should it deem such a vote necessary. There is also provision for a special conference of the party if 200 members call for one – something they have done on two occasions, once to object to Liberal Democrat peers' choice of representative on the FPC and once on Europe.

Those thinking of joining the party won't know all these details, but they are told on the party's website (one which, since March 2019, now allows people to sign up as registered supporters rather than members if they want to) that 'you'll have the power to change things and all our members, from [our leader], right down to our newest member you get the same vote', allowing you to '[d]irect and advise on our Party's manifesto for the next General Election, whenever it comes'. Liberal Democrat members also have the right, if, that is, they can persuade 75 local parties to meet and vote for such a course of action, to trigger a leadership contest. The latter, like elections for the party president, are conducted by an all-member ballot using the Alternative Vote (which is the party's preferred system for single vacancies).[4] The nomination requirements, however, are considerably less permissive than the Greens': candidates have to be MPs, nominated by at least 10 per cent of their colleagues in the Commons and supported by 200 members from at least 20 local parties. Party members also enjoy extensive rights in selecting candidates for party and public office, although, when it comes to the latter, their freedom of choice is often qualified by quotas designed to ensure diversity on grounds of gender, ethnicity and disability. Members can also attempt to deselect their MP at his or her reselection meeting, although any MP who loses such a vote has the right to demand a postal ballot of all party members in the constituency.

The Labour Party

Labour Party members, too, have the right to deselect a sitting MP should a third (reduced in 2018 from a half) of all the party units (usually 'branches') or 'affiliated organizations' (mainly unions) that make up their Constituency Labour Party (CLP) each vote individually not to recommend reselection to the party's National Executive Committee (NEC) in a 'trigger ballot'. If that occurs, then the sitting MP, presuming they thought it worth carrying on the fight, would have to battle it out with other candidates in a fresh selection contest conducted under the normal rules, namely, an elimination (sometimes called a 'preferential') ballot consisting of all nominees (who need to have been Labour members for at least 12 months) shortlisted by the elected officers of the CLP. The party's councillors are easier to unseat than MPs because, in their case, only a majority of individuals, as opposed to branches, is required to force reselection – one reason why attempts by the

Corbyn-supporting left to wrest control from so-called moderates or centrists first focused on local government rather than the parliamentary party.[5]

Grassroots members can also remove a sitting Labour leader but only after some 20 per cent of MPs (and, prior to Brexit, MEPs) nominate a challenger. Such a challenge then initiates a contest in which the incumbent (as was the case when Jeremy Corbyn was unsuccessfully challenged by Owen Smith in 2016) is not required to pass the threshold for nominations – a threshold which the conference in 2018 decided should stay at 10 per cent of MPs but would be supplemented by a requirement for a contender to garner 5 per cent of CLP nominations or (much to the disappointment of many members) the backing of three affiliated organizations making up at least 5 per cent of the affiliated membership (a proviso widely seen as giving the big unions a major say on who could run). In 2014, following a scandal involving heavily criticized attempts to recruit new members by trade union left-wingers hoping to influence the selection of their favoured candidate for the Falkirk constituency, the party abandoned its 'electoral college system' for leadership contests. Since then, votes of all those entitled to take part, be they individual members, members of affiliated socialist societies or trade unions or registered supporters (who all pay a reduced rate to belong), are counted together (although tallied separately) in an elimination ballot, which can either be won in the first round by a candidate winning over 50 per cent (as Jeremy Corbyn did in 2015 and 2016) or after subsequent rounds have eliminated their competitors from the race.

Labour members also get to elect other posts in the party – nationally as well as locally. The deputy leader is an elected position, as are a number of seats on the body charged with the party's governance and strategic direction, the 39-member NEC. Nine of those seats (after the CLP section was boosted by three additional seats in 2018) are elected (after nomination by CLPs) via a combination of online and postal ballots of individual members. Individual members can also vote for two further members of the NEC if they are members of socialist societies or Black and Minority Ethnicity (BAME) Labour fora and for another one if they are aged between 14 (the minimum age for a Labour party member) and 26 and therefore (automatically) enrolled in Young Labour, the party's youth wing. It is the NEC, rather than the membership, which chooses Labour's general secretary, who looks after the organizational side of the party, although its recommendation is subject to approval (which is usually pretty well guaranteed) by its annual conference.

The NEC has a role in policy formulation but the latter is also in the hands of a much larger (critics would say amorphous) National Policy Forum, 55 members of which are nominated by CLPs and elected by a regionally based postal ballot of individual members. Any member can propose policies (and policy changes) to the NPF (or to local policy forums) and to its delegated policy commissions – indeed, there is now an online portal for this. However, the final say on policy lies with the party's annual conference. By no means all members can attend the latter: CLPs can send a small number of delegates, with the exact number determined by their size and having regard to gender balance. Those delegates' votes on policy or rule changes can be (although they certainly don't have to be) decided by votes taken prior to the conference at CLP meetings. But their influence on outcomes, even after ordinary members were granted more speaking slots from 2017 onwards, is potentially outweighed by affiliated trade unions wielding their bloc votes for or against various motions and amendments. Each CLP can submit either a 'contemporary motion' (relating to the event following a specific date, usually around six weeks before Conference starts) or a 'rule change' to Labour's constitution. The Conference Arrangements Committee (CAC), two of whose members are chosen by a ballot of all individual members over the summer, then groups together contemporary motions by category and presents these topics on the 'priorities ballot' on the first day of Labour Party Conference. Delegates and union delegates can then vote for four topics which they believe are a 'priority' for the conference to debate; the eight most popular topics (four in the members' section, four in the unions) will then be debated. Normally, rule change amendments – unless deemed by the NEC to be urgent – are not discussed until the following conference.

Many Labour members were furious when they were denied what they regarded as a proper debate and vote on Brexit at the party's Brighton conference in 2017, although this was not down to some sort of skulduggery by the CAC. In fact, the CAC included it on the ballot (how could it not, given how many CLPs wanted it debated?), but the powerful left-wing ginger group Momentum was able to persuade delegates who shared its desire to prevent the conference from obliging Mr Corbyn to support a soft Brexit (or even no Brexit) not to make it one of just four urgent motions that (before 2019, when the number will increase to ten) CLPs and affiliated organizations (in the main trade unions) were each allowed to put forward. The same trick could not be pulled off at Liverpool in 2018; however, there, the tradition of 'compositing' motions ensured that the one which went forward on Brexit gave the leadership the leeway it needed (for a few months at least) to avoid explicitly calling for a second referendum (or People's Vote) – something our research (see Chapter 4) suggested three-quarters of members wanted it to do. That said, manipulation by the CAC, in consultation with the leadership and powerful trade unions, has gone on (and presumably will carry on) for decades. This has not stopped the party from inserting into an appendix in its rulebook the following, which ranks as one of the most positive statements about membership coming from any of the UK's six biggest parties:

> We value the role of our members and our affiliated members as progressive campaigners, community activists and social entrepreneurs who forge positive change in their own neighbourhoods as well as shaping and promoting national policy. . . . Together our members and affiliates can create a Party that is truly reflective of the communities we serve; a Party able to turn outwards and find innovative and flexible ways to encourage contact and support from local communities, drawing in those who share Labour's values, and therefore bringing a local Labour presence in every constituency, and in being an agent for change locally, nationally, and internationally.[6]

On the other hand, it is clear that Labour, like some other parties (in particular, UKIP, which, notwithstanding its recent flirtation with Islamophobic white nationalism, still insists that applicants for membership swear that they are 'not and have never been a member' of various far-right parties and movements), is concerned about the possibility that some of those who want to join it risk bringing it into disrepute. This is presumably why its website makes clear to potential new joiners that they will have to agree to 'pledge to act within the spirit and the rules of the Labour Party in [their] conduct both on and offline, with members and non-members and . . . stand against all forms of abuse'.

The Scottish National Party

The SNP values its membership and, as long as they are over 16 and therefore full rather than 'associate members', it provides them with rights that are at least on a par with those provided by Labour – indeed probably more so since, although the SNP does invite membership by affiliated organizations (a BAME Members Network, a Disabled Members Group, a Federation of Student Nationalists, Out for Independence, Scots Asians for Independence, a Trade Union Group, and Young Scots for Independence), they play nowhere near the role that the trade unions play in the Labour Party.

SNP members join nationally, at which point, in common with members of most other parties, they agree to endorse their party's aims and accept its constitution, rules and standing orders. But – unless they prefer not to be, in which case they can join the 'Headquarters Branch' – they are then allocated a local branch, each of which then sends delegates to a constituency association. Any member of the party is entitled to join the SNP's National Assembly, which is a forum for policy discussion that may go on to produce resolutions and statements for consideration by the party's Policy Development Committee, composed of the deputy leader, a policy development convenor, and 16 regional reps elected by the Annual National Conference. The latter also elects two parliamentarians and sixteen regional members to the SNP's NEC, the rest of which is formed by representatives of the party's parliamentary groups, councillors and affiliated organizations, together with a dozen 'National Office Bearers' and the party's leader. The National Executive is responsible for the SNP's overall organization (including the establishment or dissolution of any branch), as well as its political direction and strategic management. The executive also draws up a list, with an eye to gender balance, of approved candidates, after which candidates are chosen and (where lists need to be drawn up) ranked by the members living in the area concerned. The SNP's Annual National Conference, to which branches send delegates according to branch size, is, at least in theory, the party's supreme decision-making body. As well as helping to elect the national executive, it also elects the committees which investigate any alleged breaches of the party's code of conduct by members. Every full member is entitled to vote in leadership contests, with candidates, excepting the incumbent should he or she be challenged, requiring nomination by 100 members drawn from at least 20 local branches.

The Conservative Party

Grassroots members of the Conservative Party enjoy relatively few rights and privileges compared to their counterparts in other parties – and according to some campaigners the situation has got worse rather than better.[7] Yet they are not completely without influence, particularly when it comes to candidate selection and leadership contests. Indeed, one could argue that Brexit may never have happened without the Tory rank and file. After all, their decision in 2001 to back the utterly uncharismatic Eurosceptic Iain Duncan Smith over the more obviously electable but unrepentantly Europhile Ken Clarke may have done nothing to improve the party's electoral chances, but it did a great deal to ensure that the increasingly Eurosceptic tone set by William Hague after 1997 would become the party's default stance. So, too, did the determination of constituency associations up and down the land to select prospective parliamentary candidates who (whether they believed what they were saying or not) promised faithfully, if not to bash Brussels, then at least to resist any slide toward a federal superstate. And once those candidates became MPs, the fact that they could rely on their constituency associations either to support them if they defied the whip to call for an in–out referendum, or to urge them to do so if they did not, helped, along with the rise of UKIP, to push an initially reluctant David Cameron to promise to hold one.[8]

The role of ordinary Tory members in choosing the party's leader is of very recent vintage, coming about as the result of the so-called Fresh Future reforms introduced by William Hague after the party's crushing defeat by Tony Blair's New Labour in 1997 – reforms fuelled at least in part by the hope that giving the grassroots more of a say might both reverse a precipitate decline in membership and assuage their palpable sense of having been let down by a deeply divided and sleaze-ridden parliamentary party. The system introduced by Hague (which incidentally survived an attempt to abolish it in 2005) nevertheless allowed MPs to retain a gatekeeping function by limiting the rank and file's choice to whichever of the leadership hopefuls could make it through to the last two in a series of successive secret ballots at Westminster organized by the 1922 Committee of Tory backbenchers. They would then tour the country drumming up support and appearing at hustings while ordinary members were issued with postal ballots, with the winner elected by a simple majority of votes cast, irrespective of the turnout. Even then, however, all was not quite what it seemed. In the event that the parliamentary party decided on just one candidate without a contest (as happened when Michael Howard replaced Duncan Smith in 2003) or only one candidate was left standing after all their opponents fell by the wayside or else withdrew from the Westminster stage of the contest (as happened when Theresa May took over from David Cameron in 2016), then the grassroots would lose any formal say in the party's choice of leader. The qualifier 'formal', however, is important: there can be little doubt that in casting their ballots – or indeed in deciding to avoid a contest altogether – Tory MPs take a view on how likely the various candidates on offer would be to find favour with their local parties. It is also a little-known fact that there is provision in the party's constitution for any leader who finds him- or herself offered the crown without a contest in the country to hold a post hoc ballot of the grassroots in order to confirm their position – although whether anyone would actually deign to exercise that option is surely doubtful: even if the risk that such a ballot would see members reject the parliamentary party's choice is probably small, a poor turnout could still cast deeply embarrassing doubt on their legitimacy.

The involvement of rank-and-file Tories in selecting their party's parliamentary candidates goes back much further than their role in choosing its leaders and remains perhaps their most jealously guarded privilege – one normally exercised at a meeting open to all local party members voting in a secret ballot. Again, however, that privilege is not absolute. Candidates must normally be chosen from an approved list of candidates chosen by an unelected Candidates Committee. And even then, over the years, party leaders (often via Central Office, now known as Conservative Campaign Headquarters or CCHQ) have made exceptions, intervening – sometimes officially, sometimes informally – to help get favourites selected and/or block people seen as troublemakers, occasionally even removing them from the list altogether. Associations' rights to draw up their own shortlists can also be formally set aside, for instance, in the event of a by-election or a snap election. The Conservative Party's constitution is the subject of an ongoing consultation process which many worry will lead to more central control over candidate selection, but even as it currently stands, it contains the following statement: 'The Board shall have the power to do anything which in its opinion relates to the management and administration of the Party' – effectively an all-purpose get-out clause and one which was used in the run-up to the 2017 general election to allow CCHQ to impose parliamentary candidates or shortlists on the constituencies.[9] Associations have also been, if not obliged, then encouraged (e.g., via 'the Priority List' created in the early years of David Cameron's leadership) to choose candidates whose selection would supposedly signal the party's desire to break with its 'stale, male, and pale' image. The party has experimented, too, with open primaries, allowing a constituency's voters, as well as its Tory party members, to take part in the selecting from the association's shortlist. However, it is highly unlikely to repeat the experiment. The turnout at non-postal primaries was woefully low, while postal primaries proved phenomenally expensive and, in 2010, produced the famously independent-minded MP for Totnes Dr Sarah Wollaston, who eventually left the party with two of her parliamentary colleagues in early 2019. Associations do, it should be noted, have the right not to re-adopt incumbent MPs as their parliamentary candidate, although should their executive do this, said MP then has the right to trigger a postal ballot of the association's entire membership. As is the case with all other votes on party matters (including leadership contests), a member's eligibility to take part depends on them having been a member for at least three months before ballots close.

The Tory grassroots' influence on the Conservative Party's power structure and policy is far less direct. It should not be discounted completely, however. When it comes to the former, ordinary members get to elect most of their local association's officers (who collectively form its executive) at their annual general meeting, although, because many associations are now too small to maintain functional ward branches, those officers are less likely than they were to represent a geographical spread of the constituency. The most important of these posts is the association chairman (the masculine noun used irrespective of the incumbent's gender) who, *ex officio*, all belong to the party's approximately 800-member National Conservative Convention. The convention is supposed to represent the interests of members, although its officers (a chairman, a president and three vice presidents) are elected not by the membership as a whole but by area committees which in practice means by a few hundred Association chairs and deputy chairs. The convention elects four (albeit only 4 out of a possible 19) members of its top administrative body, the Party Board. Associations' Annual General Meetings (AGM's) also elect two representatives each to area councils, which have, among other things, a disciplinary role, having a right to recommend suspension or expulsion of individual members to the Party Board (whose decision, incidentally, is binding and not subject to any review). Associations get to send their chairman (and deputy chairman) to the party's annual conference, although, in reality, attendance by members is so low nowadays that any almost any individual member who wants to (and can afford to) attend can probably do so. That conference, however, has no formal say on party policy, which, the constitution makes clear, is the preserve of the leader, albeit 'having regard to the views of Party Members and the Conservative Policy Forum'. Members, however, do not elect anyone onto the CPF, which is composed entirely of people appointed and co-opted to it. Members could, if they wanted to try to, change all this by proposing an amendment to the party's constitution – either indirectly via the National Conservative Convention, on which all chairmen sit, or by gathering 10,000 signatures to a petition submitted to the Party Board. Given such a petition would require around one in ten mostly inactive members to sign it, the likelihood of that happening seems remote, and even if it were to happen, any amendment would need passing by a three-way constitutional college made up of the convention, MPs, and officers and frontbench spokesmen in the Lords.

UKIP

On the face of it, UKIP members have a better chance of achieving formal changes to the way their party is run than their Conservative counterparts. In theory, it only takes twenty or more local associations (which in UKIP's case means constituency parties or branches covering more than one constituency) to write to the chair of the party to trigger a ballot of the entire membership on amending its constitution, although each has, firstly, to show that its request follows a vote for such action at a properly constituted AGM or emergency general meeting and, secondly, to make a contribution to the cost of such a ballot. In practice, this has never been achieved, however, and, even if it were to happen, any change to the constitution would need to be approved by a two-thirds majority of those members voting. Still, UKIP's grassroots can hardly complain that they have not been consulted about the direction of the party in recent years, having been called on to vote – via a postal ballot, as laid down in its constitution – in no less than three leadership contests in as many years, all of which have ended either badly or farcically or both. That same constitution provides for a leadership contest to be held every four years, albeit one in which the incumbent is allowed to stand. It also makes clear that the party's NEC, which is elected by the membership, can vote no confidence in UKIP's leader, after which an emergency general meeting open to all members either accepts or rejects its decision, acceptance leading to the dismissal of the leader and rejection leading to their continuation and the holding of fresh elections to the NEC.

UKIP members would also appear, at least at first glance, to have more of a say on the party's policies than their Tory counterparts. A subcommittee of the elected NEC recommends policy – often policy first generated by the leader and their appointed spokespersons – to that body, and members, as long as they've been full (as opposed to an ill-defined category of 'associate') members for at least 28 days, can vote by simple majority to approve policy motions at UKIP's annual confer-ence. Once again, however, all is not quite as it seems: according to the party's constitution, such motions only have advisory force, with the NEC obliged only to discuss rather than implement them.

On the other hand, when it comes to selecting parliamentary candidates, UKIP members seem to have a fairly free hand, with each of them chosen by balloting members at a specially convened meeting following hustings addressed by the run-ners and riders. That said, those runners and riders do have to be on an approved list, while candidates for local authority elections are selected by the local party's branch officers rather than the membership, although, since the former are chosen by the latter at local annual general meetings, this can hardly be called undemocratic.

British parties in comparative perspective

So, given the above exactly how 'democratic' are British political parties? We can actually get a sense of how they compare to parties in other parliamentary democ-racies by drawing on some recent academic work which tries to gauge the internal democracy of parties by reference to members' representation on key bodies such as executive committees, and by party decision-making procedures on selecting candidates for office, choosing their leaders, and formulating policy.[10] This distin-guishes between two types of democratic procedure, which the authors refer to as 'assembly-based' and 'plebiscitary'. They argue that these stem from two funda-mentally different logics of decision-making and construct separate measures for each type.

The first is the *Assembly-based IPD index (AIPD)* and covers policy formulation, personnel selection (leaders and candidates), and organizational structure. As the authors put it,

> [i]n a nutshell, the AIPD index measures the inclusiveness of decision-making inside parties that is based on discussions within party bodies and assemblies . . . A higher index score indicates that a more inclusive party

body has the final say on decisions over personnel and policy, and intra-organizational power is less top-heavy.[11]

The second is the *Plebiscitary IPD index (PIPD)* and measures the degree to which parties allow for decision-making on their programme and their personnel based on the plebiscitary logic of one-member-one-vote. As the authors put it,

> plebiscitary decision-making disconnects the process of discussion and deliberation from the actual decision which is eventually taken by the lone party member at his or her desk or computer screen. We contend that this is a fundamentally different logic as there is no way to deliberate and reach compromise (frequently through repeated rounds of voting). It is the politics of 'either/or'. Even though formally the members decide, it is dichotomous politics which arguably gives a lot of power to the leaders.[12]

When seen in a comparative perspective, it is interesting to observe that the main British parties actually rank as highly democratic in terms of both measures. Out of 122 parties spanning 19 different parliamentary democracies, Britain's parties generated the highest national average score on the AIPD index and the second-highest PIPD score. On the AIPD index, the Green Party of England and Wales had the second highest score out of all 122 parties, while the Liberal Democrats were seventh equal, the Conservative and Labour Parties were both in the top 20, and the SNP and UKIP in the top 30. On the PIPD index, the Greens had the ninth-highest score out of 122, while the Liberal Democrats, Labour, Conservatives and SNP all came joint 12th, and UKIP joint 44th.[13] As a rule, parties tend to emulate their national competitors in their organizational structures and procedures, so the clustering of some of these scores is not surprising but it is nevertheless striking. Still, is it enough to satisfy their grassroots members?

You got the power?

We asked respondents in each of our membership surveys a number of questions about internal party processes. Tables 7.1 and 7.2 report these. In the first of these tables, we start by focusing on the extent to which members feel that the membership has enough influence over the formulation of party policy. Respondents were asked to choose between three possible options: that the members should have more influence over policy, that the leadership should have more influence, or that the current situation was about right. The table reports the percentage opting for the first of these, since this can be taken as a desire for greater intra-party democracy, at least in respect of policy-making.

The overall sample percentage across the parties who feel that members should have more influence over policy is almost identical in 2015 and 2017: 37 per cent and 38 per cent, respectively. To this extent, one might conclude that a little over one-third of party members feel that their leaders should be more responsive to the

TABLE 7.1 Members' attitudes regarding their position within parties, 2015 and 2017

Statement	Conservative		Labour		Liberal Democrat		UKIP		Green		SNP		All parties			
	2015	2017	2015	2017	2015	2017	2015	2017	2015	2017	2015	2017	2015		2017	
Members should have more influence over policy	32.3	54.6	58.3	55.8	36.6	27.5	33.6	53.9	27.1	23.4	26.3	31.4	36.6	$V = 0.199$	37.7	$V = 0.241$
The party leadership respects members	81.5	66.7	69.6	91.1	85.0	96.3	93.3	79.0	96.0	99.4	98.4	97.0	86.2	$V = 0.230$	88.8	$V = 0.277$
Approve of registered supporters' schemes	55.7	43.2	46.2	48.6	43.8	43.0	43.6	38.5	42.0	50.0	31.1	36.7	44.4	$V = 0.094$	43.2	$V = 0.065$
Experience as a member has fully lived up to expectations	44.1	25.2	32.4	47.9	44.2	33.7	53.2	28.2	50.2	42.8	75.7	60.0	49.4	$V = 0.183$	40.2	$V = 0.176$

Note: Figures represent percentage of respondents agreeing or agreeing strongly with statements; V = Cramer's V measure of association between party and attitude; eta^2 = measure of association between party and attitudinal scale. All relationships significant at $p < .001$.

TABLE 7.2 Members' attitudes regarding candidate-selection procedure, 2015 and 2017

Statement	Conservative		Labour		Liberal Democrat		UKIP		Green		SNP		All parties	
	2015	2017	2015	2017	2015	2017	2015	2017	2015	2017	2015	2017	2015	2017
Open postal primary	10.2	5.2	9.1	15.1	9.3	10.8	10.8	12.3	10.9	11.8	9.5	12.4	9.9	10.7
Open primary	20.6	9.1	12.1	11.1	11.9	8.6	14.2	15.5	11.3	10.0	8.3	8.0	13.5	9.5
Closed postal ballot	34.5	59.3	52.3	58.3	54.1	66.7	39.1	46.0	59.7	64.6	64.3	61.8	49.9	61.6
Closed ballot	34.7	26.4	26.5	15.6	24.7	14.0	18.1	26.2	18.1	13.6	18.0	17.7	26.7	18.3

Note: Figures represent percentages; Cramer's V = 0.135 (2015) and 0.102 (2017). All relationships significant at $p < .001$.

grassroots when it comes to policy development. However, there are some notable variations by party, some but not all of which are presumably a function of how much formal power members actually have. For example, grassroots Conservatives may actually have more influence than might be assumed, especially if they live in a constituency with a Tory MP: as one of those MPs put it,

> if you get a lot of members and supporters in your association saying 'I've got a problem with this' then I think that does translate through to people being more concerned about it. . . . And people at the top of the party do ask, 'Well, what are your members saying about x, y, and z?'. . . so they do have an informal influence in that way.[14]

This is confirmed by an interviewee with extensive parliamentary and local association experience, who noted that the latter had become so small now that it only took an MP to fall out with, say, a dozen prominent activists, to make their lives very uncomfortable, and anyway

> [i]f you think about it, when an MP goes back to their constituency, Friday/Saturday/Sunday who do they have the most contact with? They're going back to their constituency office which is run by . . . local members. They'll go out canvassing – with party members. All the events they go to – dinners, raffles and things – the vast majority of them are organized by party members. And so in . . . 50 to 75 per cent of the stuff they're doing, they're always corralled by party members. If you surround yourself with people like that then you . . . become part of the bubble. . . . You're surrounded by the same like-minded people. You don't necessarily hear the other side of the story. Or if you do, you might mention the other side of the story and immediately you're surrounded by the views of other people who immediately take the other side. . . . It's peer pressure isn't it?[15]

However, the Conservative rank and file's *formal* say is frankly negligible – and they know it, which, in an era where deference has all but broken down and consumerism is on the rise, is likely to engender a fair amount of dissatisfaction. By the same token, then, it is hardly surprising that it is their counterparts in the Green Party, who seem to be most satisfied, in that only about a quarter of their members seek even greater membership influence over policy. Green members were more or less matched in terms of the percentage who sought more membership influence in the SNP in 2015 (but not 2017) and by the Liberal Democrats in 2017 (but not in 2015). That the Liberal Democrats should find themselves in a similar position to the Greens on this score again fits well with what we know about their party's commitment to democracy in deciding policy and picking people – a commitment which, according to staffers we interviewed, is in and of itself a big draw for many who join the party.[16]

The two parties which experienced very significant increases in the proportions wanting greater membership influence over policy in the short two-year period from 2015 and 2017 are UKIP and the Conservatives. In each case, there was an increase from about a third to about half of members wanting more influence. In the case of the Tories, one might surmise that this has much to do with the way in which the governments of David Cameron and Theresa May struggled to cope with the challenge of Brexit: a highly Eurosceptic membership was, presumably, less than fully impressed by the leadership's performance. By the end of 2018, the membership was split almost exactly evenly between those who felt Theresa May was generally doing well as leader and those who felt she was doing badly; 59 per cent opposed the deal that the prime minister had negotiated on the UK's exit from the EU, and 68 per cent felt that the government was handling the negotiations poorly.[17] In the case of UKIP, this was a tumultuous period, in which the party soared to new heights of electoral success (2015), achieved its defining mission (2016) and then sank back electorally (2017) while, as we have noted, undergoing several chaotic changes of leadership. In such a context, it is perhaps little surprise that the members felt that need for greater influence over their leaders.

Interestingly, the party whose members appear most dissatisfied with the level of membership influence over policy is Labour. In both surveys, more than half of them wanted a greater say for the grassroots. Intra-party democracy has always been a contested and complex concept in Labour's case, not least because of the role played in its internal processes by external bodies – most obviously the trade unions– from its foundation onwards.[18] Throughout its history, the party has striven to balance the roles and powers of the parliamentary elite, the extra-parliamentary membership, and the affiliated organizations that created it and have always done so much to provide it with resources. In reviewing this history, it is hard to avoid the impression that the members have often struggled to make their voices heard over those of the other two elements of this triad. Perhaps, then, it is not surprising to find that approaching three-fifths of them desire greater influence over party policy – and, of course, they can only have been encouraged by the election of a leader who promised them exactly that in 2015. The figures for the 2017 survey suggest, however, that he was not widely felt to have delivered on this promise during his first two years as leader – an impression only strengthened by subsequent developments: by 2019, there were unmistakable signs of growing discontent among an over-whelmingly anti-Brexit membership at the way Jeremy Corbyn was dealing with this issue. Thus, 29 per cent of members opposed Labour's stance on Brexit, and over half of these claimed to have considered leaving the party because of it. More than 70 per cent of members wanted a new referendum to be held on Brexit, and nearly 90 per cent said they would vote to remain if given such an opportunity.[19] Yet the leadership continued to hold out for as long as possible against committing to a 'People's Vote', and even when the party appeared to shift towards backing one at its 2018 annual conference, many observers saw it more as a ploy and a promise it was hoping never to have to keep than a genuine conversion to the cause.[20]

Before then, however, as the second row of Table 7.1 shows, Labour's membership overwhelmingly considered themselves to be respected by the leadership; indeed, there is a notable jump (from 70 per cent to over 90 per cent) between 2015 and 2017. The Greens, Liberal Democrats and SNP feel similarly positive about their leaders' attitudes; once again, though, there are clear drops in the percentage of UKIP and Tory members who feel this way about their leaders. In the former case this change is, admittedly, from a very high baseline in 2015 (93 per cent) and still amounts to a four-fifths satisfaction rate with their leadership's attitude. For the Conservatives, however, there is greater cause for concern. By 2017, only two-thirds of members feel respected by the leadership; true, this remains a clear majority, but it is a notably lower proportion than in any other party, and a clear drop from the 81.5 per cent who felt so positively just two years earlier. In view of the parallel growth in the number of Tory members wanting a greater say over policy, this seems to indicate a pattern of greater dissatisfaction with the leadership in the Conservative Party than in any other.

As we have seen, parties such as Labour have introduced a registered supporters scheme in recent years. Perhaps ironically, given the fact that its introduction in that party has coincided with, and may even have facilitated, the rise to power of the left) the idea that it would (both by making it cheaper and appearing to involve a lower level of commitment) help parties attract more 'normal people' into politics (thereby offsetting the influence of zealots supposedly determined to make things awkward for more pragmatic leaders) has been around for some time.[21] We were therefore curious to know how full members felt about this. On the face of it, the granting of rights (such as the ability to vote in leadership elections) to such supporters might be taken as something of an affront to existing members who pay a higher subscription, although the very limited research which has been undertaken to date does not necessarily point to any clear pattern in this respect.[22] We therefore asked our respondents if, irrespective of whether their party ran one, they approved of such schemes or not. Table 7.1 reports the percentages saying approve or strongly approve. In every case, more members approve than disapprove, although only in two instances (the Conservatives in 2015 and the Greens in 2017) does this amount to an absolute majority. In most cases, about 40 to 50 per cent approve of registered members schemes, although the figure for SNP members is nearer to a third. We might sum up by saying that there is tentative but limited approval for the idea of a registered supporters' scheme – and by implication, for officially promoted 'multi-speed membership' models of party organization.[23]

Picking the right people (and kicking out the wrong ones)

We also asked our respondents about attitudes towards candidate selection. This, as we have noted, has traditionally been one of the most prominent functions of party members in British political parties. In our surveys we presented four different models of membership involvement in the process of selecting candidates for Parliament, and asked which they preferred: *open postal primary*, where anyone in the constituency, whether or not they are a party member, can vote by post to help select the candidate; *open primary*, where anyone in the constituency, whether or not they are a party member, can turn up to a meeting held to select the candidate and cast a vote; *closed postal ballot*, where members of the local constituency party can vote by post to help select the candidate; or *closed ballot*, where members of the local constituency party can vote at a meeting held to select the candidate. The primary models are, of course, only rarely used by Britain's political parties, so the closed ballots restricted to party memberships are the normal methods deployed. The results of Table 7.2 suggest that a membership-only ballot remains the favoured option of members in the country – especially if it only requires the posting of a letter rather than turning up to a meeting. To this extent, the parties are generally doing the right thing by their grassroots memberships – excepting those occasions when the central party organizations impose their own candidates, something which does happen on occasion, as for example at the 'snap' 2017 general election. It should also be said that support for primaries is by no means negligible, typically standing at 20 to 30 per cent, although there seems to have been a distinct fall in support for primaries among Tory members in 2017.

While addressing the issue of parliamentary candidates, we also asked our samples about the types of candidates they favoured (Table 7.3). To the extent that they indicate a clear preference for more candidates of certain types than currently exist, we might infer a level of dissatisfaction with the outcome of current selection procedures. The table suggests a quite pronounced demand for several types of candidates – most obviously for more candidates from 'the areas that they represent'. This is true of all parties, most obviously the Greens and Labour (in 2017). Interestingly, Tory members are slightly (albeit only slightly) less keen on local candidates than are members of other parties, perhaps because they continue to believe very strongly in picking candidates 'on merit' – something which, suggested one Conservative well versed in observing selection contests all over the country, was because, although local roots were certainly an advantage, '[t]he Tory Party is essentially a group of managerial people and their wives' who, ultimately, will vote for whoever they think will be 'the best potential MP'.[24] That said, the idea that where a candidate comes from is important was used as a counter to attempts under David Cameron to lever more women onto shortlists and into the final round of voting.

There would also seem to be a clear demand among members as a whole for more female MPs: again, this is true of all parties, although there is almost certainly a degree of variation by ideological outlook here. Clearly members of the four left-of-centre parties have absorbed the message that the situation needs changing, with the Greens (whose only representative in the House of Commons is a woman) not unexpectedly in the vanguard. Equally predictably, members of UKIP, which tends to reject anything that smacks of 'political correctness', think very differently. Possibly more interesting is the response of Tory members. As we know from previous research, the leadership still has some way to go to persuade the grassroots that things have to change on this front, but it does appear to have made some progress over the years: although they are clearly not as keen on the idea as their counterparts on the left of the political spectrum, about half of Tory members would like to see more women MPs.[25] The obvious enthusiasm of Liberal Democrat members is worth noting since the Party has a very poor record of getting women into

TABLE 7.3 Members' attitudes regarding types of MPs they would prefer, 2015 and 2017

Statement	Conservative		Labour		Liberal Democrat		UKIP		Green		SNP		All parties	
	2015	2017	2015	2017	2015	2017	2015	2017	2015	2017	2015	2017	2015	2017
From area they represent	69.6	71.5	80.8	86.2	78.1	85.0	87.2	84.4	90.0	87.9	84.5	84.4	81.0 $V = 0.121$	82.8 $V = 0.107$
Working class	35.6	33.5	87.2	87.5	65.7	71.9	62.2	48.8	92.7	90.6	83.3	79.7	70.4 $V = 0.241$	69.0 $V = 0.231$
Women	51.9	43.7	85.4	85.3	86.7	85.1	39.8	29.2	93.3	90.2	84.2	76.8	73.3 $V = 0.237$	72.2 $V = 0.230$
Disabled	38.3	41.2	83.0	87.0	50.4	79.6	37.5	28.3	90.4	91.5	78.7	74.9	67.4 $V = 0.237$	70.1 $V = 0.231$
Young people	28.7	30.1	62.8	84.4	58.7	75.3	31.5	18.1	79.6	86.1	76.9	78.3	55.7 $V = 0.206$	65.8 $V = 0.262$
Ethnic minority	36.8	32.2	75.4	87.0	77.9	82.4	20.2	10.5	88.5	85.9	74.2	76.6	61.8 $V = 0.253$	67.8 $V = 0.286$
Christians	23.9	21.9	11.2	7.3	12.9	8.8	31.9	33.0	5.0	6.4	14.3	14.7	16.6 $V = 0.165$	13.8 $V = 0.162$
LGBT	19.4	22.1	58.7	76.6	54.5	62.9	14.6	14.2	76.9	79.1	55.8	56.2	46.1 $V = 0.235$	53.9 $V = 0.249$
Muslims	18.7	17.9	44.7	72.5	45.4	56.5	7.9	5.2	54.8	65.1	44.1	49.6	35.6 $V = 0.197$	45.8 $V = 0.237$
Graduates	20.8	18.9	10.5	18.9	13.3	21.2	16.6	12.4	11.3	15.0	10.6	17.3	14.0 $V = 0.093$	18.0 $V = 0.097$

Note: Figures represent percentage of respondents saying that they would like to see a lot more or slightly more MPs from these backgrounds than are currently at Westminster. V = Cramer's V measure of association between party and attitude. All relationships significant at $p < .001$.

winnable seats – so much so that at the 2015 election, at which it performed particularly disastrously, it failed to return a single female MP to the Commons.

Sex is one thing; sexuality and gender, another. Although the House of Commons can boast one of the biggest proportions of openly gay MPs of any legislature in the world, some would argue that it has some way to go before it becomes fully representative in this respect – and there are no transgender MPs at Westminster. Green members would obviously like to see this change – as would the majority of members of the parties to the left of centre. Once again, however, members of the right-of-centre parties don't feel this is particularly important, and indeed, in UKIP's case there are more members who would like to see fewer LGBT people in Parliament than would like to see more, although the plurality would be happy with things staying as they are. The latter is also true of Tory members, although in their case there are slightly more who would like to see more LGBT MPs than there are who would like to see fewer.

On the question of ethnic minority representation, we see, once again (and as we do when it comes to MPs with disabilities), the by-now familiar pattern. Green members, living up to their image as socially liberal, are, as expected, most enthusiastic about the idea of having more MPs from minority backgrounds, with members of the other left-of-centre parties not so very far behind. Conservative members, once again, are much less keen, although their lack of enthusiasm is not as marked as their counterparts in UKIP. Not for the first time, if one drills down below the headline figures in Table 7.3, the number of UKIP members saying they would like to see more of a particular section of society represented in parliament (at 10 per cent in the case of ethnic minorities in 2017) is lower than the number (32 per cent) saying they would like to see fewer MPs coming from that background. That said, it is vitally important to note that about half of all UKIP, as well as Conservative, members would be content to see things pretty much as they are in this respect.

UKIP members' decidedly lukewarm response to the idea that the UK should have more ethnic minority MPs is more than matched by their response to the idea that there should be more Muslim MPs – indeed, the number of UKIP members who feel there should be more (at just 8 per cent in 2015 and 5 per cent in 2017) is dwarfed by the number (45 per cent and 56 per cent, respectively) who say there should be fewer – an indication perhaps that by no means all UKIP members would object to calls by some of their number to appeal more explicitly to Islamophobia. That said, it is worth noting that members of other parties aren't as keen on there being more Muslims as they are on there being more MPs from other minorities – and even the majority of Green members who think there should be is, at 55 per cent in 2015 and 65 per cent in 2017, relatively low.

Perhaps unfortunately, given how high-profile the issue has become for Labour, we didn't ask about Jewish MPs. But we did ask members whether they would like to see more Christian MPs. Interestingly, this is the one minority where the number of members of the left-of-centre parties, especially the (presumably anti-establishment, highly secular) Greens, saying they would like to see more of them in Parliament was exceeded by the number saying they would like to see fewer of them (although it should be said that the most frequent answer was 'about the same'). Indeed, the normal pattern is reversed when it comes to Christian candidates: this time Tory and UKIP members are notably more likely to want to see more Christians in Parliament, perhaps because, as the country's established religion, Christianity serves as a marker of tradition and identity for them.

Asking whether party members would like to see more or fewer MPs with university degrees is the only time we see the number who reply 'fewer' outstripping the number who say 'more', although we should stress that the most common response by far to this question is 'about the same'. Nevertheless, the differences between members of the six parties are interesting if fairly predictable. UKIP members are far less likely to have a degree than their counterparts in other parties, so it may not be too surprising that they aren't particularly keen on a House of Commons packed full of graduates. Labour (and Green) members, however, are well educated, suggesting that their lack of enthusiasm stems more from their egalitarian ideology than from their demography. And Conservative Party members (very probably as a function of their age) aren't as well educated as members of most of the other parties, but they don't seem to have too much of a problem with graduates on the green benches – perhaps because many of their children (and grandchildren) will have gone to university even if they themselves didn't.

If anyone imagined, however, that Conservative Party members might at least pay lip service to the idea that more working-class people should be elected to Westminster, where they are now far less in evidence than used to be the case when many Labour MPs had backgrounds in manual labour, they would be wrong. Tories may or may not regard such people as the salt of the earth but they're clearly not the sort of people they actually want in charge. This stands in marked contrast, once again, with attitudes among the members of the left-leaning parties. While Green and Labour members are generally pretty middle class and very well educated, they are keenest to see more working class people in Parliament – a measure of their values-based commitment to equality or their kneejerk 'political correctness', depending on one's point of view.[26] Interestingly, members of UKIP, fall some way between the Tories and the left-of-centre parties in this regard: in spite of its reputation for representing the 'left-behind' and challenging 'the elite', they do not seem as bothered about working class representation as one might expect.

Time and space prevented us asking members of all parties about deselection rather than selection, but it was something we addressed in our 2016 survey of members of the Labour Party who joined it in the wake of the general election held the previous year, many of them to support Jeremy Corbyn. 'Only' a third (32 per cent) of them perhaps aware of the past voting record of Mr Corbyn and Mr McDonnell, said that 'Labour MPs who continually vote against the party's agreed line in Commons votes should be deselected'. But another 29 per cent neither agreed nor disagreed with that statement, which presumably means they might be persuaded to back action. However, Labour's new members seemed much, much keener to discipline MPs who lay into Corbyn himself. A clear majority (55 per cent) believed that 'Labour MPs who persistently and publicly criticise the leadership in the media should be deselected' – a proportion that rose to two-thirds (68 per cent) of those who joined after Corbyn was elected. There also appeared at least among Labour's post–general election 2015 membership, to be majority support (59 per cent vs 25 per cent) for the introduction of mandatory reselection of all Labour MPs.

Interestingly, when two years later, in December 2018, we surveyed both Labour and Conservative members on Brexit and asked what they thought about local parties deselecting MPs who rebelled on the issue, some 60 per cent of Labour members were opposed to the idea, with only 25 per cent agreeing. There was, however, considerably more support for the idea among their Conservative counterparts: although 50 per cent were opposed, that left 41 per cent (and 43 per cent of the majority who voted leave) in agreement. This was a precursor perhaps of some of the motions of no confidence in their 'remainer' MPs then passed by local associations, including one in the Beaconsfield constituency of former Attorney General and campaigner for a second referendum, Dominic Grieve: his association voted no confidence in him in late March 2019 after a campaign led by one of its members who, at the 2017 general election, had stood against him as UKIP's candidate. Some saw this as evidence of the influence of what one former Tory MP, Anna Soubry, famously called 'Purple Momentum' – UKIP entryists in the Conservative Party.[27] However, it is just as likely to have been a reflection of the hardening of attitudes among existing members between the summer of 2015 (when 65 per cent of them were prepared to see what David Cameron could negotiate with Brussels before making up their mind how to vote in the referendum) and Christmas 2018 when Tory members (some 77 per cent of whom said they voted for Brexit) told us that they would prefer a 'No-Deal Brexit' to Theresa May's proposed withdrawal agreement by a margin of 64 to 29 per cent.

Party meetings

Another way of gauging members' satisfaction with the way their party is organized is to tap into their experience of party meetings. We therefore asked our respondents if they had attended any local party meetings in the past 12 months and, if so, what their impressions of them were. Specifically, we asked if they found them interesting or boring on a scale of 1 to 5 (with 4 and 5 rated as interesting), easy or difficult to understand (with 4 and 5 as easy) and friendly or unfriendly (with 4 and 5 as friendly). Table 7.4 reports the proportion of responses falling into these 'interesting', 'easy to understand' and 'friendly' categories. The overall averages across these three items are positive, in that they all fall above 50 per cent for both 2015 and 2017, but, of course, there is some variation by party and by category.

Keeping meetings interesting would seem to be the biggest challenge facing parties: overall, only 56 per cent of members give them a score of 4 or 5 on this scale in 2015, although 67 per cent of them do so in 2017. Labour, Liberal Democrat and Green Party members seem least inspired by party meetings in 2015 (each group returning averages below 50 per cent), but they all evidence notable upturns

TABLE 7.4 Members' attitudes regarding local party meetings, 2015 and 2017

Statement	Conservative		Labour		Liberal Democratic		UKIP		Green		SNP		All parties	
	2015	2017	2015	2017	2015	2017	2015	2017	2015	2017	2015	2017	2015	2017
Interesting	56.2	65.5	47.5	63.0	45.1	68.6	68.3	75.2	48.3	67.6	70.1	77.1	55.9	67.3
													$V = 0.140$	$V = 0.092$
Easy to understand	71.4	79.9	64.3	76.1	65.5	82.8	77.0	87.4	53.7	76.8	77.3	87.1	68.3	81.7
													$V = 0.104$	$V = 0.086$
Friendly	68.6	73.5	60.6	71.9	65.4	84.3	76.2	86.7	58.2	81.4	79.4	87.3	67.8	80.4
													$V = 0.128$	$V = 0.126$

Note: Figures represent percentage of respondents scoring 4 or 5 on scales where 1 'boring/hard to understand/unfriendly' and 5 = 'interesting/easy to understand/friendly'. V = Cramer's V measure of association between party and attitude; All relationships significant at $p < .001$.

in 2017; by then, around two-thirds of their party members claim that they found meetings interesting. UKIP and SNP members are most inclined to have found meetings interesting, with some three-quarters falling into this category.

On the whole, members were highly likely to claim that they found their party meetings friendly and easy to understand. True, only 54 per cent of Green members find party meetings easy to understand in 2015, but this figure jumps to 77 per cent two years later. Likewise, only 61 per cent of Labour members find their meetings friendly in 2015, but this figure increases to 72 per cent in 2017 – something that might surprise some observers in view of the fairly public infighting that had occurred in some local parties after the election of Jeremy Corbyn. Certainly, we were told by a number of interviewees that the atmosphere at some branch and CLP meetings had become 'poisonous'. For instance, one Labour staffer, who is also heavily involved at the local level, put this down to the fact that 'meeting activists' (as opposed to 'campaign activists'), many of whom, in his experience, were recently retired, well-educated, relatively affluent public-sector professionals who had re-joined after leaving in the 1990s, were now using a combination of invective and their intimate knowledge of the party's proce-dures to wrest control from those who had stuck by it (and often represented it as councillors) through thick and thin.[28] That said, our data show only a slight tendency for Corbyn supporters to be more likely to find party meetings friendly: 75 per cent of those who voted for him in the 2015 leadership election and 73 per cent of those who voted for him in 2016 found the meetings friendly, while the respective figures for those who supported his opponents were 68 per cent in 2015 and 67 per cent in 2016.

Overall, these relatively positive figures are consistent with the argument that we make elsewhere in this book about the importance of the activism of members being embedded within local social networks. For those who engage with their local parties, it seems that there is a good chance they will find the experience posi-tive and so join in campaigning at election time.[29] The challenge for parties is to get members to engage in this way. In 2015, almost all our respondents claimed to have attended a party meeting in the past year, but in 2017, only 67 per cent did. By 2017, of course, several parties had enjoyed notable boosts to their membership, so one possibility is that significant numbers of these new members might have declined to engage actively at the local level. Alternatively, there may have been a generalized loss of interest in attending meetings across all parties – something which, in fact, the figures seem to suggest: by party, the numbers claiming to have attended at least one local meeting in the 12 months prior to June 2017 are 79 per cent for UKIP, 75 per cent (SNP), 69 per cent (Labour), 65 per cent (Conserva-tive), 62 per cent (Liberal Democrat) and 60 per cent (Green). It is worth noting, however, that if we compare these responses to the ones given by party members to researchers in the 1990s – namely, Labour (64 per cent in 1990, 46 per cent in 1997 and 39 per cent in 1999), Conservative (34 per cent in 1992), Liberal Democrat (47 per cent in 1999) – then there doesn't appear to have been any overall decline; indeed, quite the opposite.[30]

Expectations – met or dashed?

Finally, we asked our survey respondents a very general question about whether or not they felt that the experience of being party members had lived up to their expectations. Of course, one has to be careful about exactly what to infer from the answers, given that they depend on what people expected of party membership in the first place – something we're not in a position to know. Nevertheless, it provides an interesting insight into overall satisfaction. In the last row of Table 7.1 we report the percentages who feel that the experience has fully lived up to expectations, and they are arguably quite worrying for the parties. On average fewer than half of all party members are willing to say that it had, whether we're looking at 2015 or 2017. Indeed, for every party bar Labour, there was a fall in the percentage stating that membership had fully lived up to expectations. The most positive case is the SNP, where the drop was from a very high baseline (76 per cent) to a respectable 60 per cent. For Labour the figure is not as high (48 per cent), but it represents a move upward from 2015 (when it was 32 per cent), presumably reflecting the enthusiasm of the new Corbynista recruits. The figures are less positive for the other parties. By 2017, two-fifths of Green members, one-third of Liberal Democrats and barely a quarter of UKIP and Tory members say that the experience of party membership has fully lived up to expectations.

Conclusion

While there is a good deal of positivity around, then, Britain's party members are far from wholly satisfied with their experience. Overall, only two-fifths feel that membership has fully lived up to expectations, while a third want more influence over the policy-making process. In part, this might stem from the unrealistic expectations of some members as to how politics works, and the sheer impossibility of leaders managing to satisfy 'all of the people all of the time'. But it might also reflect genuine dissatisfaction with at least some aspects of internal party procedures. A majority approve the closed ballots that parties typically use to pick their parliamentary candidates, although as many as a fifth of grassroots members would like to see the use of open primaries. This might in part stem from a widespread wish to see some changes made to the kinds of people who represent their parties in Parliament – or at least, from the clear demand for more candidates from a greater variety of social backgrounds. The general preference for maintaining the special position of full members in candidate selection is also reflected in the fact only two-fifths are keen on the idea of registered supporters' schemes. Most of those who attend party meetings find them positive experiences, but one third admit to not engaging in this way – and stimulating a greater willingness to take part is surely one of the key challenges that parties face, and perhaps have always faced. But it is to another perennial challenge that we now direct our attention, namely, the fact that many people who decide to join parties sooner or later decide to leave them.

Notes

1 Liberal Democrat staffer, interview 25 February 2015.
2 For an explanation of STV, see Farrell, David (2011) *Electoral Systems: A Comparative Introduction* (Basingstoke: Palgrave Macmillan), Chapter 6.
3 Green politician, interview 4 June 2016.
4 See Farrell, David (2011) *Electoral Systems: A Comparative Introduction* (Basingstoke: Palgrave Macmillan), Chapter 3.
5 See Edwards, Peter (2017) 'Is there a hard-left "purge of moderates" going on in the Labour Party?', *LabourList*, 28 November, available online at https://labourlist.org/2017/11/is-there-a-hard-left-purge-of-moderates-going-on-in-labour/.
6 Labour Party (2018) *Labour Party Rule Book* (London: Labour Party), Appendix 1, available online at http://labour.org.uk/wp-content/uploads/2018/04/2018-RULE-BOOK.pdf.
7 Strafford, John (2019) 'The Conservative Party no longer belongs to its members. No wonder it faces an existential crisis', *ConservativeHome*, 3 February, available online at www.conservativehome.com/platform/2019/02/john-strafford-the-conservative-party-faces-an-unprecedented-existential-threat.html. Mr Strafford runs the Campaign for Conservative Party Democracy (Copov): see www.conservativepartydemocracy.com/ and http://copov.blogspot.com/.
8 See Bale, Tim (2016) *The Conservative Party From Thatcher to Cameron*, 2nd Edition (Cambridge: Polity Press). See also Bale, Tim (2018) 'Who leads and who follows? The symbiotic relationship between UKIP and the Conservatives – And populism and Euroscepticism', *Politics*, 38 (3), pp. 263–277. See also Conservative activist, interview 13 September 2015.
9 See Wallace, Mark (2017) 'EXCLUSIVE: Draft new Conservative Party Constitution revealed – Including further candidate selection centralisation', *ConservativeHome*, 29 November, available online at www.conservativehome.com/thetorydiary/2017/11/exclusive-draft-new-conservative-party-constitution-revealed.html.
10 von dem Berge, Benjamin and Poguntke, Thomas (2017) 'Varieties of intra-party democracy: Conceptualization and index construction', in S. Scarrow, P. Webb and T. Poguntke (eds.) *Organizing Political Parties: Representation, Participation and Power* (Oxford: Oxford University Press), pp. 136–157.
11 von dem Berge, Benjamin and Poguntke, Thomas (2017) 'Varieties of intra-party democracy: Conceptualization and index construction', in S. Scarrow, P. Webb and T. Poguntke (eds.) *Organizing Political Parties: Representation, Participation and Power* (Oxford: Oxford University Press), p. 144.
12 von dem Berge, Benjamin and Poguntke, Thomas (2017) 'Varieties of intra-party democracy: Conceptualization and index construction', in S. Scarrow, P. Webb and T. Poguntke (eds.) *Organizing Political Parties: Representation, Participation and Power* (Oxford: Oxford University Press), p. 144.
13 Bolin, Niklas, Aylott, Nicholas, von dem Berge, Benjamin and Poguntke, Thomas (2017) 'Patterns of intra-party democracy across the world', in S. Scarrow, P. Webb and T. Poguntke (eds.) *Organizing Political Parties: Representation, Participation and Power* (Oxford: Oxford University Press), pp. 177–180.
14 Conservative MP, interview 18 April, 2016.
15 Conservative activist, interview 13 November 2015.
16 'Our members consistently say that internal democracy is something that they value. [The leader's] vote is as equal to the vote of somebody who joined the party an hour ago.' Liberal Democrat staffer, interview 1 February 2017. According to another staffer, internal research on what was important to members suggested that 'the Number One thing that came out was the ability to decide policy' – something that does have its downsides: 'One of the constant challenges for Lib Dem leaders is 'How do I get the members not to land me with some policy that I hate?' Liberal Democrat staffer, interview 9 February 2016.
17 All figures taken from Party Members Project survey of the Brexit-related attitudes of Conservative Party members in December 2018, available online at https://d25d2506sfb94s.

cloudfront.net/cumulus_uploads/document/veyvny2qzz/QMULResults_181222_Con-Members_Brexit_w1.pdf.

18 Webb, Paul and Bale, Tim (2017) 'No place else to go: The Labour Party and the trade unions in the UK', in Allern, Elin H. and Bale, Tim (eds.) *Left-of-Centre Parties and Trade Unions in the Twenty-First Century* (Oxford: Oxford University Press).

19 All figures taken from Party Members Project survey of the Brexit-related attitudes of Labour Party members in December 2018, available online at https://d25d2506sfb94s.cloudfront.net/cumulus_uploads/document/btqj6dwsvl/QMUL Results_181221_LabourMembers_Brexit_w1.pdf.

20 See, for example, MacShane, Dennis (2019) 'Jeremy Corbyn's referendum pledge is a fragile fix for a splintering Labour Party', *The Independent*, 26 February, available online at www.independent.co.uk/voices/corbyn-labour-second-brexit-referendum-final-say-tig-europe-a8797356.html.

21 Getting more 'normal people' involved not only was one of the intentions behind Tony Blair's recruitment drive in the 1990s but was also very much in the minds of those who, during Ed Miliband's leadership, helped to set up the registered supporters scheme that eventually helped elect Labour's most left-wing leader since the mid-1930s. 'The registered supporters were always seen as the antidote to the left. . . . The whole idea was that you would get nice ordinary people who want to turn up once a year to a barbeque and be on the MP's Christmas card list' as opposed to the 'polytechnic, bearded people – the likes of Jeremy Corbyn – sitting in their bedsits and going to CLPs in Lambeth and Islington'. Labour staffer, interview 9 August 2017.

22 Garland, Jessica (2016) 'A wider range of friends: Multi-speed organising during the 2015 Labour leadership contest', *Political Quarterly*, 87 (1), pp. 23–30. See also Garland, Jessica (2018) 'Loosening the bonds? The causes and consequences of multi-speed membership in the British Labour Party 2011–2018', Unpublished PhD thesis, University of Sussex. Back in 2006 YouGov conducted a small-scale survey of party members on the issue and found that, while a quarter of members thought 'supporters' should be able to participate in policy making, only one in ten thought they should have a share in deciding policy; one in ten said they should play a role in choosing candidates, and the same proportion was in favour of allowing supporters to vote in leadership elections; just over half, however, objected to giving them any of these rights – a feeling shared even more strongly (and perhaps ironically in light of what came to pass in 2015) by members on the left of the party. See Gauja, Anika (2017) *Party Reform: The Causes, Challenges, and Consequences of Organizational Change* (Oxford: Oxford University Press), pp. 174–175.

23 Scarrow, Susan E. (2015) *Beyond Party Members: Changing Approaches to Partisan Mobilization* (Oxford: Oxford University Press).

24 Conservative Peer, interview 15 August 2016.

25 Childs, Sarah and Webb, Paul (2012) *Sex, Gender and the Conservative Party: From Iron Lady to Kitten Heels* (Houndsmills: Palgrave Macmillan).

26 Labour's NEC has agreed £150,000 for bursaries to support disabled candidates or candidates from working-class or low-income backgrounds. Trade unions affiliated with the party also make great play of wanting to get more people from ordinary backgrounds into parliament. However, recent research strongly suggests they are, in fact, rather more interested in supporting the candidature of aspiring politicians because they share their ideological perspective rather than because they are working class. See Hill, Eleanor (2018) 'It's not what you know, it's who you know: What are the implications of social networks in UK politics for electoral choice?', Unpublished PhD thesis, University of Manchester.

27 See Gilligan, Andrew and Wheeler, Caroline (2019) 'Caught between deselection and infiltration – Not Labour, this is the new Tory party', *Sunday Times*, 24 February. See also Wallace, Mark (2019) 'Blukip! Purple momentum! But . . . the big problem with Tory entryism claims is that there's no evidence that they're true', *ConservativeHome*, 22 February, available online at www.conservativehome.com/thetorydiary/2019/02/

blukip-purple-momentum-but-the-big-problem-with-tory-entryism-claims-is-that-theres-no-evidence-theyre-true.html.

28 Labour staffer, interview 27 July 2017. We were also told, among other things, about Momentum members in CLPs caucusing prior to ward and constituency meetings and about Jewish members being made to feel unwelcome because of the insistence on the part of other members that accusations of antisemitism were primarily motivated by a desire to undermine Jeremy Corbyn. See Labour activist, interview 10 September 2018.

29 Interestingly, the generally positive experience most of the members we surveyed stands in marked contrast to what a study of young members in six countries revealed that 8 out of 10 of the 500 or so young members that were interviewed 'mentioned that in some branches of the party, the atmosphere is extremely unpleasant' and not just because they felt they weren't listened to by their elders but because of each other: the researchers observed 'many professional-minded young party members blaming lazy, utopian free riders at the very same time that they are themselves targeted by many moral- and social-minded young partisans for their apparent ambition, careerism, and hypocrisy'. See Bruter, Michael and Harrison, Sarah (2009) *The Future of Our Democracies: Young Party Members in Europe* (Basingstoke: Palgrave), pp. 152, 160.

30 Seyd, Patrick and Whiteley, Paul (1992) *Labour's Grass Roots* (Oxford: Clarendon), p. 226; Whiteley, Paul, Seyd, Patrick and Richardson, Jeremy (1994) *True Blues* (Oxford: Oxford University Press), p. 246; Whiteley, Paul, Seyd, Patrick and Billinghurst, Antony (2006) *Third Force Politics* (Oxford: Oxford University Press), p. 44.

8

QUITTING

Why members leave their parties

Research on party membership has focused almost exclusively on why party members *join* political parties rather than on why they *leave* them.[1] Yet people quit parties all the time. And it matters. Obviously, it has a big impact on the many parties in advanced liberal democracies which are losing rather than gaining members over time.[2] But it also makes a difference to those parties which are, for the moment at least, bucking the trend and attracting people to their colours. Just because their net membership is growing doesn't mean that no one is leaving – only that, for the moment at least, more people are joining than are departing. For instance, the surge in UK Labour Party membership since 2015 might have looked even more impressive had the party been able not only to bring in hundreds of thousands of new members but also managed to hang onto the tens of thousands who, according to media reports anyway, left it in the meantime.[3] And even in cases where a party's membership seems to be fairly stable, we know that there is an awful lot of turnover and churn below the surface.[4]

Fortunately, our study helps us look at this question in more depth than anyone else has been able to do before. In the early summer of 2015, we surveyed the members of six of the biggest parties in the UK – the Conservatives, Labour, the Liberal Democrats, the SNP, the Greens and UKIP. Some of them told us that they had previously left and then re-joined and were happy to tell us why – as were some of those who responded to an additional survey we ran in 2016 of people who'd joined the Labour Party since the 2015 election. Together, their explanations helped us to design a survey aimed at people who used to be, but were no longer, party members – a survey we went on to field in the summer of 2017. Some of those 'leavers' who took that survey were people who'd taken the original survey in 2015, which meant we could compare and contrast leavers with those who, like them, had filled out the original survey but who, unlike them, hadn't quit in the meantime.

We wanted to understand why those ex-members had left, both by finding out what they thought had motivated them and by looking back to our earlier surveys to see if there was anything about them that, in retrospect, might have allowed us to predict that they, and not others, would be the ones to leave. In so doing, we weren't flying completely blind since some previous studies have touched on the question, albeit in most cases not quite as directly as we were able to.

For one thing, the apparent long-term decline of membership in Europe's political parties, while by no means as universal and linear as some imagine is, as we noted in Chapter 2 and Chapter 5, both well documented and in many ways persuasively explained. As a result, political scientists think they have a pretty good idea as to why, overall, fewer people in the twenty-first century are keen to invest their time and money in belonging to a political party than was the case in the mid-twentieth century. Whether we are talking about people who did belong to parties but no longer do so or about people who never bother joining in the first place, representative politics no longer offers them what it once did; meanwhile, whatever that was can now be found in a whole host of alternative activities and organizations, some of which simply weren't around during the so-called golden age of membership.

Nevertheless, it remains the case that previous studies are for the most part talking about aggregates and broad structural and cultural changes rather than the myriad micro-decisions taken by individuals. As the editors of a fascinating comparative collection on party members (which is aware that 'divorce' is part of what they call 'the dynamics of membership involvement' even if none of the contributions is actually able to deal with the issue) put it, 'looking at party membership decline alone does not say anything about who is staying and who is leaving'.[5]

To begin to do that, we can turn to a few pieces of existing research, a couple of them conducted in countries other than the UK. Probably the most sophisticated is a study from Austria which uses that country's election study (and the fact that party membership remains relatively high in that country because it can still be the passport to a state-funded job) to tease out differences between current and former members.[6] It found that, when asked to pick from a range of options presented to them, the most frequent explanations given by ex-members for leaving were 'Ideological differences between me and the party' (27 per cent) and 'Membership no longer [materially/instrumentally] useful to me' (22 per cent), followed by 'Too little time for the party' (16 per cent) and 'Too little influence on the party line' (13 per cent), with 'I am engaged in other voluntary work' (9 per cent), 'Parties cannot change anything in society' (8 per cent) and 'Membership too expensive' (7 per cent) bringing up the rear.

Interestingly, former and current members of Austria's parties did not seem to differ socially or demographically. However, the study did find that '[p]eople who have left a political party have lower levels of political interest, are less likely to think that politicians care about what people like them think and are less worried about failing to turn out to vote' – although whether they became like that while they were members or were already like that when they joined, we cannot, of course, tell. Meanwhile, in spite of 'getting involved in alternative forms of participation' being cited as a reason for leaving by one in ten of those who left, it did not actually appear to make party members more likely to leave their party. Nor, interestingly, did material/instrumental benefits. Ideology, however, appeared to matter as much as respondents themselves thought it did: the research found that the more strongly members feel about it, the less likely they are to leave, unless they perceive a mismatch exists (or has developed) between themselves and their party – something echoed incidentally in a study of Swedish party members which shows that those who are more out of step with their parties are more likely to consider joining another one.[7]

Political disagreement with one's party also comes across as important in a bigger study from Denmark, albeit one that could talk not about members who had left but only about existing members who'd thought about doing so – something that appears to be fairly common.[8] As in Austria, demographics hardly mattered. And nor, incidentally, did the desire to hold office. On the other hand, both dissatisfaction with intra-party democracy and falling out with one's party over policy/ ideology appeared to be just as important as motives for (possible) exit in Denmark as they were for (actual) exit in Austria. Conversely, being an active rather than passive member seemed to discourage people from thinking about leaving, as did (interestingly) the extent to which members felt an emotional attachment to their party and whether they evaluated party activities as interesting and as a chance to mix with the kind of people they liked.

In addition to these two, relatively recent studies from overseas, we can turn to the work of two pioneers in the field of party membership in the UK. In the follow-up to their seminal books on Britain's three biggest parties, Whiteley and Seyd were primarily concerned with explaining declining activism among those who stuck with their party – in this case, Labour – for which they were able to construct a panel study over the 1997–1999 period.[9] But they were also curious as to whether their General Incentives Model could also provide an explanation for why some members left it altogether. They found, broadly speaking, that it could. Although social class appeared to have some effect on exiting (with working-class members marginally more likely to leave than middle-class members), the effect was not strong – and certainly not as strong as disappointment with the party's performance in government, which they also found to be significant (unlike, rather interestingly, dissatisfaction with its leaders). Getting involved appeared to be important as well, with *in*active members more likely to leave than their active counterparts. Ideology seemed to matter: 'with [Labour's] left-wingers being more likely to exit the party than [its] right-wingers', who, it should be said, were at that time clearly in control. But so, too, did (other) selective incentives (the weakening of which was associated with a greater likelihood of exit) and expressive incentives (measured by strength of partisanship) with 'strongly attached members . . . much less likely to leave', even when other factors might have pushed them into doing so.

Whiteley followed up this work with some research that in some ways prefigured our own by comparing the demographic details of 1,230 respondents from a larger British Election Study survey who were currently members of political parties with

2,288 respondents who used to be. There were some differences, which Whiteley, rather than attempting to link with reasons for leaving, preferred to associate with changes over time in each party: the comparison suggested, for instance, that Labour's membership was 'becoming more professional . . . , more affluent and more male', that Conservatives were slightly more likely to be retired than they used to be, and that Liberal Democrats were more likely to be graduates and younger than before. But the main finding was that, overall, 'the profile of ex-members is rather similar to the profile of [current] members', suggesting, once again that, when it comes to leaving, anyway, demography isn't destiny. What mattered more, the data suggested, was politics: by looking at when people had left their parties, it was obvious that many former Labour members had quit after 1997 and especially after 2001, very possibly in the wake of the Iraq War; on the other hand, it seemed that it wasn't just being in government that cost parties members – departures from the Tory Party peaked in 2006, which may well have been a reflection of grassroots opposition to David Cameron's supposedly 'liberal Conservative' modernization project.[10]

Why did you leave? A first cut

We turn first to the write-in explanations collected in our 2015 (all six parties) and 2016 (Labour new joiners) surveys, from respondents who told us that, rather than being continuous members of their parties, they had left them and since re-joined. All in all, those 'left-and-re-joined' party members constituted some 17 per cent of our 2015 sample, although the proportions differed significantly according to party, from 28 per cent of Labour members to 23 per cent of Tory members, 19 per cent of Liberal Democrat members, 11 per cent of SNP members, 8 per cent of UKIP members and 7 per cent of Greens. Although some of the self-reported reasons for leaving given by these 'left-and-re-joined' members in 2015 and 2016 were impossible to convincingly classify because they were simply too idiosyncratic, it was nevertheless possible to group them, and therefore reduce most of them to a range of options capable of capturing the majority of responses.

Interestingly, those original write-in responses did throw up some variation (possibly predictable, possibly not) between members of different parties, although the big differences in the number of respondents from each party mean they are presented merely as a matter of interest rather than because they can be relied upon. Table 8.1, which presents the results of a hand-coding exercise carried out on those write-in responses, illustrates some of them. For instance, UKIP and (albeit to a lesser extent) Tory members seemed rather more inclined simply to have forgotten to renew – which may say something either about their motivation and their memories or about the relative inefficiency/ineffectiveness of their parties' reminder systems. Green Party members, on the other hand, were much more likely than members of other parties to say that they'd let their membership lapse due to a lack of funds – which may or not be related to variations in income and wealth.

However, the stand-out difference from the 2015 survey (and the additional survey of Labour 'new members' in 2016) was between those who had left Labour and

TABLE 8.1 Coded write-in reasons for leaving given by 2015/16 members who had left and re-joined their party

	Conservative	Labour 2015	Labour 2016	Liberal Democrat	SNP	Green	UKIP	All parties
I was just too busy	13	7	1	13	13	11	11	8
I just forgot to renew (or just didn't get round to renewing) my membership	17	5	3	14	10	14	21	10
There was a problem with the direct debit/ standing order I used to pay my subscription	0	0	0	2	0	4	0	0
I needed to save money	6	10	2	6	10	30	9	8
I started a job which required me to be politically neutral	3	1	2	2	6	0	4	2
I developed health problems	0	0	0	1	3	2	0	1
I moved house	9	5	2	7	13	4	4	7
I was particularly disappointed and/or disillusioned with the leader of the party	6	13	21	6	1	2	7	10
I disagreed with the general direction the party seemed to be taking	8	13	28	16	7	7	7	14
I disagreed with a specific policy the party had adopted	5	24	26	10	2	2	4	14
I fell out with people in my local association/ branch	2	0	0	2	2	0	2	1
I just went off politics altogether	2	3	3	2	4	2	2	3
I didn't really feel I was contributing anything by belonging to a party	0	1	2	0	2	0	0	1
I disliked the conflict and factionalism I found in the party	1	2	0	1	1	2	4	1
Abroad	13	4	0	5	10	4	0	6
None of the above	15	12	8	15	19	18	28	14

Note: All figures are percentages.

those who had left other parties. If we add up the percentage of members whose responses suggest they had a broadly ideological or principled reason for leaving their party (in other words, putting together disagreement with its leader, its general direction and specific policies that it adopted), then it explains the (temporary) departures of just less than a fifth of Tory and UKIP members and about a tenth of Liberal Democrat, SNP and Green members. But about half of those 28 per cent of Labour members who said they had at one time or another left the party when we surveyed them in 2015 had walked out over ideology or principle – a proportion that rises to an amazing three-quarters of those Labour 'left-and-re-joined' members who took up membership of the party after the 2015 general election and were surveyed by us the following year. This suggests that the stereotype of Labour members as people who take their politics rather more seriously (or, at least, ideologically) than some of their counterparts in other parties may contain at least a grain of truth. It may also provide further support for the idea that many (although not, of course, all) of those who flocked to join the party to support Jeremy Corbyn in 2015 and afterwards were people who saw it as an opportunity to rescue their party from 'Blair', 'neo-liberalism' and 'Iraq', all of which came up again and again (and again) in their responses.[11]

The 2017 leavers' survey

We used these write-in responses from the nearly one in five members in our 2015 surveys who had previously left their party and re-joined it (as well as the responses from Labour Party members we surveyed in 2016 who had done the same thing) to design a survey aimed at people who had left parties and, at the time of asking, had not re-joined them. This time we asked respondents to pick an answer from a fixed menu of choices, albeit with the opportunity to say 'Don't Know' and to expand on their answer.

While this 'leavers' survey' contains some 1,760 respondents, not all of them were surveyed by us in 2015 or 2016: some ex-party members will have joined the You-Gov panel since then, for instance. However, we will, first of all, compare all those party members who responded to our survey in 2015 (some 5,500 people) with those who also responded then but who left their party thereafter, numbering just under 600 people. In one or two cases, we are able to take this latter figure to just over 600 by adding in people who responded to our 2017 leavers' survey and who also took part in our 2016 survey of post-2015 general election Labour Party members. Even then, however, the number of twice-surveyed respondents this produces is still insufficiently large to allow us to meaningfully break our findings down by party; accordingly, we have not attempted to do so.

What we are effectively asking is whether we can 'retrodict' who would have left by looking to see if there is any obvious difference between the answers they gave in 2015 (or 2016 if they were 'new' Labour members) and those given by all party members at the same time. Note that there is no indication that those who left their parties between our two surveys in 2015 and 2017 were any more 'flakey' or 'flighty' than the average member: some 17 per cent of them told us in 2015 that they had previously left their party and re-joined – which was exactly the same proportion of the total sample who had done the same. In other words, we do not seem to be talking to or about 'inveterate leavers'.

First, we compare our 2015 (and, in this case, our 2016) respondents with our 2015–2017 leavers on the basis of demographics (Table 8.2). In line with previous research, there appears to be no great difference, suggesting that the 'resource model' referred to in studies of joining, in particular, and participation, in general (see Chapter 5), cannot tell us much about leaving. Put another way, like the handful of other scholars who have looked at this issue, we could not have predicted, by looking at their gender, age, class or education, who was going to leave rather than stay with their party.

As we have seen, previous research, building on the social-psychological model of participation suggests that what political scientists refer to as 'political efficacy' and 'civic duty' may be important, with those displaying lower levels of such qualities more likely to leave than those displaying higher levels. Table 8.3 hints that, at least when it comes to efficacy, that may very well be the case. This is especially clear in the responses to the statement that 'politicians don't care what people like me think'; leavers display a notably higher level of political disillusionment in this regard.

Next, we turn to those drivers which play a big part in the research on why people join political parties, not least those that feature in the influential General Incentives Model (see Chapter 5). If, as previous work on leaving has tended to assume, leaving is the mirror image of joining, then we should expect to see those who eventually leave their parties less driven by some or all of the supposed motives that lead people to enrol in the first place. Table 8.4 lists our leavers' responses to the questions designed by the pioneers of party membership studies to tap into those motives.

TABLE 8.2 Demographic comparison of 2015–17 leavers and all party members

	Members 2015 (N = 5,654)	2015–17 Leavers in 2015 (N = 563)
Male %	65	68
Age (mean)	51	54
ABC1 %	76	74
Graduates %	45	45

TABLE 8.3 Efficacy and civic duty: 2015–17 leavers and all party members

		Members 2015 (N = 5,654)	2015–17 Leavers in 2015 (N = 581)
Politicians don't care what people like me think	Agree	26	35
	Strongly Agree	12	19
	Total Agree %	**38**	**54**
Every citizen should get involved in politics if democracy is to work	Agree	46	46
	Strongly Agree	23	19
	Total Agree %	**69**	**65**

TABLE 8.4 General incentives motives to join: mean scores of members and 2015–17 leavers

Type of general incentive	Joined party to . . . (0 – 10)	Members 2015 (N = 5,654)	Leavers in 2017 (N = 581)	Difference in means (members – leavers)
Collective positive	Support policies	9.2	8.2	1.0
Collective negative	Oppose policies	7.8	6.4	1.4
Expressive	Attachment to party's principles	9.2	7.9	1.3
Selective outcome	For career reasons	2.1	0.6	1.5
	To become an elected politician	2.5	0.9	1.6
Selective process	Mix with like-minded individuals	5.8	3.8	2.0
Social norms	Because of influence of friends and family	3.0	1.4	1.6
Expressive	Because of belief in party leadership	7.9	6.8	1.1

Note: All scales run from 0 (unimportant as a reason for joining) to 10 (very important as a reason for joining).

Turning first to what can be broadly described as 'purposive' or 'collective policy' incentives, it looks as if (as per previous research) those who eventually left their parties were not quite as committed in this respect as the average party member. Turning next to 'selective incentives', and, in particular, those related to progressing at work or within the party itself, a difference is also visible: leavers are even less likely than the average party member to say they enrolled for what we might term instrumental reasons. A difference is also observable when it comes to so-called solidary (or 'social process') incentives: leavers are less likely than the average member to have joined for social reasons. They are also, it would seem, less likely to have been attracted into the party by a particular leader.

We can also look at the extent to which those who we surveyed in 2015 but then left their parties felt less close to them, ideologically, than the average member – something that previous studies have suggested may well be significant. We do this simply by comparing where respondents placed themselves on average on a 0-to-10 left–right scale and where they placed their parties on the same scale. The difference between leavers and the average member in this mean ideological distance between member and party is small (1.02 for all members and 1.42 for leavers) but nonetheless tangible.

We move next to experiences of party life itself, some aspects of which might – if they are negative or if they dash expectations (e.g., about levels of consultation,

TABLE 8.5 Experience and expectations: 2015–17 leavers and all party members

		Members 2015 (N = 5,654)	Leavers in 2017 (N = 580)
Party activism often takes time away from one's family	Agree	47	51
	Strongly agree	11	11
	Total agree	**58**	**62**
Working for the party can be pretty boring at times	Agree	24	24
	Strongly agree	3	4
	Total agree	**27**	**28**
The party leadership doesn't pay attention to ordinary party members	Agree	14	12
	Strongly agree	4	4
	Total agree	**18**	**16**
Respected by leadership	A lot	43	46
	A fair amount	44	42
	Not very much	10	8
	Not at all	1	2
	Net Yes	**76**	**78**
Party members should have more influence over policy		35	34
How far have your experiences as a party member lived up to your initial expectations?	Fully	45	42
	Partly	39	37
	Not really	7	9
	Not at all	1	1
	Net lived up	**76**	**69**

influence and involvement) – push people toward the exit. These are addressed in Table 8.5.

While those who eventually left were very slightly more likely than the average member to think doing things for the party took time away from family, there appears to be next to no difference in their takes on how boring membership could sometimes be – or their feelings about how much the leadership listened to or respected party members. And those who left don't appear to have been any more inclined to say that party members should have more say over policy. Yet, on an overall measure of satisfaction (namely, the extent to which their experience was living up to their expectations) there does seem to be an appreciable difference. Either because they had higher expectations that were therefore more easily dashed or because their experience was somehow more negative, those who eventually left their parties were, on balance, less likely to say things were quite what they had hoped for.

One possible explanation is that those who left were disappointed or even dismayed by what they found when they went to a local party meeting. However, as Table 8.6 shows, this does not appear to be the case. True, the views of leavers, as

TABLE 8.6 Views on local party meetings: 2015–17 leavers and all party members

Meetings were . . . (1–5)	Members 2015 (N = 5,654)	2015–17 leavers (N = 580)
Old-fashioned/modern	3.4	3.3
Boring/interesting	3.7	3.6
Unfriendly/friendly	4.0	3.9
Divided/united	3.8	3.6
Hard to understand/easy to understand	4.1	3.9
Badly run/efficiently run	3.5	3.4

TABLE 8.7 Leavers' general impressions of the members they met

Other party members were . . . (1–5)	Leavers (N = 1,575) mean score
Unfriendly & unwelcoming/friendly & welcoming	3.8
Extreme/moderate	3.3
Cliquey/inclusive	3.2
Thought very differently to me/like-minded	3.5
All the same/a diverse range of people	3.5
Judgmental and prejudiced/tolerant and open-minded	3.5
Working class/middle class	3.2
Sexist/equal treatment irrespective of gender	3.9
Racist/equal treatment irrespective of colour	4.0
Mostly interested in the social side/very into politics	3.6
Ideological/pragmatic	2.7
Boring/interesting	3.4

Note: Results reported only for those leavers who answered all questions in this section.

expressed by their ratings on a 1–5 scale with a negative on one end and a positive on the other, are always just a shade less positive than those of the average member, but they are nevertheless strikingly similar.

We also asked all those in our leavers' survey (which, including both those who had and had not participated in our 2015 and 2016 members surveys, totalled well over 1,500 respondents) what they thought of the people they had interacted with while they were members, again using a 1–5 scale at either end of which were positive and negative evaluations. Interestingly, as Table 8.7 shows, their feelings were in the main fairly positive (i.e., members were, on balance, friendly and welcoming, diverse, tolerant and open-minded, not sexist or racist, into politics and reasonably interesting), although on some measures (moderate rather than extreme, inclusive rather than cliquey and, especially, ideological rather than pragmatic) slightly less so. This suggests that the bulk of leavers probably weren't pushed into resigning or put off renewing their membership by their fellow members.

Of course, a party member's feeling about other members will depend on how much they interacted with them, which will, in turn, depend on how active they were in various aspects of party life. We measured this by asking people in 2015 about different activities they were involved in over the previous five years. Their answers are displayed in Table 8.8.

In keeping with previous research in other countries, it looks as if those British party members who end up leaving are rather less involved – particularly 'on the doorstep' not only in relatively high-intensity activities like canvassing and delivering leaflets but also in selections – than the average member. They are also, again in keeping with previous work, less likely to have stood for party or elective office. This table may, of course, be read as a harbinger of the decision that leavers were destined to make within the next two years; their lower level of commitment to the party was reflected in their relative disinclination to campaign actively for it.

We also tried to tap into a broader sense of identification with the party and (relatedly) into how prepared members were to act as 'ambassadors in the community' for it (see Table 8.9). When it comes to the latter, there does seem to be a difference between leavers and the average member, but it is not huge. It does look as though leavers are rather less likely than the average member to see the party as 'theirs'; with the benefit of hindsight, this might once again be seen as an early sign of relative lack of commitment that was destined to end in the decision to exit the party.

Finally, we asked leavers outright to tell us why they had left. This was done by presenting them with a list, from which they could choose three in rank order. We also gave them an opportunity to elaborate by expanding on their answers in writing. Table 8.10 gives the results of this exercise for all those in our 2017 leavers' survey.

TABLE 8.8 Differences in activity between 2015–17 leavers and average member

	Members 2015 (N = 5,654)	Leavers in 2017 (N = 580)	Difference (members – leavers) percentage points
In the last 5 years I frequently . . .			
Displayed poster	28	20	8
Donated money	25	17	8
Signed a petition	37	34	3
Delivered leaflets	32	20	12
Attended party meeting	28	19	9
Helped at a party function	15	7	8
Canvassing	19	8	11
Stood for office	11	5	6
Stood for elective office	11	6	5
Taken part in selection of PPC/leader	20	9	11
Formulation of policy	8	3	5

Note: All figures percentages. PPC = Prospective Parliamentary Candidate.

TABLE 8.9 Members' and leavers' sense of affinity with their party and willingness to act as an ambassador in the community

		Members (N = 5,654)	Leavers (N = 580)
When I speak about the party, I usually say "we" instead of "they".	Agree	38	38
	Strongly agree	31	21
	Total 'agree'	69	59
If you are in a social situation, or at work, and the talk turns to politics, which of the following best expresses what you usually do?	I get involved but don't say I'm a member	28	32
	I get involved and I say I'm a member	59	56
	I prefer not to get involved	10	10

Note: All figures percentages.

TABLE 8.10 2017 leavers' top-three reasons for quitting (N = 1,760)

	1st	2nd	3rd	Total
Disagreed with general direction of party	9	14	9	32
Disappointed/disillusioned with leader	14	10	8	32
Decided I supported a different political party	14	7	6	26
Didn't feel I was contributing anything	7	9	8	24
Disagreed with specific policy	11	6	6	23
Disliked conflict and factionalism	6	7	7	19
To save money	10	5	4	13
Forgot to renew	7	4	2	13
Too busy	3	5	4	12
Went off politics altogether	2	2	3	7
Moved house	2	2	2	6
Health problems	2	2	1	5
Fell out with people in my association/branch	2	2	1	5
Job required me to be politically neutral	1	1	1	3
Problem with direct debit/standing order	1	1	1	3
None of the above	9	3	5	17

Note: All figures percentages.

Their answers would appear to confirm much of what we have already found even if, especially when one reads their write-in responses, they reveal a good deal of variation and complexity. 'Ideology' (measured by disagreement with the general direction of the party and with particular policies) is prominent. Related to this, perhaps, is members realizing that, in fact, they were in the wrong party – something that serves as a reminder that parties operate in a market place for members as well as voters.[12]

Similarly related may be the second-most commonly cited reason for leaving, namely, disappointment or disillusion with the party leader: write-ins certainly suggest that this is rarely solely personal or tactical; rather, it has to do with that leader personifying a particular direction for the party in question, be it left or right, socially conservative or liberal. Also important, in line with previous work on leaving, is the feeling that one isn't contributing anything, to which we ought to add, perhaps, people admitting that they have just gone off politics altogether – something that may or not be related to some of the other reasons they give for quitting. Dislike of conflict and factionalism, for instance, may have played a part and is fairly frequently mentioned, although, interestingly, very few members claim or admit to having actually fallen out with people locally.

Practical reasons are not that frequently cited either: although nearly a fifth of leavers mention the need to save money and more than one in ten confesses to simply being too busy, health problems, house and job moves and administrative glitches are not that frequently mentioned. That said, about one in seven leavers admit that simply forgetting to renew was a factor – something that parties might want to bear in mind. It is also the case that, since, for most people who join anyway, their subscription comes out of their disposable income, any conscious decision not to renew on financial grounds is likely to reflect at some level a feeling that their membership (the 'product', if you like) is not providing value for money – at least compared to the other organizations they belong to or even entertainment services (film-streaming services, pay-TV channels, etc.) that they sign up to. As one of the party's staffers who was privy to its internal research on non-renewals put it to us, '[i]magine if you've got a direct debit to the Lib Dems and to the RSPCA and you have to cancel one of them. People are going to go for the political party, frankly, because it's less clear what difference we make'.[13]

Tell me more: write-in responses to the 2017 leavers' survey

Having looked at leavers' responses to a predetermined list of options, we can also look at what they said when we invited them to expand upon their reasons for quitting. To anyone doing that, it soon becomes obvious that what one British prime minister, Harold Macmillan, famously termed 'events, dear boy, events' often impact on individuals' decision to quit. Sometimes, those events are important in and of themselves: an obvious instance of this would be the Liberal Democrats' decision to form a coalition with the Conservatives in 2010, which, in fairly short order, precipitated the departure of thousands of (often quite active) members – to the evident frustration of some of those members who stayed, including one staffer we interviewed:

> I think it's fucking pathetic, frankly. I mean we're obviously going to end up in coalition at some point. . . . How can that possibly mean we only believe in coalition with Labour? It's just stupid. Spineless, useless, quitters.[14]

Other events are more like straws that break the proverbial camel's back – the proximate rather than the underlying cause, if you like, of someone deciding to leave their party: an example might be David Cameron pushing marriage equality legislation through the Commons, providing yet more proof to socially conservative Tories that he was not one of them.[15]

We already know from our post-2017 leavers' questionnaire (and indeed other studies) that the most common reason for leaving volunteered by ex-members is disagreement with the ideological/policy direction their party seems to be taking. Figures 8.1 through 8.4 explore what happens if we investigate this further by categorizing the reasons given by former members when we invited them to expand on their answers in writing.

It is immediately apparent that this qualitative analysis (which admittedly still throws up all sorts of sometimes idiosyncratic reasons for leaving, subsumed under 'other') supports the idea that ideology and leadership do indeed matter, but often in combination with one or two very obvious 'events'. Just over half of those who gave their reasons for leaving UKIP, for instance, said they did so because Brexit meant the party had fulfilled its purpose and because their hero, Nigel Farage, had stepped down (Figure 8.1) – one reason why, unless EU withdrawal is delivered to their satisfaction, at least some of them may consider re-joining UKIP or, perhaps more likely, Farage's new Brexit Party.

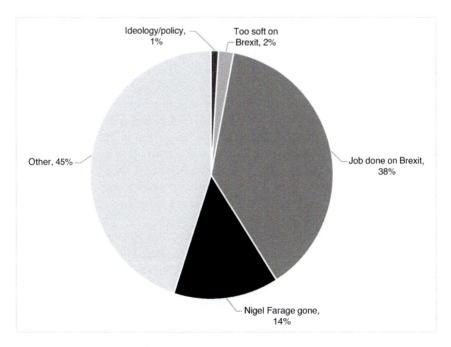

FIGURE 8.1 Ex-UKIP members (*n* = 154)

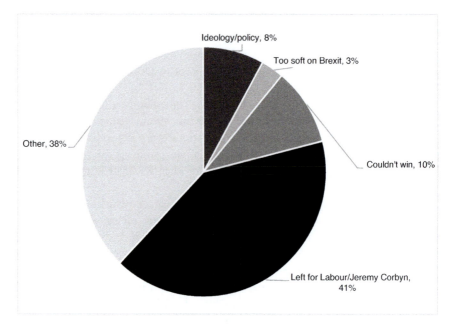

FIGURE 8.2 Ex-Green members ($n = 152$)

Brexit doesn't seem to have driven many Greens to leave (see Figure 8.2). But Labour's big swing to the left under Jeremy Corbyn clearly persuaded some that the grass was redder on the other side. According to our panel data, over a third of those who left the Green Party of England and Wales after 2015 did so in order to join Labour and Jeremy Corbyn's leadership was specifically mentioned by many of them. Typical reasons given included 'Corbyn offered a reinvigorated Labour Party that was unashamed, proud and built to succeed!' and 'I joined the Greens to show Labour I wanted them to be more left-wing. When JC became leader, I felt the Labour Party was finally back on track'. Another frequent refrain was the possibility of power: 'I thought with Jeremy Corbyn as leader there was a historic chance to make a real difference on a national scale. Green policies are important, but Labour has a better chance of implementing them under Corbyn.'

For over a quarter of those who told us why they'd left Labour, however, Corbyn was a push – rather than a pull – factor, although for a third of them what they saw (at the time anyway) as the party's failure to fight Brexit was the final straw (see Figure 8.3).

Interestingly, fewer than one in five of those who explained their reasons for leaving the Conservative Party (see Figure 8.4) blamed its pursuit of a hard Brexit, suggesting that the widespread commitment to the latter among Tory members that we noted in Chapter 4 did not necessarily come about as a result of Tory remainers and soft Brexiteers deserting the party *en masse*.

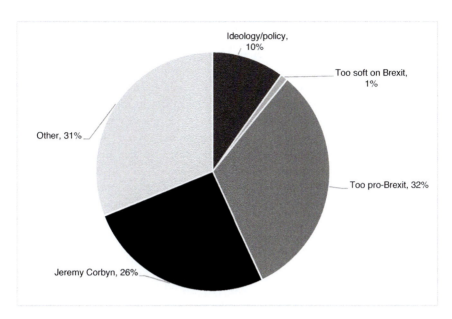

FIGURE 8.3 Ex-Labour members (*n* = 261)

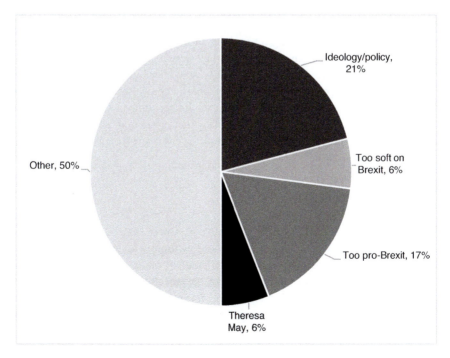

FIGURE 8.4 Ex-Conservative members (*n* = 139)

Final pass: a statistical analysis

Both our findings and those of others who've studied quitting suggest that we should expect dissatisfaction with a party's ideological position, its leadership or its intra-party processes to increase the odds of exit, while active commitment to and embeddedness in the local party network should work in the opposite direction, functioning, if you like, as a constraint on exit. So far, at least when it comes to our data, we have only made some very basic comparisons between members as a whole and members who left. But we can do slightly better than that. Because some 2088 of our 2017 respondents were people who we also questioned in 2015 and because 114 of them had left their party during the intervening two years, we have what social scientists call 'panel data'. And we can use more advanced techniques – in this case, binary logistic regression – to see if the expectations outlined earlier hold good. More technically-minded readers may like to refer to the results of this statistical model in Appendix 2. But we can summarize its findings here.

First, and importantly, none of the various demographic control variables included in the model prove to be significant: gender, education and social class made no difference to how likely someone was to have left. So what does? Well, although the association isn't quite as strong as we might have expected, it does look as though the further people feel that they are (in either direction), ideologically speaking, from their party, then the more likely they are to leave it. What may well matter more, however, is the extent to which that sense of distance or mismatch grows worse over time: the greater the change, the more likely someone is to leave. It also seems pretty clear that the less impressed someone is by their party's leader – something we judged by asking them about their leader's performance during the election campaign – then the more likely they were to leave. The extent to which people feel that their leader respects the party's membership (which perhaps serves as a proxy for how they feel about the party's internal processes more generally) also makes a difference. Finally, it turns out that the longer someone is a party member and the more active they are, then the less likely they are to quit, which suggests that the more people are effectively embedded at the local level, then the more likely they are to stick around.

Conclusion

We cannot tell for sure, of course, whether the relative lack of involvement, dissatisfaction and ideological alienation displayed by those who leave their parties are a symptom or a cause of their leaving – whether, in other words, they are simply early signs of detachment or actually one of the drivers of the latter. Nor can we guarantee that those ex-members will never re-join their party or, for that matter another party: anyone trawling through the write-in responses from members and ex-members may well be surprised at the extent to which people who are sufficiently ideologically motivated to join a particular party can later decide that they actually prefer one of its rivals.

Emphasizing this, as well as pointing to the churn that all parties experience, risks implying that their members are somehow easy-come, easy-go. This would be a mistake. If there is one thing that our research suggests it is that the decision to quit is one people make primarily for political and ideological reasons rather than as a function of, say, personal animosities or as a reaction to life events, even if the latter are sometimes bound to play a part. Many people who leave their parties are leaving something that once mattered to them and should therefore matter to us, and to the parties themselves. Like any voluntary organization (or, indeed, any business firm or public service), parties are presumably as interested in retention as they are in recruitment. Whether our findings can help them to persuade more of their members to stay remains to be seen. Why parties want to do that – and what they want from members, new and old – is the subject of our next chapter.

Notes

1 So much so, indeed, that there would appear to be only a handful of papers (not all of them published) ever written on the topic, at least in English. For an interesting discussion of the phenomenon, see van Haute, Emilie (2015) 'Joining isn't everything: Exit, voice, and loyalty in party organizations', in Richard Johnston and Campbell Sharman (eds.) *Parties and Party Systems: Structure and Context* (Vancouver: UBC Press), pp. 184–201.

2 See van Biezen, Ingrid, Mair, Peter and Poguntke, Thomas (2012) 'Going, going . . . gone? The decline of party membership in contemporary Europe', *European Journal of Political Research*, 51 (1), pp. 24–56; Kölln, Ann-Kristin (2016) 'Party membership in Europe: Testing party-level explanations of decline', *Party Politics*, 22 (4), pp. 465–477; and Webb, Paul and Keith, Dan (2017) 'Assessing the strength of party organizational resources', in Scarrow, Susan E., Webb, Paul and Poguntke, Thomas (eds.) *Organizing Political Parties: Representation, Participation and Power* (Oxford: Oxford University Press), pp. 32–35.

3 See, for example, Wheeler, Caroline and Shipman, Tim, (2019) '150,000 members desert Labour in Brexit backlash', *Sunday Times*, 20 January 2019 and Press Association (2017) 'Labour Party has lost nearly 26,000 members since mid-2016, report claims', *Guardian*, 3 March, available online at www.theguardian.com/politics/2017/mar/03/labour-party-lost-members-mid-2016.

4 See for example Voerman, Gerrit and van Schuur, Wijbrandt (2011) 'Dutch political parties and their members', in Emilie van Haute (ed.) *Party Membership in Europe: Exploration Into the Anthills of Party Politics* (Brussels: ULB), pp. 77–94.

5 van Haute, Emilie and Gauja, Anika (2015) *Party Members and Activists* (Abingdon: Routledge), pp. 4, 199, 201.

6 Wagner, Markus (2017) 'Why do party members leave?', *Parliamentary Affairs*, 70 (2), pp. 344–360.

7 Kölln, Ann-Kristin and Polk, Jonathan (2017) 'Emancipated party members: Examining ideological incongruence within political parties', *Party Politcs*, 23 (1), pp. 18–29.

8 Kosiara-Pedersen, Karina (2016) 'Exit. Why party members consider leaving their parties', Paper presented to *the ECPR General Conference*, Prague, September 2016.

9 Whiteley, Paul and Seyd, Patrick (2002) *High-intensity Participation: The Dynamics of Party Activism in Britain* (Ann Arbor: University of Michigan Press).

10 See Whiteley, Paul (2009) 'Where have all the members gone? The dynamics of party membership in Britain', *Parliamentary Affairs*, 62 (2), pp. 248–250.

11 Whiteley, Paul, Poletti, Monica, Webb, Paul, and Bale, Tim (2019) 'Oh Jeremy Corbyn! Why did Labour Party membership soar after the 2015 general election?', *British Journal of Politics and International Relations*, 21 (1), pp. 80–98.

12 See van Haute, Emilie (2015) 'Joining isn't everything: Exit, voice, and loyalty in party organizations', in Johnston, Richard and Sharman, Campbell (eds.) *Parties and Party Systems: Structure and Context* (Vancouver: UBC Press), pp. 190–191.
13 Liberal Democrat staffer, interview 9 February 2016.
14 Liberal Democrat staffer, interview 25 February 2016.
15 In spite of numerous anecdotal reports to the effect, no one knows quite how many members left over this issue: some of the Tories interviewed confirmed that some members did go but also noted that more talked about going but didn't. If they did, then they may well have been among those whose concerns about Cameron taking the party in too liberal a direction we identified in an early pilot survey. See Webb, Paul and Bale, Tim (2014) 'Why do Tories defect to UKIP? Conservative Party members and the temptations of the populist radical right', *Political Studies*, 62 (4), pp. 961–970.

9

THE DEMAND SIDE – HOW PARTIES SEE MEMBERSHIP

> The centre probably views membership as a necessary bloc which, outside of an election, is quite possibly a difficult group to manage. So, I think there's a mixed view: they obviously want people to be involved politically; but I think they find the demands of the membership quite tiring. But come an election they realise they need the footsoldiers.[1]

Before the recent surges in membership experienced by some of Great Britain's political parties, it was all too easy to conclude that the latter were at least partly to blame for decade after decade of decline in the number of people committing to join them and work on their behalf. Parties, one could argue, were no longer interested in attracting members – especially the kind of demanding, active members who sometimes seem to delight in causing trouble for their leaders. Funding could supposedly be had from elsewhere and elections won not by locally driven grass-roots campaigning in the constituencies but on national television and via centrally directed polling, advertising, and direct mail.[2]

The historical record, however, tells a different story. A dive into their archives reveals that parties have never stopped taking the local effort seriously, have long worried behind closed doors about losing members, active as well as passive, and have occasionally launched campaigns – most, but not all, of them unsuccessful – to turn the situation around.[3] Meanwhile, detailed studies of individual constituencies over time, while they confirm that 'a decrease in the number of other activists has led to the contemporary situation in which [local government] councillors now comprise a much larger proportion of the activist population', nevertheless show that activism tends to fluctuate in line with membership itself and clearly suggest 'that the falling supply of individuals prepared to become politically involved is more important than the changing demand of parties for activists'.[4] Similarly detailed studies of other constituencies nevertheless show that, at least during the post-war 'golden age' of membership, when folk positively flocked to become members, conscious and concerted efforts by parties to recruit people were still capable of boosting their numbers even further.[5]

So, what about now? The last time anyone took a really close look at the demand for party members in the UK was in the mid-1990s – a very long time ago in terms of how digital technology has transformed everyday life for millions of people, at work, at home, and at play.[6] How, in this new era, do parties – specifically those who are elected to represent them at Westminster and staffers who work for them at HQ – see members? Are they seen as so vital that it's worth setting targets for how many you want to recruit? Or are they simply nice to have but no longer strictly necessary? Are they thought of as assets or liabilities? Or perhaps a bit of both? How easy is it to attract more of them and to hold on to them? How many can be persuaded to volunteer their time as well as hand over their money? And what exactly is it that they are needed for anyway? Can't whatever that is be done just as well by people who support the party but don't want to go so far as to join it? Perhaps the whole idea of parties as mass membership organizations is hopelessly outdated – a relic of the twentieth (or even the nineteenth) century that's no longer fit for purpose in the twenty-first? This chapter attempts to answer those questions, largely by letting the parties speak for themselves.[7]

Assets, not liabilities

First up, it is apparent from talking to them that virtually every party sees members as very much an asset. Most obviously, they are valued as a vital source of free labour, or else a massive help in paying someone else to do the job instead. As one Tory MP puts it, there are essentially two ways to deliver a constituency annual report to 46,000 letter boxes: 'You get your volunteers to do it, or you pay the Royal Mail to do it . . . at about three-and-a-half grand a pop', but even if you choose the latter option, 'you then need people to come to your association dinners, your supper clubs and so on' to be able to afford it.[8] But it's also about more than that. Many MPs, for instance, value members as a link to their locality and sometimes as a source of helpful (even if seemingly trivial) counsel – and that's true even if they are adamant that they make up their own minds about policy rather than bowing to pressure, and even if they have had to spend time they don't really have in managing the petty disputes that occasionally break out between their local activists. As one Labour MP insists, '[t]hey're not just footsoldiers. You have got incredible teachers, nurses, care-workers, business people, who give you advice about stuff'.[9] Or, as a Tory MP goes on to say, thinking of the time when they first moved into the constituency as a candidate:

> I found my membership . . . invaluable in being able to connect me to people because they were plugged into the community: they were in congregations; they were in voluntary organizations; they were school governors. So, I think they act as a bit of bridge, a link, between you and the community. And, of

course, I was single . . . [So] some of those that I'm closer to play the role for me that perhaps a wife or a partner would in telling me 'You should have worn a tie at that', 'You were a bit brusque with X', or 'So and so has died; make sure you drop a note.'[10]

The fact that this kind of close understanding can develop is not, of course, entirely surprising since, as is sometimes too easily forgotten, many parliamentarians started out as grassroots members themselves, progressing from delivering leaflets and knocking on doors, through taking on roles as officers and local councillors, to becoming (perhaps after a few failed attempts) parliamentary candidates and then MPs. Indeed, having some sort of track record can contribute enormously not just to their initial selection but also to their ability to persuade 'their' members to work for their election, as well as to their ability (as long as they continue to work hard themselves) to motivate and effectively manage those members for years thereafter.[11] It can also make a big difference to leaders: one Liberal Democrat insider puts some of former leader and deputy PM Nick Clegg's problems with his party down in part to the fact that, unlike his successor, he wasn't seen by members to have done 'the activist slog'.[12]

Such shared experience, and members knowing that their representative is prepared in the words of one Labour MP, 'to bust a gut for them', does not, however, mean all is sweetness and light.[13] For example, some MPs quite like the fact that a fair few of their most active members (indeed, some of their local party officers) also represent the party on local authorities, believing that it grounds them in reality and gives them an appreciation of the trade-offs and compromises that responsible politics inevitably involves. But others worry that it turns local meetings into a series of reports on what the council is up to rather than a welcoming space for discussion and for building the party and maintaining its campaigning edge. Moreover, especially in the Labour Party of late, discussion is not always as comradely as it might be – one reason why some of the party's MPs are keen to keep their members' focused on campaigning, an activity which, as well as helping them to get re-elected, hopefully takes up time and energy that would otherwise be spent on ideological infighting, as well as bringing so-called keyboard warriors (presuming they turn up for canvassing sessions) into what, in their experience, will be chastening contact with 'real voters'.[14]

Parties also continue to take members seriously not just as campaigners and a link to local communities but also as a source of finance, although – perhaps predictably – the extent to which they do so varies between parties, as Table 9.1 reveals. For the Conservatives, members' subscription payments, while they are of course welcome, make up a relatively small (indeed tiny) slice of the party's income – at least at the national level, the vast bulk of which is made up of donations from businesses and 'high net worth' individuals, just as Labour's coffers have traditionally been filled in the main by union money.[15] That said, as one or two Conservative MPs note, things are a little different at the local level – especially in the vast majority of constituencies that don't have fairly large associations (which means

TABLE 9.1 Sources of parties' central income 2017 (percentages)

	Conservative	Labour	Liberal Democrat	UKIP	Green	SNP
Member subs.	1.80	28.97	13.17	32.18	36.34	40.77
Other donations	74.50	32.73	63.19	54.91	49.16	24.54
State grants	1.22	13.31	4.45	0	0	3.05
Other	22.48	24.99	19.19	12.91	14.50	31.64

Source: Political Party Statements of Account 2017, as remitted to the Electoral Commission.

Note: All percentages relate only to *central* party income emanating from stated sources. Each party has different rules on how much of its income as a whole stays with or goes straight to its local branches, so these figures can only suggest (because they almost inevitably, therefore, understate) how much of their *total* income comes from their members. Moreover, the figure for *donations* also includes money that members donate in addition to their annual subscriptions, which can – if parties are successful at appealing to them – be quite substantial. Note also that there is a long tradition of local parties under- or overstating their membership for financial reasons: for instance, Conservative associations are supposed to send CCHQ a fixed amount of the subscription for every member they recruit locally; understating their membership means they keep more of the money.

600 members plus, apparently).[16] Away from Westminster, as one puts it, 'membership income is still important in just providing a bedrock on which all the rest of it can be built'; getting a few more people to commit to paying the annual fee, and perhaps to forking out a few quid more at various fundraising events (one wag refers to raffles as 'the Tory tax') can come in quite handy, especially if, say, the constituency office or income-generating rental property needs refurbishment that year. Those fundraisers, of course, still go on in seats (often safer seats) where there are more members, although there, apparently, they are as much to do – and this applies to Labour as well as the Conservatives – with raising and maintaining morale as they are with raising cash.

For the Liberal Democrats, however, the money that membership fees bring is much more important and has often been absolutely vital. After all, the party – and the same is true for most smaller parties, including, for instance, the Greens and the SNP – cannot count on large gifts from rich institutions or individuals. True, each member costs something to service but, now that processes are so much more automated than they once were, those costs are (as presumably they are in most other parties) easily covered by their annual subscription. Moreover, the party knows that members, as well as being more inclined than mere supporters to hit the streets and the phones and to stand as candidates at election time, are also more inclined to respond to requests for donations. As one staffer puts it, in many ways echoing our findings in Chapter 6:

> If I get you to do something [for me] once, you're more likely to do it again: Psychology 101, right? Getting someone to be a member means that they are disproportionately more likely to say yes to anything else because they're part of the gang.[17]

In this, Liberal Democrats are not untypical: most parties do find they are able to go back to their members (even if some of them sometimes resent getting yet another begging letter) and persuade them to part with small, supposedly one-off sums over and above their annual subscription. As a Green Party staffer observes, 'the fact that you wear a badge and you say you're a member' allows you to commit more of your finances than if you weren't going to put your badge on'.[18]

But the demand for members goes beyond the merely instrumental, beyond 'leaflets, phoning, money' (the brutally succinct summary provided by one Labour MP) or the fact that, as a Liberal Democrat staffer puts it, 'they're going to defend you in conversations with other, 'normal people' – something that, for a party which doesn't have much support in the press, and can't afford lots of advertising and direct mail, is essential to getting its message out.[19] Indeed, many of those politicians and staffers we interviewed were nonplussed at the very notion that a party could exist without members – some to the point that they clearly regarded such a scenario as almost morally unconscionable. Members, in their view, were the heart and the marrow of the party – indeed, in the words one activist who has served on Labour's NEC,

> they *are* the party . . . Without them, we wouldn't exist, we wouldn't have people taking our message out on the ground, we wouldn't win any elections, we just wouldn't function at all . . . You wouldn't have *anything* without the members.[20]

A Green politician echoes that sentiment: 'Members *are* the party. The party is not some collection of stuffed shirts meeting in closed meetings. The *members* are the party. If we took the members away, we'd take the energy of the party away.'[21] So does a Liberal Democrat staffer: 'If you don't have members, you'd just turn into a PR company for a bunch of people who want to run the country . . . There's no *soul* to that. It becomes a purely transactional thing.'[22]

For some, all this means that members simply cannot be seen as a liability. However, most MPs and staffers recognize that they potentially present their party with some challenges, although not ones, they believe, that an effective national or local leader should really find too hard to cope with. As one Labour MP put it, members are 'a massive asset – if you lead them and manage them properly!'[23] The most obvious case in point, perhaps, is when a party's grassroots make policy demands that, if acceded to, could saddle it with a commitment that it decides it can't fulfil in government (as happened to the Liberal Democrats over tuition fees) or else pull in the opposite direction to its voters and especially the voters it needs to win over. 'It's always the case', another Labour MP admits, 'that your party is in a slightly different place to the public . . . but it can get very difficult.'[24] Members can also say and do things which can embarrass their party in the media but which their party struggles to disown: they are, after all, the words and actions of a card-carrying member and can all too easily be spun, especially if they hold even minor office in the party, as somehow representative by journalists on the hunt for a story – even though those journalists are well aware that it is all but impossible for parties to thoroughly vet people in advance of them becoming members. Social media only compounds the risk by ensuring that stuff which in years gone by would have been seen and heard by just a few diehard activists sitting in a drafty community centre now reaches an audience of thousands all around the country. Moreover, the fact that mainstream media outlets then pick up on it may well oblige the party to act and be seen to act, thereby amplifying an issue it had hoped to play down and causing even the average voter (who generally doesn't pay much attention to politics) to wonder whether, to take two recent instances (and with no small justification), Labour really does have a problem with antisemitism or the Tories with Islamophobia.[25]

Members only?

All of this obviously risks inflicting serious reputational damage on parties. Yet as far as they are concerned, that risk is more than outweighed by the benefits members bring. Moreover, they are, in the main, convinced that it is worth trying to recruit paid-up members rather than relying on supporters – people who vote for the party, who may even be persuaded to give money to it and do things for it at election time but who for some reason are reluctant (or perhaps just too busy) to sign up as fully-paid-up members. As noted earlier, most parties are convinced – with some justification, our research suggests – that members were likely to do (and probably to give) more than supporters invited along on what one Tory MP calls a 'turn up, you don't have to belong to be involved' basis. And the payment of a relatively inexpensive but 'meaningful' annual subscription, another MP feels, signifies (and perhaps encourages) an 'emotional commitment' and, as another puts it, a 'genuine relationship'. That said, parties were clearly more than happy to accept practical assistance from people who aren't members but are, say, prepared to hand over their details for inclusion on a locally held database of potential helpers. A Labour MP even goes so far as to say that when out canvassing with volunteers 'I would have no idea who was a Labour Party member and who wasn't. . . . Our qualifying criterion is are you prepared to do some work?'[26] A Tory MP puts it this way: 'I'd rather have twenty people out delivering leaflets and helping me to knock on doors than I would have a hundred people paying twenty pounds a year and turning up and whinging', while another confesses,

> I'm far less bothered about who my membership is; what I'm bothered about is how many people do stuff. . . . To me, actually, someone who delivers two hundred leaflets a month is more valuable than someone who gives me £15 a year.[27]

On the other hand, Conservatives, in particular, are wary of moving from that to an institutionalized 'registered supporters' scheme. Indeed, their recent decision to do so, announced by Party Chairman Brandon Lewis in the spring of 2019, runs counter to a widespread belief among Tories that what they see as a hard-left takeover of the Labour Party stemmed at least in part from its decision to begin such a scheme in the wake of the abolition of its electoral college in 2014 in reaction to the alleged attempt by left-wing trade unionists to fix the selection contest in Falkirk the year before.[28]

It was assumed that this move, as one Labour staffer who was closely involved at the time wryly notes, would see an influx of the same kind of supposedly moderate, not overly political 'normal people' who, legend had it, had been attracted to Labour in the early to mid-1990s, when back-garden barbeques, as opposed to ideological infighting, were apparently all the rage.[29] Not that the party under Ed Miliband was overly concerned about growing, mind. True, as that same staffer notes, Miliband's immediate circle were concerned (perhaps much more so than they should have been) with how policies would go down with 'left-liberal' opinion in outlets like the *Guardian* or the *New Statesman*. But worried about how things would play with the grassroots? Not so much. 'I don't think there was ever a feeling that the Labour membership wouldn't knock on doors because you had a tough-on-immigration mug', they recall, while party management and policy formation, in their recollection, was all about Westminster and the trade unions (and, of course, voters) rather than Constituency Labour Parties (CLPs). Besides, 'everybody was aware of the limitations of Ed's appeal and therefore there were limits as to how much you could expect to grow' in terms of membership. Moreover,

> after the slight Cameron rise in opposition, you had the continuing hollowing out of the Tories and a very significant hollowing out of the Lib Dems . . . It's easy to forget [in hindsight] when 223,000 looks pretty pathetic . . . but actually it didn't look that bad, because everyone else had been losing and you'd stabilized.

At least in part then, parties' views on increasing their membership vary over time – both according to how realistic they think such a goal might be (which may well involve an assessment of the pulling power of their leader) and how well they think they are doing compared to their rivals.

Even in the light of Labour's experience with registered supporters and members since 2015, however, there is a tentative acknowledgement among a minority of Conservatives that some kind of tiered membership, taking into account different levels of commitment, might still work in the long term and perhaps bring in more people overall. And this is presumably why (along with the fact that Brexit was a much bigger preoccupation at the time) their chairman's plans for a 'Conservative Community Network' of registered supporters, did not attract much criticism, or even attention, at the time – possibly because it was followed soon after by the Liberal Democrats' decision to set up their own scheme.[30] But even among those prepared to suck it and see, the assumption is that, ultimately, real rights and privileges must be limited to full members in order to provide sufficient incentives for them to join. This is an assumption shared across the political spectrum: as one

Green politician put it, '[t]here's got to be some advantages to being a party member to encourage people to actually join'.[31]

Rewards

As to what those incentives should be, there is less consensus. Parties are well aware that people join them for a variety of reasons. In their view anyway, personal ambition and simply enjoying organizing things influence only a small (albeit often relatively active) minority, with the same going for the simple desire for friendship. But by far the most common motive, they believe (and our research backs them up), is a desire to express support for the party's values and to help in some small way to get it elected. It is therefore fairly obvious, they feel, that members need to believe that they have some kind of influence on the direction the party takes and who represents it. However, on the nature and scope of that influence, views vary markedly according to party, with the Conservatives the obvious outlier.

For those working for and representing the Liberal Democrats, for instance, giving members a big (indeed ultimately determinative) influence on policy is not only right in principle but essential to the party's ability to recruit and retain them. In marked contrast to the Conservatives and Labour, it cannot (and does not want to) claim to represent particular socio-economic groups or 'sectional' interests. Values, and by extension policies, are therefore incredibly important, and the party's internal research shows that they are also members' number one priority – one reason why it recently decided to allow any member who wants to attend and vote at its formally sovereign annual conference to do so rather than limit the right to elected delegates. The same goes for the Greens: as one of its staffers puts it, '[w]hat's attractive about giving some money to the Green Party is still that ability to have your say, the fact that you're putting something into being part of a whole . . .'[32]

For Conservatives, however, there is a widespread presumption that most members and potential members neither want, nor should be given, a formal say on policy – partly because, as one MP holding a marginal seat (not altogether surprisingly perhaps) observes, 'policy should be pitched to where we think floating votes are and not pitched to where our core membership is'.[33] Interestingly, however, there is a feeling among some MPs that the party may have gone too far in seeking to limit members' influence, not least by getting rid of the debates on Constituency Association motions that were also a feature of its annual conference for most of the twentieth century. That yearly get-together, many believe, has, since its move away from seaside resorts to the cities of Manchester and Birmingham, come to be seen by grassroots members as the unaffordable preserve of would-be politicians, lobbyists, pressure groups and the media – 'a complete corporate junket' that is 'totally, utterly coordinated and an exercise in wannabe MPs getting their two-minute slot', as one (actual) MP puts it.[34]

Making more of an effort to at least consult members would also, some believe, pay dividends: as one senior Tory MP notes ironically, '[m]aybe if you start asking people what they think, . . . perhaps they'd like to join!'[35] Few in the party, however, express much faith in the ability of the party's official Conservative Policy Forum to make any real difference to its platform: as one Tory MP confides: 'I have never seen a policy come out of that process; it's an exercise in Marie Antoinette membership management – "let them eat cake".'[36] They also note that, while the ability of ordinary members to select council and parliamentary candidates, as well as to choose the party leader, may to some extent make up for this lack of policy influence, it is not always as unfettered as it might be. Perennial concerns about CCHQ interference were heightened in the early years of David Cameron's leadership by the introduction of the 'Priority List' and were reinforced by candidates being effectively imposed on some Constituency Associations in the run-up to the 'snap' election of 2017 – an election called by a prime minister, note, who had become Tory leader without, in the end, the grassroots being given a vote.[37] And in any case, as one Conservative MP notes, if you live in a safe seat with an incumbent who has no plans to go anywhere soon, then even your chance to select a Prospective Parliamentary Candidate (PPC) doesn't exactly come round very often.[38]

That doesn't, of course, prevent the Tories' website – in the list of things joining the party enables you to do – mentioning candidate and leadership selection.[39] The list – often accompanied by pictures of the ethnic minority members who in reality make up a tiny proportion of Tory members – also mentions the chance to '[m]eet like-minded people and make a difference to our country' and to [s]upport local campaigns and attend social events with members just like you'. Top of the list, however, is the admirably direct (if not necessarily entirely accurate) 'Help us win elections – all of your subscription goes towards our campaigns', with the rather vague 'Influence Party policy – by giving feedback on policy briefs' coming a little further down. The list also promises 'regular member updates' from 'inside the party' (normally, it seems, emails from the chairman, some of which laud the government's achievements, most of which slam its opponents and all of which invite donations). And finally, it reminds visitors that 'members have the opportunity to stand for election as Conservatives. So, if you decide that you want to take part in our democracy, you can!'

Masters of their own fate?

Given the limits on what the Conservative Party can, or is prepared, to offer its members and what many see as its consequent difficulty in attracting and holding onto them in recent years, it is not altogether surprising that it is less keen than some of its rivals on setting aspirational targets for recruitment and retention. Indeed, beyond hoping that its ongoing move to a centralized membership system will allow it to make an improved offer to existing and would-be members living in areas in which fellow Tories are thin on the ground and/or who are not particularly keen on getting active, the party seems unconvinced that there is really much it can do – at the national level anyway – to significantly boost recruitment (although it believes retention, at least, should improve).[40] This near fatalism is resisted, of course, by some Conservatives: after all, as one Tory MP puts it,

> You need as many members you can get for that membership to represent a reasonable cross section' [of the country the party is trying to represent and] 'it needs more of them in areas that we still need to fight back in. . . . the Manchesters, the industrial heartlands, the Midlands, the north.[41]

But that fatalism fairly widespread, standing in marked contrast to the belief (and the experience) of other parties that growth is possible and, not only that, but they can help make it happen. Interestingly, this is not a belief confined to the two parties that have seen the biggest surges in membership in recent years, the SNP and Labour. It is also strong in the Liberal Democrats and the Greens – possibly even stronger because there is an extent to which they, more than their counterparts on the (centre) left, whose growth owed a great deal to 'events' (to wit: an independence referendum and a leadership contest) may have made more of their own luck.

The Liberal Democrats, it is true, enjoyed a surge in membership that, ostensibly anyway, owed itself to two events over which they had little control. The 2015 general election came after they'd spent five years in what, for many of their erstwhile supporters, had been a counter-intuitive coalition with the Conservatives – a coalition that had seen tens of thousands of disappointed members leave the party. Predictably enough, the election turned out to be a disaster for the Liberal Democrats. Yet, whether it was through a sense of guilt at not having come to the aid of the party before it was too late, or just a sense that it hadn't really deserved quite such a pasting, large numbers of often young, first-time members joined in the summer of 2015. Another big boost to numbers came after the British people voted to leave the EU a year later. In reality, however, the story of those surges is not only a little more complicated but also a testimony to the fact that parties are not simply the passive recipients of good (or, in some cases, bad) luck.

With the appointment in 2012 of a new chief executive, as well as a new membership team with extensive (and in some cases commercial) experience of building and maintaining subscription-based organizations, the Liberal Democrats made a conscious effort to commit both time and money to developing their offer and modernizing their systems – to move membership from very much a back-office function that nobody really owned into a key component of the party's strategy, with targets and incentives to match.[42] Up until then, according to those involved, there was little understanding that 'we're selling a product and maintaining a relationship'.[43] Both the offer and the systems were bolted on, almost as an afterthought, to a tradition of essentially local recruitment and involvement. They were consequently, indeed embarrassingly, poor: as one insider recalls, if you expressed a wish to join, you couldn't be sure you'd be contacted and, even if you were, 'we'd send you this crap paper card which would disintegrate; the new members pack was photocopied and we'd despatch it weeks and weeks after you'd joined'.[44] As a result, retention was appalling: 'of the people who joined, 70 per cent we lost in the first year' and numbers were, not surprisingly, stagnant or falling. Yet for a long time the party 'didn't see it as something they had any control over – the number of members was an externality; it was like the weather; it happened to you, as opposed to you being able to control it'.

The aim, then, was not only to move membership up the organization's agenda but to change this mind-set, to challenge the fatalism that assumed decline and not growth was the norm – a pessimism that only the Tories, able to spend so much more than any other party on the targeted digital advertising and direct mail that could maybe make up for lack of members, could really afford.[45] The aim, too, was to make it as easy as possible to join (and, just as important, to renew) at a national level, and via devices like smartphones and tablets, at the same time as preserving members' sense of connection to their locality for which the Liberal Democrats – pioneers of 'pavement politics' in Britain – are famous. Following the example of Obama's campaigns in the US – and probably in a way that might now be impossible under the General Data Protection Regulation (GDPR) – potential supporters' contact details were captured locally as well as nationally and then swiftly turned into hopefully persuasive communications.

As a result, from halfway through their time in coalition with the Conservatives – a period where voters were in short supply and their leader (someone most parties rely on to encourage people to join) plumbing new depths of unpopularity – the Liberal Democrats, albeit without many observers noticing, managed not only to stem but to begin to turn around the loss of members that began soon after Clegg and Cameron got together in Downing Street. And by the time the 2015 election (and likewise the EU referendum) came around, the party, having invested a fair amount of money and having, in the words of one staffer, 'scenario-planned the hell out of both of those events,' was ready with social media campaigns to take advantage of the situation. Those campaigns were clearly boosted by the commitment on the part of Tim Farron, the winner of the post–2015 election leadership contest, to grow membership to 100,000. But, in a clear example of one party learning from another's experience, they were very much inspired by what happened to the SNP during and after the independence referendum of 2014 – by the realization, in other words, that events can prompt people to ask themselves, 'What do you believe in?' creating 'moments where people want to stand up and be counted' and are therefore especially likely to respond positively to an invitation to join.[46]

That 100,000 target was reached by the Liberal Democrats in 2017, even if, according to the party's accounts submitted to the Electoral Commission, it ended up just below it by the end of that year. Whether it can be maintained at that kind of level, of course, is a moot point. It is worth noting, however, that the party has in recent years also made significant strides in *retention* as well as recruitment, primarily by trying to improve its membership offer or 'journey'. As one staffer puts it,

> [p]eople might spontaneously see a politician on TV and say 'I feel something. I want to help those people.' . . . But you're going to be very lucky if that

moment occurs 365 days later. So, the real test is. . . . , after a year, do they go, 'Actually, the forty quid I spent there, or whatever it is: yeah, I feel good about that.'[47]

That said, simple efficiency does no harm – and that goes beyond the fact that many people now sign up to parties via (what is in some cases an annually increasing) direct debit: indeed, as the same staffer notes, the latter can be much of a curse as a blessing since, especially with rise of internet and mobile banking, anyone wishing to cancel their subscription can now do so at click of a keypad or a swipe of a screen. Retention actually has more to do with the fact that members who have not renewed are now routinely re-contacted, both by HQ and at the local level, and assiduously encouraged – just as they would be by a business – to do so. All this, along with a rule change that now allows any member who is able to attend a genuinely welcoming annual conference that has an important say on policy (see Chapter 7), may account for the fact that in recent years, the Liberal Democrats have been able to post retention rates well over 80 per cent.[48]

The Greens' membership surge also owed something to 'events'. First there was the election of their first MP (Caroline Lucas representing Brighton Pavilion) in 2010. Then there was the coming to power that same year of a Conservative–Liberal Democrat coalition bent on cutting public spending while facing a Labour Party that couldn't wholeheartedly oppose either austerity (because it was desperate to appear 'responsible' on the economy) or the government's restrictive immigration policies (because it was itself determined not to be seen as 'soft' on the issue). Again, however, if one looks behind the scenes it becomes clear that, like the Liberal Democrats (with whom they share a reliance on members' donations and subscriptions), the Greens made a conscious decision in late 2013/early 2014 to professionalize their membership, funding and digital operations.

The party's systems were streamlined and enhanced so as to create something of a virtuous circle whereby more members led to more income, which was, in turn, invested in more staffers, whose skills helped the party further smarten up its web offer, social media and internal communications. This then helped it recruit even more members by ensuring that, as one insider puts it, 'when you had all that enthusiasm, it wasn't dampened by the idea that "Well, the Greens can't organize themselves"'.[49] Moreover, all this was rushed into place just as the 2014 European Parliament elections were affording the Greens more visibility. Their unexpectedly strong performance that May (they had a few months previously been expected to lose seats but actually moved up from two to three) then lent them an all-important sense of momentum, resulting in a doubling of membership over the course of a few months. At that point, however, those responsible for the changes (many of which had initially been welcomed by local parties who knew they could do with some help) encountered a degree of pushback against what some activists clearly perceived as an attempt to pull the party away from its radical roots in consensus decision-making and local autonomy. This and, of course, the fact that (as we noted in Chapter 8) so many members fell prey to the charms of Jeremy Corbyn after 2015, meant that the Green surge proved a rather more temporary phenomenon. This suggests that a party's attempt to position itself to make the most of the good times doesn't necessarily mean it can do much to stem losses when times turn tougher. Nevertheless, it is a similarly useful reminder that parties are not simply passive recipients of fortune even if they are far from wholly masters of their own fate.

All politics is local

There are limits, however, to how much party HQs can impact what goes on at the local level, and the latter can make a big difference to recruitment, retention and, of course, levels of activism.[50] This is particularly the case, as we have already noted for the Greens: staffers at the national level did a great deal in the last parliament to improve the party's systems so that local parties had the means to communicate better with their members, potential and actual, but ultimately, they could not ensure that the will to do so demonstrated in some places was matched in others. Nor, given limited resources, were the digital platforms developed to aid communication as interactive, intuitive, and indeed welcoming as many had hoped.[51] These limits to national influence also characterize other, much bigger and ostensibly far better-resourced parties, including perhaps the richest of them all, the Conservatives. As one Tory insider notes, 'direct mail from [the leader] can engage people and they will write a cheque or send a credit card donation [but] I don't think the centre . . . is suitably equipped to then engage those people on an ongoing basis'.[52] Moreover, notwithstanding ongoing efforts to capture all members on a national database, there is a long (and some would say dogged or even cussed) tradition in the party of constituency association independence from 'the centre'. As a result, as both politicians and staffers note, an awful lot depends upon the people involved – in particular, the officers (from the association chairman down) and, assuming the association has the resources to pay for one (which is by no means guaranteed nowadays), the agent/organizer. That said, to quote one of the latter:

> As membership has declined and the job has changed with technology, there isn't actually enough work to keep one agent fully occupied with one constituency. There are still some constituencies with one agent [but] . . . they probably spend about 70 per cent of their time raising money to keep themselves employed – and 30 per cent of their time complaining about people not working hard enough![53]

Candidates and, more so, MPs may be able to help manage their local party, especially if they make a point of attending and hosting its events and/or maintaining communication with their local members, which many do electronically nowadays – and not just by 'old-fashioned' means like email but also via services like WhatsApp. That said, the ability of an MP (even one with what one of them terms good 'soft management skills' and a track record of hard work) to set a positive tone is inevitably limited. Time is one big constraint. So, too, is the fact that what one MP euphemistically refers to as a local party's 'strong characters' can sometimes be its hardest workers – even its backbone. Especially in constituencies with small memberships, this can lead MPs to tolerate self-perpetuating cliques and behaviour which they might otherwise prefer to tackle even though they know that it is off-putting to other members or potential members. Occasionally, HQs can try to knock heads together or even work to remove the offending characters from positions of influence. But, as one veteran insider notes of the Conservative Party, it finds it much easier to do so when its leader is enjoying electoral (or at least opinion polling) success and when the party chairman is perceived by activists to be 'one of us' in the sense of having come up through the ranks (which, to be fair, is the norm) rather than someone effectively parachuted into the job from nowhere, as many believed was true of Andrew Feldman, one of David Cameron's later picks for the job and allegedly the high-up who famously referred to some of the Tory grassroots as 'swivel-eyed loons'. Nevertheless, according to the same source, the fact that Cameron was able to get the party back into contention, and the fact that one of his earlier picks, Eric Pickles, knew the party inside out meant that, by that time, some 'seriously problematic people' (some of them prominent in local government) had already been quietly persuaded to go.[54]

A good organizer (which is what agents are generally known as these days) can also make a difference to the culture of the local party and to its ability to recruit and retain new members. Indeed, many MPs rely heavily on them to do just that, assuming, that is, that they have or share, an organizer in the first place – and that he or she is not only employed full-time but also capable and competent, not least when it comes to information technology (something the Conservatives in particular really struggle with).[55] The very best organizers are not content merely with upping their grassroots' game when it comes to campaigning at parliamentary and local elections. They also want to build the party, both in terms of members and in terms of activism, although it is worth noting that, for most parties, being able to call some 10 to 15 per cent of members activists is seen as, in the words of one staffer, 'doing really, really well – that tends to be the benchmark'.[56] Perhaps few organizers go so far as one of our interviewees, who will not only place adverts in the local press for people who might be interested in standing for the council but who will, if they see someone they don't know has written a letter to the editor that suggests some sympathy with their party's position, try to contact them and ask them to think about joining.[57] However, many try hard to create a community-group-style atmosphere at social events to which existing members will feel comfortable inviting their friends in the hope that they might be persuaded to join (or at least donate). And, like their MPs and candidates, most organizers are aware that, once people have joined or at least thought about joining, it is crucial not to try to get them to do too much too soon: suggesting they help with canvassing, for instance, has to be handled particularly carefully because new members often worry – unnecessarily it turns out – that voters on the doorstep will expect them to know their party's policies inside out; it is also much easier to get someone to commit to delivering leaflets to a street or two once in a while than to suddenly try to land them for the responsibility for an entire ward. That said, as one Liberal Democrat staffer puts it, it's not always about so-called 'small asks first', it's also about 'smart asking', which partly depends on timing.[58] That's why a lot of the 'surge members' who joined the party straight after the EU referendum were immediately asked (and proved happy) to help out straight away in the tactically important (because high-profile) Richmond by-election held in December 2016.

Yet the balance between local campaigning and party building can be a difficult one to strike. And, as one insider notes, the increasing number of often quite young graduates who are drafted in as 'campaign managers' on temporary contracts from one election to another, and who perhaps see the job as 'a stepping stone' to higher things rather than a calling in itself, are understandably tempted to prioritize the former over the latter.[59] Although this may well help win elections in the short term – one Tory insider is absolutely convinced that it did an awful lot to help the Tories to their surprise overall majority in 2015 after being 'outgunned' by the out-going Labour Party in 2010 – it can also come back to bite you later on.[60] Another insider, thinking back to the way the party's efforts to make up for its shortage of members by organizing 'road trips' to marginal constituencies by activists eventually backfired as allegations of expenses-fiddling and bullying surfaced, notes wryly that 'if we'd spent more time rebuilding the grassroots, we probably wouldn't have had . . . to bus people round the country'.[61] On the other hand, to quote his more enthusiastic colleague again: 'If you win the seat then you have someone who provides a fulcrum around which you can operate the year after; whereas if you don't win the seat, you haven't.'[62]

Facing the (digital) future

For all this, however, while both politicians and staffers have in no sense given up on trying to attract new members to their parties and encouraging them to campaign for it, the feeling that their organizations are not quite fit for purpose in the twenty-first century is actually quite widespread.[63] Admittedly, they get a little fed up with what they see as facile comparisons with campaign groups and/or charities with burgeoning memberships and bank balances, not least because as one Labour Party insider observed, NGO's don't have to do 'boring' and 'bad' stuff as well as good stuff. After all, while Britain's biggest membership organization, the Royal Society for the Protection of Birds provides, like the National Trust or English Heritage, a useful reminder to parties that even in the digital era tangible, touchable benefits like a quality membership card and a glossy magazine shouldn't be dismissed out of hand (if, that is, they can be afforded), 'the RSPB doesn't have to read the minutes out to members and doesn't have to select councillors'.[64] But many would share the conviction of a Conservative MP, who himself came up through the ranks having joined the party as a teenager, that

> [i]t's about how technological change and social change today needs to be reflected in the way we do business. If any review sets off to look at how we

try and turn the clock back, and reinvent an era of mass membership, I don't think we've got a prayer.[65]

In short, parties – or at least many of their MPs and staffers – are well aware that society has changed much more than they have and that they need rapidly to adapt to those changes, not least because the battle for people's attention, let alone their time and money, is just so intense nowadays: as one Liberal Democrat put it, '[t]he competition is not the Tories or Labour; the competition is Netflix'.[66] Some insiders, of course, would go further than others, depending in part (but not wholly) on which party they represent or work for, be it large or small, democratic or autocratic, ageing or relatively youthful. It is probably no coincidence, for example, that it was a Green Party staffer who told us,

> You need to have an online voting system . . . [U]nder each policy, you can create a discussion and a mechanism of voting on some of those ideas. We need interim ways of getting people involved . . . So, for example, someone might put forward an idea and you could get people to vote on it on the members' website . . . So it's all about digital democracy . . . It becomes relevant to people when they see it online.'[67]

Likewise, even had we shorn the extract of some of its giveaway terminology, many readers might well have been able to guess that the following thought-provoking contribution came from a Liberal Democrat:

> That gets to a question which is the most fundamental question facing political parties. What is the purpose of a political party in the 21st century? And it's not one they like asking – or they like being asked. Because the purpose, to a lot of the existing people, is 'To do what I do. I get to be the leader of a council or to sit on the Federal Executive or whatever, and the purpose of the party is to allow me to do that thing.' Whereas actually what the Lib Dems should be is 38 Degrees [the largely online campaigning organization] with two things: 1) some sort of moral core, as opposed to just 'We will campaign for whatever you want' . . . and [2] real agency through the political process. But what 38 Degrees *have* done is that they have created a ground-up thing which makes people feel empowered. . . . [Although] they can't think of a second trick . . . and they will struggle from now on, we should take a step back and say, 'What works about them?'. Well, it's free/easy to join. Members have genuine power. And the tone in which they do it . . . So, if you could just bottle that and say, 'OK there is some consistent set of values across this (community empowerment is a big one . . .) but . . . we are going to stand for political positions as well, both locally and nationally', then actually you will have invented a political party for the 21st century . . . based on a digital-first idea. Whereas the Lib Dems' problem is how to go from a door-knocking local, village politics organisation and make that suitable for people who join

online, [for whom] politics is national, [and who] don't have a sense of community in a geographic sense.[68]

Yet those who recognize that the future has to be digital also realize, then, that the virtual has somehow to be fused with the real, the online with the offline.[69] As we noted in earlier chapters (especially when considering what encourages people to go beyond simply joining a party to actively campaign for it and to stick with it), face-to-face interaction at a local level continues to matter: one reason, perhaps, why at least one party needs to worry – if, that is, it takes the words of one of its activists as seriously as it surely should do:

> We're not very welcoming . . . If someone was asking how do they get involved, the last thing I would tell them to do is to go to a constituency party meeting: 'Just don't go! Maybe further down the line; but take friends with you!' At all levels of the party it just needs to be a bit more social, more fun, friendly. Then, when you get them involved initially, there needs to be a culture change because we lose people through the sexism, the antisemitism – the antisemitism has been more of a problem recently, the sexism has been there the whole time. It puts people off. [S]eeing people being abused, it doesn't make you want to have a career in politics, it doesn't make you want to be involved in this nasty world.[70]

Conclusion

It seems clear that parties are as keen as ever to continue to recruit members – indeed, they find it difficult, if not impossible, to imagine how (or even why) they would exist without them. Members are definitely seen as an asset. On the basest level they are seen as a source of finance, and, at the local level anyway, this is true even of parties for whom subscription income is not (as it is for smaller parties who cannot rely on wealthy donors) that important nationally. Their contribution to campaigning is unsurprisingly seen as crucial, but they are also seen as a link with the community and sometimes as a source of advice and wise counsel. Moreover, many (some say too many) members represent their party on myriad local bodies. If members are seen as a liability it is not so much because they represent a huge constraint on staffers and politicians but because they have the potential to embarrass their party in public – particularly on social media.

Since they recognize that there are limits to how many people can be persuaded, in this day and age, to formally join them, parties are open to the idea of recruiting 'supporters' – as their recent willingness to try out schemes designed for precisely that purpose attests. But they see those supporters as complementary (rather than as an alternative) to members, not least because they believe (with good reason, we would argue) that the latter offer them a higher level of commitment across the piece. For most parties, especially those in the centre and on the left, the price (if that is the right word for something they don't naturally regard in transactional terms) they pay for that commitment is a meaningful, even definitive, say on policy and candidate and leadership selection. Conservatives recognize that, since their members' rights extend only to the latter (and even then can be limited), they may be at a disadvantage in this respect. However, there seems to be little or no appetite for changing things – apart perhaps from making consultation procedures and the party's annual conference rather more meaningful than they are currently. This may reflect a more general fatalism in that party about growing its membership – something that stands in marked contrast to, say, the Greens and the Liberal Democrats.

Something that all parties seem to share, however, is an acknowledgement that, whatever steps they take centrally to boost recruitment and retention, much of their capacity to campaign on the ground relies on local factors. An inspiring national leader can help and winning does no harm. They can also provide resources, particularly in the form of paid campaign managers and/or agents. But a lot of it comes down to personalities which either gel or clash, and get going or get lazy. As a result, while at least some parties are trying to think hard about the future, and particularly about how to survive and thrive in a digital, more consumerist era, they know that, in upping their game in the virtual space, they have to integrate the online and offline worlds.

Notes

1 Conservative organizer, interview 27 July 2016.
2 Norris, Pippa (2002) 'Campaign communications', in Lawrence LeDuc, Richard G. Niemi and Pippa Norris (eds.) *Comparing Democracies 2* (London: Sage Publications), pp. 127–147.
3 The Tories, for instance, launched several more or less successful membership drives in the 1950s: see Bale, Tim (2012) *The Conservatives Since 1945: The Drivers of Party Change* (Oxford: Oxford University Press), pp. 60–61. Tony Blair also made it his mission to increase Labour's membership after he became leader in 1994: see Pemberton, Hugh and Wickham-Jones, Mark (2013) 'Labour's lost grassroots: The rise and fall of party membership', *British Politics*, 8 (2), pp. 181–206.
4 Cohen, Gidon, Mates, Lewis and Flinn, Andrew (2012) 'Capture-recapture methods and party activism in Britain', *Journal of Interdisciplinary History*, 43 (2), p. 274.
5 Cohen, Gidon and Mates, Lewis (2013) 'Grassroots conservatism in post-war Britain: A view from the bottom up', *History*, 98 (330), p. 220.
6 See Scarrow, Susan E. (1996) *Parties and Their Members: Organizing for Victory in Britain and Germany* (Oxford: Oxford University Press).
7 After careful consideration, we decided to treat all interviews as off the record and therefore retain the anonymity of all our interviewees equally. Where possible we give an indication of their role, although in some cases we have had to avoid being too specific so as not to give away their identity. For instance, so few Greens are elected to public office that in their case we simply refer to them generically as 'politicians'. The term *staffer* applies to people working at party HQ. We should also issue several caveats. We were unable to conduct formal interviews with *staffers* from the Labour, the SNP, UKIP and the Conservative Party, although we did have meetings, correspondence and informal conversations with some of them and these have also informed this chapter. Nor were we able to conduct interviews with *politicians* from the SNP or UKIP. Fortunately, both parties and their memberships are the subject of ongoing detailed studies from other research teams.

8 Conservative MP, interview 24 February 2016.

9 Labour MP, interview 20 April 2016.

10 Conservative MP, interview 24 February 2016.

11 One or two MPs, mainly on the Conservative side, expressed in passing a slight concern that some of their more recently elected colleagues had 'been fast-tracked due to background or experience' and had not come up through the ranks in quite the same way. As a result 'they don't have the same understanding of all of the upsides' of their activists, 'as well as some of the rubbing downsides', and were therefore likely to find it more difficult to manage those activists – and to stand up for themselves on policy when their local party disagreed with them.

12 Liberal Democrat staffer, interview 25 February 2016.

13 Labour MP, interview 20 April 2016.

14 Labour MP, interview 8 March 2016.

15 The Conservative party's end of year accounts covering 2017, submitted to the Electoral Commission, suggested membership receipts made up less than 2 per cent of its total income, although the party hit back at subsequent criticism by suggesting, among other things, that this understated the true picture because a large proportion of the take from subscriptions is held at the local level and therefore did not show up in the party's national accounts. See https://twitter.com/JamesCleverly/status/1032311091181887494.

16 Conservative organizer, interview 27 July 2016.

17 Liberal Democrat staffer, interview 9 February 2016.

18 Green staffer, interview 26 May 2016.

19 Labour MP, interview 17 August 2016. Liberal Democrat staffer, interview 9 February 2019.

20 Labour activist, interview 7 April 2016.

21 Green politician, interview 5 April 2016.

22 Liberal Democrat staffer, interview 9 February 2016.

23 Labour MP, interview 8 March 2016.

24 Labour MP, interview 20 April 2016.

25 See 'A guide to Labour Party anti-semitism claims', *BBC*, 3 March 2019, available online at www.bbc.co.uk/news/uk-politics-45030552 and 'Islamophobia: "No place" for it in Conservative Party says chairman', *BBC*, 19 March 2019, available online at www.bbc.co.uk/news/uk-politics-47633067.

26 Labour MP, interview 17 August 2016.

27 Conservative MP, interview 13 April 2016 and Conservative MP, interview 24 February 2016.

28 Tory activist, interview 13 November 2015. Stevens, John (2019) 'Tory recruitment drive to let "activists" join for free', *Daily Mail*, 2 March, available online at www.dailymail.co.uk/news/article-6762799/Tories-push-supporters-amid-talk-Brexit-deadlock-lead-general-election.html. On Labour's introduction of registered supporters under Miliband, see McHugh, Declan (2015) 'Why did Labour use this system to elect its leader?', *New Statesman*, 8 September, available online at www.newstatesman.com/politics/elections/2015/09/why-did-labour-use-system-elect-its-leader and, more generally, Bale, Tim (2015) *Five Year Mission: The Labour Party Under Ed Miliband* (Oxford: Oxford University Press).

29 Labour staffer, interviews 27 July 2016 and 9 August 2016.

30 For details, see the report by Liberal Democrat activist and blogger, Mark Pack, 'A week in', 24 March 2019, available online at www.markpack.org.uk/158035/a-week-in-the-early-signs-are-very-promising-from-the-lib-dem-registered-supporters-scheme/.

31 Green politician, interview 6 April 2016.

32 Green staffer, interview 6 May 2016.

33 Conservative MP, interview 12 April 2016.

34 Conservative MP, interview 12 April 2016.

35 Conservative MP, interview 13 April 2016.

36 Conservative MP, interview 12 April 2016. Who knows if they are right, though? The new Conservative Policy Commission and Conservative Policy Network set up in 2018 may surprise the sceptics by turning out to be more than merely cosmetic exercises. See www.conservativepolicyforum.com/ and in particular www.conservativepolicyforum.com/news/feedback-conservatives-values-policy-commission.

37 On the Priority List, see Childs, Sarah and Webb, Paul (2012) *Sex, Gender and the Conservative Party: From Iron Ladies to Kitten Heels* (Houndsmills: Palgrave Macmillan), p. 76ff. On 2017, see Wallace, Mark (2017) '6 Our CCHQ election audit: The rusty machine, part two. How and why the ground campaign failed', September, available online at www.conservativehome.com/majority_conservatism/2017/09/our-cchq-election-audit-the-rusty-machine-part-two-how-and-why-the-ground-campaign-failed.html.

38 Conservative MP, interview 15 March 2016.

39 www.conservatives.com/join We last accessed this on 5 March 2019 so the content – visual and verbal – may of course change over time.

40 Retention desperately needs improving: see Wallace, Mark (2018) 'The minister who only just became a Conservative', *ConservativeHome*, 3 October, available online at www.conservativehome.com/thetorydiary/2018/10/the-minister-just-became-a-conservative.html, for an amusing if rather shocking tale that illustrates just how poor the party's membership systems were (and very possibly still are).

41 Conservative MP, interview 24 February 2016.

42 Liberal Democrat staffer, interview 29 October 2018.

43 Liberal Democrat staffer, interview 9 February 2016.

44 Liberal Democrat staffer, interview 9 February 2016.

45 Liberal Democrat staffer, interview 29 October 2018.

46 Liberal Democrat staffer, interview 29 October 2018.

47 Liberal Democrat staffer, interview 9 February 2016.

48 Liberal Democrat staffer, interview 1 February 2017.

49 Green staffer, 6 May 2016.

50 For an excellent extended discussion of all this, based on interviews with local organizers from a number of parties, see Pettitt, Robin (2019) *Recruiting and Retaining Party Activists: Political Marketing at the Grassroots* (London: Palgrave).

51 See Dommett, Kate (forthcoming) 'Roadblocks to interactive digital adoption? Elite perspectives on party practices in the United Kingdom', *Party Politics*, available online at https://doi.org/10.1177/1354068818761196.

52 Conservative organizer, interview 27 July 2016.

53 Conservative organizer, interview 27 July 2016.

54 Conservative peer, interview 15 August 2016.

55 See Wallace, Mark (2015) 'The computers that crashed. And the campaign that didn't', *ConservativeHome*, 16 June, available online at www.conservativehome.com/thetorydiary/2015/06/the-computers-that-crashed-and-the-campaign-that-didnt-the-story-of-the-tory-stealth-operation-that-outwitted-labour.html.

56 Liberal Democrat staffer, interview 1 February 2017.

57 Conservative organizer, interview 27 July 2016.

58 Liberal Democrat staffer, interview 1 February 2017.

59 Conservative organizer, interview 27 July 2016.

60 Conservative peer, interview 15 August 2016.

61 Conservative organizer, interview 27 July 2016.

62 Conservative peer, interview 15 August 2016.

63 For more on this, see a recent report compiled by academics for the think tank *Involve*: Dommett, Kate and Temple, Luke (2019) *What people want to see in parties today* (Sheffield: University of Sheffield), available online at www.katedommett.com/uploads/1/1/2/7/112786573/final_-_what_people_want_from_parties_today.pdf.

64 Labour staffer, interviews 27 July 2016 and 9 August 2016. See also Liberal Democrat staffer, interview 29 October 2018.

65 Conservative MP, interview 24 February 2016.
66 Liberal Democrat staffer, 9 February 2016.
67 Green staffer, interview 6 May 2016.
68 Liberal Democrat staffer, 9 February 2016.
69 For an interesting discussion of this and other challenges facing parties – especially those 'platform parties' that actually start out digital – see Gerbaudo, Paolo (2018) *The Digital Party Political Organisation and Online Democracy* (London: Pluto Press).
70 Labour activist, 7 April 2016.

10

CONCLUSION

The parliamentary/extra-parliamentary balancing act

So what, then, have we learned about party membership in twenty-first-century Britain? Perhaps the best way of answering that bigger question is to break it down into a series of smaller questions, summarizing our responses to each of them in turn. Having done that, we finish with a reminder that, although membership matters, so, too, does leadership – parties, to be successful, need to strike a balance between the two.

Who are they?

Hundreds of thousands of people belong to Britain's political parties today, and they come from all walks of life. It remains the case, however, that they are far from being a representative sample of the public – or even of those sections of the public that tend to vote for the party they belong to. In keeping with other work on party members both in the UK and in other countries, our research shows they are relatively old, relatively well-off and relatively well educated. It also shows that there are significantly fewer women than men amongst them, as well as far fewer people from ethnic minorities than there are in the population as a whole – something the parties surely need to work on if they want to look anything like the increasingly multicultural country that most of them aspire to represent and govern.

But if there are few differences between the parties on that score, there are on others. Some of those differences are perhaps predictable, depending on one's prejudices. For example, it will no doubt come as a source of satisfaction, but not surprise, to readers who are no fans of theirs that UKIP's members are the least educated of any parties' members or that the Conservatives' members seem to have the highest incomes and are tend to be located in the south of England, making it easy for their opponents to cast doubt on their claim still to be the party of 'One Nation'. Equally, those with more right-wing sympathies will no doubt smile when they see that so many Labour Party members work in the public sector, read the *Guardian*, and, like them, live in Southern England – an awful lot of them, outside London anyway, in parliamentary constituencies that their party has little hope of winning.

Stereotypes aside, however, we have shown that those parties on the left of centre, and especially the Greens, tend to have slightly younger members than those on the right. The average age of Conservative members, for example, may be under 60, but it is still the case that nearly one in four of them is around or above retirement age. The parties that like to think of themselves as 'progressive' are also significantly more gender-balanced, not least the Labour Party, which has seen many more women joining it in the last four or five years – in marked contrast to a Conservative Party that seems to have really struggled over the last decade or two to recruit and retain female members. As for class, all parties have memberships that are, on the whole, more middle class than their voters. But the gap is less marked in Liberal Democrats and the Greens, many of whose voters are middle class anyway, and in the SNP, which has a relatively (although only relatively) large number of working-class members. UKIP, on the other hand, attracts a comparatively high share of working-class voters, making for quite a mismatch with its generally middle-class membership. That same mismatch between members and voters will become increasingly evident in the Tory Party if it continues, as it did in 2017, to attract more support from socially conservative and nationalist working-class voters but alienates some of its more liberal, cosmopolitan, middle-class voters. If Labour, as it appears to be doing, does the opposite, then, as already seems to be happening, any mismatch between its members and voters will decrease as its voter base looks more and more like its middle class, degree-holding membership.

What do they think?

We are most used to thinking of politics as a matter of right and left, with positions on that continuum being defined by attitudes towards how much of the economy should be in the public or the private sector and how much government should tax and spend, as well its priorities – welfare or defence, redistribution or deregulation? However, there are many other things that matter, not all of which are best subsumed or collapsed into that familiar, horizontal dimension. Many argue, for instance, that what are sometimes labelled 'cultural' (as opposed to 'economic') issues – migration and multiculturalism, law and order, national sovereignty, morality, the environment even – constitute a distinct second dimension, even if that in itself is a simplification. If we bear this in mind when we move from the demography to the ideology of party membership in Britain, then some clear patterns emerge.

Although they may have begun to cool a little on austerity, the Conservative rank and file are by some distance the most right-wing in economic terms, while members of the other five parties we focus on are generally left of centre – indeed, quite far to the left in the case of Labour and the Greens. Most interestingly, per-haps, this includes members of UKIP, not least because, while they are not that keen on the idea of redistribution and are not quite so overwhelmingly anti-austerity as the members of more conventionally left-wing parties, they are very suspicious of big business – all of which is very much in keeping with the so-called welfare chauvinism (i.e., support for a comprehensive safety net provided for, but limited to, nationals) evinced by those who vote in Western Europe for populist radical right parties.[1] UKIP members, however, are much more socially conservative and anti-immigration than the members of any other party, including rank-and-file Tories, while – equally predictably perhaps – Green members are the most socially liberal and pro-immigration. These attitudes are, we suspect, fairly stable across time but a large influx (or, by the same token, a large-scale exodus) of members can make a difference: Labour's membership, for example, was pretty socially liberal even before the Corbyn era, but it is even more so now. This, of course, dovetails with the fact that, among party members as a whole (and irrespective of party), youth, a university education and a middle-class occupation (especially if it's in the public sector) tend to go hand in hand with socially liberal values, although interestingly gender has a much less clear-cut influence.

If we combine the two dimensions – the economic and the cultural, left/right and socially conservative/socially liberal – and look at how each party's membership fits into the resulting clusters, it is striking quite how far apart the members of Britain's two biggest, supposedly mainstream parties actually are. Around seven out of ten Labour members are on the socially liberal left, whereas seven out of ten Tories are on the socially conservative right. Only three out of ten UKIP members are there with them, compared to six out of ten who could be described as on the socially conservative left. Around a third of Liberal Democrat members are socially liberal left-wingers, but nearly half of them are in what one might call the centre – a space that interestingly is occupied by only around 15 per cent of the members of most other parties.

The biggest gap by far, however, between the four self-styled progressive parties (Labour, the SNP, the Liberal Democrats and the Greens) and the other two (UKIP and the Tories) is on Brexit. A year before the 2016 referendum, there were actually a surprising number of Conservatives who were not wholly convinced that leaving the EU was such a great idea, especially if their then leader could negotiate improved terms of membership. Two-and-a-half years afterwards, the Conservative membership was overwhelmingly not only pro-Brexit but also keen on a hard or even a 'no-deal' Brexit. Meanwhile, on the other side, members of Britain's main opposition party were equally adamant (like members of other left-leaning parties) that it should not go ahead. Both parties, however, were more equivocal – something that may prove deeply problematic in the long run.

How and why do they join?

People wanting to join political parties tend to make the first move rather than respond to any direct (or at least obvious) invitations on the part of the parties. Although a fair number approach their local party in the first instance, most initial contacts are made with the national party, quite often after checking out its website, possibly after seeing one of its broadcasts. The personal touch, however, is also important, with significant numbers of members having been persuaded to join after talking to friends and family. Social media, perhaps surprisingly, seems relatively unimportant so far, but this may well reflect the fact that many members would have joined before it achieved such prominence.

The reasons why people join political parties do not seem to have changed much since they were first investigated by the academic pioneers in the field back in the 1990s. As a result the General Incentives Model developed then still seems to hold good today. First and foremost, people join a political party because they are attracted by its principles and very often by its leader and because they are keen to see its policy platform implemented and to stop rival parties bringing in or continuing with policies they dislike and think are damaging. They also join because they believe it's important that people get involved in democratic politics. True, these expressive, collective policy and altruistic incentives are not the only ones that are important: social norms (friends and family) and selective process incentives (engaging in activities with like-minded people) also matter, but they matter less. Joining for the sake of advancing one's career (either in or outside of politics) – a selective outcome incentive – is not unknown, of course, but appears to be nowhere near as common as people who aren't members think it is. This misapprehension, it turns out, is one of several which, along with (equally misplaced) concerns about how much time membership might take up, may prevent people who strongly support parties from actually joining them. That said, it remains the case that some types of people are more likely to join parties than others: their members are not only more convinced than their supporters that they can make a difference, but they are notably more male, middle class and better educated, suggesting 'resources' are still a factor when it comes to the reasons why people join.

Party membership declined between the mid-1950s and the early 2000s – probably because of the declining value of non-political selective benefits which are bestowed by party membership (such as access to leisure and cultural activities), and the erosion of expressive incentives like class and related partisan loyalties. So why the big increase in membership we have witnessed in recent years? The answer, as we explain in more detail in Chapter 5, appears to lie in a complex mix of intra- and inter-party dynamics that were subtly different for each of the parties affected and involved a fair degree of contingency. But they once again reveal the importance of ideological, expressive and policy incentives, as well as – in Labour's case, in particular – the ability of a particular leader to embody a set of values which appealed strongly to those who rushed to join after 2015. It turns out that what one might term the 'relative deprivation' of 'educated left-behinds' (people who were not achieving the kind of rewards from life they might have expected, especially after getting a degree) was an important factor in that membership surge. However, Labour's post-2015 members are not, in the main, much less middle class, educated, and middle aged than its pre-2015 members, nor are they much more left-wing. They are, however, significantly more socially liberal (on issues like law and order, education and immigration) and are also considerably more supportive of the leadership and willing to take measures against MPs who do not share their view. Many of them are, in fact, returning members – people who abandoned the party under New Labour but now feel they have their party back.

What do they do for their parties?

Relatively few members can really be called activists. True, a few of them help out at elections, even if the numbers vary both between elections and between parties, with the Liberal Democrats often leading the way and the Tories, Greens and UKIP finding things much more difficult. But members are not the only people who campaign for their parties: non-member supporters (and in Labour's case affiliated trade union members) get involved too. That said, it is party members who play the most vital roles and take on the most intensive and demanding forms of activity – the ones that involve getting out of the house and coming face-to-face with voters. Moreover, it is normally only members who can get involved in maintaining local constituency organizations, voting on policy, and selecting candidates between elections.

The same General Incentives Model used to explain why people join also provides a useful basis for understanding why some members are more active than others: the ideological drivers that lead many people to become members in the first place also influence how hard they work for their parties once they've joined, and those who like the direction their party is taking are more likely to campaign for it than those who aren't so sure. Members hoping for a political career and/or feel part of their local parties' social networks are also more likely than others to get involved in higher-intensity activity, although it turns out – perhaps not surprisingly – that a sense of connection with one's local party is less important as a driver of online activism than it is of activities that involve getting out 'on the doorstep'.

Local context plays a part in other ways, too. For instance, the more marginal a constituency contest is, the more likely it is that party members will make an effort at elections. Anecdotal evidence also suggests that individual MPs, organizers and a determined group of volunteers, can mean the difference between a busy, buzzy local party and one where very little goes on. Interestingly, our survey evidence suggests – perhaps a little contradictorily – that, although a degree of fatigue seems to have set in between the two general elections held in short order in 2015 and 2017, members overall think they are more active now than they used to be, which at the very least calls for a reconsideration of the 'spiral of demobilization' that academics were talking about a couple of decades or so ago.

What do they think about the way their parties work?

On the whole Britain's party members feel pretty positive about the organizations they belong to, as well as the other people who belong to them. But they are far from completely satisfied, with fewer than half feeling that membership has fully lived up to expectations. Overall, they also want more influence, especially over the policy-making process – something which, along with all sorts of other rights and privileges, can vary markedly from party to party, with members of the Conservative Party having no formal say while members of the Greens and the Liberal Democrats, in particular, have the last word. Interestingly, while an overwhelming majority of Labour members clearly felt respected by the party's leadership, just over half continue to feel, in spite of the election of a leader who promised much in this respect, that the membership should have more of a say on policy. This may or may not be because there is little concrete evidence so far of those promises being delivered on, especially when it comes to Brexit. Of course, leaders are inevitably destined to disappoint or frustrate *some* of their followers on every issue: aggregating the multiple preferences of tens or even hundreds of thousands of members is a perennial challenge for organizations that purport to be democratic. The intensity with which certain groups of members protest their case can make for politically lurid headlines, but the real danger to a party's leadership is only likely to rear its head when the numbers who contest its position constitute a clear majority. Still, from Labour's perspective at least, its members remain considerably more satisfied with their membership experience than their Tory (and UKIP) counterparts, who seem to view their party's internal processes (and their overall experience) in much more negative terms than they used to – possibly because of Brexit, or possibly because one survey was conducted just after a general election campaign that saw David Cameron win an unexpected overall majority and the other after Theresa May blew that majority after what is widely regarded as one of the worst campaigns by the party in living memory.

When it comes to what has traditionally been seen as one of the major perks of membership, a majority of party members continue to support the closed ballots that parties still typically use to pick their parliamentary candidates, even if a small but significant minority would be prepared to see more use made of open primaries. And members' reluctance to dilute their say in candidate selection is arguably reflected in their relatively lukewarm response to the idea of registered supporters' schemes, especially if they involve giving those supporters any of the rights and privileges that have traditionally been the preserve of members. That said, there is a widespread wish to see some changes made to the kinds of people who represent their parties in Parliament. The scale and scope of the demand for candidates from a greater variety of social backgrounds, however, varies markedly between parties, with Conservative and UKIP members far less willing to countenance greater diversity than members of the other four parties.

Why do some of them quit?

The decision to leave one's party is driven predominantly by political and ideological disagreements rather than by life events or poor administration and communication or personal animosities – although sometimes these play a part. How much members agree with the direction their party is taking – and the leader who is taking it in that direction – matters more than, say, whether they are male or female, working class or middle class. That said, how active they are, how effective they feel, how much being a member has lived up to their expectations, also matters, as does how long they've stuck with the party and how active they are in it. Ultimately, though, what counts most is what members *think* rather than who they *are*, especially, perhaps, when it comes to those who belong to parties that have traditionally laid great stress on their principles – one reason, maybe, why so many people left the traditionally internationalist and nominally social-ist Labour Party over Tony Blair's decision to go to war in Iraq and his supposed embrace of 'neo-liberalism', and why Jeremy Corbyn's equivocation over Brexit may, in the end, cost him dearly.

And what do parties want?

One very obvious answer to this is members! Parties – even the Conservative Party, at least at the local level – continue to value the human and financial resources they represent, as well as the links into the community, and the legitimacy and the momentum they can bring. More than that, many, if not most, of those who work for and represent parties find it difficult to imagine how or even why they would carry on without members. That is not to say there is no recognition whatsoever of the downsides of membership – the constraints on the leadership, the pressure put on MPs, the capacity to embarrass the party, particularly on social media. But, by some distance, members are seen as an asset, not a liability.

As a result, while parties are (more or less warily) introducing registered support-ers' schemes in the hope that they will pull in donations of time and money from people unwilling to commit to full membership, they also recognize that those who do commit must continue to be afforded particular rights and privileges. Indeed, in the Conservative Party one can detect a degree of concern that affording its mem-bers so little formal say on policy may be putting the party at a disadvantage when it comes to recruitment and retention, even if there seems to be precious little appetite to make more than cosmetic changes in this regard.

This may well be dangerous in the long term: as one Liberal Democrat staffer put it, in the twenty-first century, 'you cannot run a membership organization . . . where your members don't have a stake in what's going on. They need to have that sense of ownership. . . . They want to get value for money'.[2] But it does reflect a pervasive fatalism concerning membership in the Conservative Party that stands in stark contrast to the more positive attitudes prevalent in other parties. They appear far more inclined to believe that they can actually grow their numbers by upgrading their systems both to improve retention and to take advantage of the recruitment opportunities particular events (most obviously elections) can offer. There is nev-ertheless a widespread acknowledgement, notwithstanding an equally widespread understanding the future will be digital, that what goes on locally still makes a big difference and that the key to success, along with providing a more welcoming environment for new and younger entrants, lies in effectively integrating members' online and offline experiences.

Past, present, future

The trouble with writing about politics is that things can change so fast. Just when you think you've got a grip on what's happening or successfully mapped the terrain, everything shifts. When we first conceived this book more than five years ago now, we assumed, like most observers, academic and otherwise, that most, if not all, of the parties we were looking at would be losing rather than gaining members. How wrong we were! True, a couple of parties that then seemed to be on the up – the Greens and UKIP – have struggled recently, although the former may be in the process of steadying its ship and even turning it around. But the SNP and Labour have enjoyed truly unprecedented growth and the Liberal Democrats haven't done too badly either. Only the Conservatives seem to be treading water, finding it difficult to recruit younger people, women and ethnic minorities in particular and arguably in danger, as a result, of becoming less and less representative of the country (although not necessarily of their own voters), both demographically and ideologically. It may or may not be true that, as one of our interviewees put it, '[t]he smaller political parties get, the more likely they are to be dominated by weirdos . . . the sort of people who zip up their anoraks right up to their necks'.[3] But right now there seems little immediate risk of that – and not just because anoraks are rarely the wet-weather gear of choice for any discerning Tory. After, all the party claims to have more than 150,00 members. And leadership contests have been known to bring in more of them, both because some people join in order to vote (many of them forgetting there are rules governing how long one has to be a member before one can do so) and because they are a reminder to potential (and indeed existing) members that membership does confer benefits.

More generally, of course, such contests are yet another reminder to those of us interested in party members of the important role a popular leader can play in encouraging them to join (predictably enough given what some see as the increasing personalization of politics) even if there is a flipside, namely, that an unpopular leader can also prompt members to leave.[4] And there is another paradox here worth noting. Incentivizing people to join parties, to become active within them and to renew their membership year after year is a perennial challenge for parties, and one that they have often sought, not least in Britain, to meet by offering their rank and file more rights and powers. However, there continues to be a pinch point when it comes to members' involvement in policy-making: the leaders they elect are in reality unwilling to act as mere delegates of their grassroots, convinced as they are (and not unreasonably) that the preferences of the latter are often at variance with the voters they most need to appeal to. Leaders need to maximize their scope for autonomous action in playing the game of party competition, while in government, the sheer impact of 'events' tends to buffet leaders and limit their ability to respond directly to member demands, even assuming that they want to.

This, in turn, raises an eternal dilemma of politics in parliamentary and representative democracies: should parliamentary elites be primarily accountable to their party grassroots or to the constituents who returned them to Parliament? The political scientist and television pundit Robert McKenzie highlighted this problem many years ago in explaining why, whatever their formal pretensions to internal democracy, parties in the UK tended to be dominated by their Westminster leaderships.[5] All of which suggests that it may be unwise for leaders to win control of their parties by promising their membership a greater say in policy matters – a promise that often holds only so long as members and leaders want the same things. This is not an entirely cynical point: the pretensions to radical democracy based on regular online consultations of members that some of Europe's newer parties maintain (think of Italy's Five Star Movement, for instance) may prove easy for leaders to manipulate.[6] To this extent, these versions of intra-party democracy can be quite vacuous, if not downright deceitful. The UK remains, for the present at least, a representative parliamentary democracy, and for that model to function effectively, political parties should be organized and structured in a way that is congruent with such a system. That congruence requires a delicate balance between the passions of enthusiastic memberships and the responsible, yet responsive, leadership that – in theory at least – should be provided by the MPs they help to select.

Notes

1 See multiple contributions to Mudde, Cas, ed. (2016) *The Populist Radical Right: A Reader* (Abingdon: Routledge).
2 Liberal Democrat staffer, interview 1 February 2017.
3 Liberal Democrat staffer, interview 25 February 2016.
4 See Cross, William, Katz, Richard and Pruysers, Scott (2018) *The Personalization of Democratic Politics and the Challenge for Political Parties* (London: ECPR Press); Rahat, Gideon and Kenig, Ofer (2018) *From Party Politics to Personalized Politics? Party Change and Political Personalization in Democracies* (Oxford: Oxford University Press).
5 McKenzie, Robert T. (1955) *British Political Parties: The Distribution of Power Within the Conservative and Labour Parties* (London: Heinemann); and McKenzie, Robert T. (1982) 'Power in the Labour Party: The Issue of "Intra-party Democracy"', in Dennis Kavanagh (ed.) *The Politics of the Labour Party* (London: George Allen and Unwin), pp. 191–201.
6 Bordignon, Fabio and Ceccarini, Luigi (2015) 'The Five Star Movement: A hybrid actor in the net of state institutions', *Journal of Modern Italian Studies*, 20 (4), pp. 463–465.

APPENDIX 1

Table A.1 reports the results of ordinary least squares regression models of positions on left-right and liberty-authority scales for 2015 and 2017. In each model we include the party that each respondent is a member of chiefly as a control variable; although this variable proves to be highly significant and strong in each model, strictly speaking we cannot interpret the direction of the relationships because the numerical coding allotted to each party carries no substantive meaning; for example, although Labour is coded '2' and the Conservative is coded '1', it does not imply that being a member of the former party is somehow 'more than' being a member of the latter party in any numerical sense. That said, we already have a very shrewd idea of how membership in the different parties pertains to positions on the two attitudinal scales anyway, and these models confirm that these relationships hold even when other demographic factors are allowed for.

TABLE A.1 Multivariate models of party members' positions on left–right and liberty–authority scales

	Left–Right Scale		Liberty–Authority Scale	
	2015	2017	2015	2017
Education	−.088***	−.094***	−.242***	−.310***
Class	−.107***	−.098***	.074***	.031
Sector	−.120***	−.025	−.107***	−.068**
Gender	−.029*	−.026	.008	.020
Age	.016	−.011	.219***	.181***
Activism	−.061***	−.086***	−.075***	−.136***
Party	−.472***	−.550***	−.159***	−.240***
Adjusted model R2	.282	.354	.204	.240
	n = 3924	n = 1457	n = 3809	n = 1414

Note: All figures are standardized regression coefficients from ordinary least squares analysis, unless otherwise stated. Education: 1=graduate, 0=non graduate. Class: 1=ABC1, 0=C2DE. Sector: 1=private, 2=public/charitable. Gender: 1=male, 2=female. Age = age in years. Activism scale from 0-9 campaign acts. Party: 1=Con, 2=Lab, 3=LD, 4=UKIP, 5=Green, 6=SNP

***p < .001; **p < .01; *p < .05.

APPENDIX 2

TABLE A.2 Binary logistic regression model: exiting party membership, 2015–2017

	B	S.E.	Sig.	Exp(B)
Subjective left–right distance from own party (0–10)	0.170	0.100	0.088	1.185
Change in left–right subjective distance from party, 2015–2017 (0–10)	0.210	0.081	0.009	1.233
How well did your leader perform in election, 2017 (0–10)?	−0.207	0.039	0.000	0.813
To what extent, if at all, does the leadership respect members? (reference = not at all)			0.017	
A lot	−1.349	0.625	0.031	0.259
A fair amount	−1.713	0.617	0.005	0.180
Not very much	−1.778	0.680	0.009	0.169
How active have you been in the party over the past five years (0–10)?	−0.105	0.037	0.005	0.901
Length of party membership	−0.060	0.012	0.000	0.942
CONTROL VARIABLES				
Gender (reference = women)	0.329	0.225	0.145	1.389
Social Grade (reference = ABC1)	0.271	0.218	0.215	1.311
Education (reference = graduates)	−0.152	0.210	0.468	0.859
Constant	0.998	0.717	0.164	2.712

Source: UK Party Members Project Panel Survey 2015–2017.

Note: Dependent variable: 1 = left party between 2015 and 2017; 0 = remained a party member in 2017. $N = 2008$.

INDEX

Note: Page numbers in italic indicate a figure and page numbers in bold indicate a table on the corresponding page.